Inner
Rhythms

Inner Rhythms

The Kabbalah of Music

DovBer Pinson

JASON ARONSON INC.
Northvale, New Jersey
Jerusalem

This book was set in 12 pt. Apollo by Alpha Graphics of Pittsfield, NH and printed and bound by Book-mart Press, Inc. of North Bergen, NJ.

10 9 8 7 6 5 4 3 2 1

Library of Congress Cataloging-in-Publication Data

Pinson, DovBer, 1971–
      Inner rhythms: the Kabbalah of music / by DovBer Pinson.
            p.   cm.
      Includes bibliographical references and index.
      ISBN 0-7657-6098-3
      1. Jews—Music—History and criticism.   2. Hasadim—Music—History
and criticism.   3. Music—Philosophy and aesthetics.   I. Title.
ML3871.P56   2000
780'.88296—dc21   99–25253
                                                                            CIP

Printed in the United States of America on acid-free paper. For information and catalog write to Jason Aronson Inc., 230 Livingston Street, Northvale, NJ 07647-1726, or visit our website: www.aronson.com

Acknowledgment

Words cannot adequately express my sincere appreciation to a dear friend Alex Goldring, whose friendship made this work a reality.

Contents

Introduction

The medieval philosophers argued as to the one absolute necessity of life. *Maimonides* offered that it is quite simple, that which is the least expensive and most easily accessible is the most necessary to life. Air, which is free and available to all, is life's most precious commodity. Likewise, water, a staple and therefore free for the taking. Food, still essential yet not as much as air and water, costs little and is easily available. More costly and slightly more difficult to procure is clothing, a necessity, yet less basic. Diamonds, the most rare and expensive of all, are not a staple in life at all, rather a luxury, not needed for sustaining life.

Following this logic, there is yet another basic necessity in life, that which sustains and nourishes, and is absolutely necessary for the continuation of the human experience. It is readily available and open to all who wish to partake of it. It is music.

Music has always been in existence. It surrounds our present, yet connects us to the past and resonates into the future.

Music is a mode of communication. It employs an indigenous alphabet, vocabulary, and organizing principles. It differs from regular communication in that it is not linguistically grounded. It emanates and touches a different place than that which is ordinarily activated in the thought process.

Human communication occurs on two levels. The verbal, consisting of an arrangement of words, may tell a lot about a person. But the way a human being "sings" those words may tell a whole lot more. The former indicates the speaker's relationship with his subject matter, while the latter betrays the quality of the person and how he relates to himself and the universe. The melody of a person says more about him than his words.

While the tune an individual sings, says much of his distinct persona, and unique journey, the in-depth study of music reveals a story of colossal proportions, the story of creation and the development of mankind through the ages. Each culture has always had its own song. It is its nonverbal language which communicates its social culture and aesthetic traditions. To understand a people, one need only study its music, for therein lie the secrets of its traditions and beliefs.

The Jewish nation, an ancient and modern people, also have their song. To understand and analyze the music of the ancient Jews is a difficult and daunting task, for there is little, if any, documentation as to its style and rhythm. While the ancient Greeks developed theories of music and spoke extensively of it, the Talmudic Sages, for reasons unknown, chose to ignore this subject. Yet, there are ways through which one can discern the music of a culture, without direct documentation regarding the music itself. One way is by studying the music of the nations and religions surrounding that culture, for music is 'contagious'. Each culture's song is inevitably influenced by its surroundings.

Another way by which the music of a culture can be studied, without direct knowledge of the music itself, is through the examination of the instrumentation utilized by that people. Each instrument has its unique musical qualities, affecting the song which it plays. These qualities tell much of the music and of the people who played it.

There has been extensive research and study done on ancient Jewish music. Those who analyzed it made use of that which was mentioned above, the surrounding cultures and the musical instrumentation. The Torah speaks of many instruments that were used in the Temple which were native to the Jewish culture, as well as, those instruments which were 'borrowed' from other nations. The Talmud speaks of the marriage of King Solomon to a princess of Egypt and of the thousand musical instruments that were given as a gift from the Egyptian ruler to the King of Israel.

What is known to us as Jewish music is actually a compilation of styles and rhythms gathered over centuries and obtained in various manners and from countless sources. However, musicologists the world over agree that the quintessential purity of the Jewish song has always been retained. The quality which makes it uniquely Jewish, regardless of the influences on it, has remained untouched and clearly identifiable.

What is this quality? What is it that makes a song sound Jewish? It is a note of longing, of a child yearning to unite with his parent, a nation pining for its homeland and lost temple, a soul on this world remembering the holiness above and longing to reunite. Each song resonates with the entirety of the Jewish experience, the devastations and victories, the separations and reunifications, and above all the constant bond with the eternal.

In the development of music, two distinct paths emerged: music which is associated with bodily movement, such as dancing, marching and the like, identified by its strict rhythm, and recitative and interpretational music. The latter is generally associated with text and is non-rhythmical, spontaneous, and free for personal expression. Ancient Jewish music seems to follow the latter path. It is Semitic-Oriental in its elements and primarily non-rhythmical and lacking harmony, although it does contain other distinguishing factors.

The study of Jewish music is vast and requires volumes to contain it. There are many who have analyzed its unique qualities and have written extensively on it. Their examination of music is essentially a lesson in history, another means of glimpsing a rich and diverse past.

There is yet another way to examine a song, and that is, to view it as an eternal message, as relevant today as it was hundreds of years ago, at the time of its composition. Each song tells its own story in the heart of the one who sings it. It evokes a unique response in each listener. A tune can touch a soul, in a way no words ever could.

The study of music as response is what I endeavor to portray in this work. Music can be used in a myriad of ways in our everyday lives. Especially today with all the gadgets that can convey music (radios, cassettes, cd's, etc.), we are bombarded by sound. Just by taking a long walk, a person changes zones of melodies, beats, and compositions of various types. Our bodies seem to vibrate to uninvited songs and noises that permeate the air around us. But invited or not it is the ambiance in which we live, and which makes it part of the human experience.

We hear music constantly, yet we often fail to listen. Each tune tells a story. The Jewish song tells a tale of the ongoing saga of survival and hope. We need to only listen closely and we may hear its eternal message.

I

An Overview of Jewish Music and Its Development

I wish to take you, dear reader, on a mystical odyssey through the corridors of Jewish song. In order to have a comprehensive understanding of the development of music and its place within Jewish tradition, I give you an overview of music and its history.

The first time the concept of music or musical instrumentation is mentioned in the Torah is when the eighth generation of mankind is being described: "Ada gave birth to Yaval; he was the ancestor of all who dwell in tents and keep herds (the first shepherd). His brother's name was Yuval; who was in turn the progenitor of all who play harp and flute."[1]

"Necessity is the Mother of Invention." This was not a time when luxury (defined as anything that does not respond to immediate existential issues) occured. Man needed to tend the sheep, and so the role of shepherd was created. Yet in the same generation, in the same family, a man invented music. Ostensibly this too was a necessity. Necessity takes on many forms. While the shepherds tended the sheep that fed the body, musicians created music to nourish the soul.

"Religious worship cannot do without music. It is one of the foremost means to work upon man with an effect of marvel."[2]

Religion, in its earliest stage of development, was responsive to man's awe and marvel and lack of comprehension of the workings of the universe. In ancient civilizations, music was generally viewed as sacred, an act of religious worship.[3] Music and religion are both phenomena that overwhelm one with a feeling beyond reason or comprehension, beyond the rational and mundane.[4]

The birth of the Jewish people began with song. The Jews left Egypt a mass of broken individuals. As they metamorphosed into a nation, they joined in song, with the greatest of men, Moses, and the simplest child, together as one body,[5] singing a song of praise to God.[6] Jewish tradition has always viewed music and song as a vehicle for expressing devotion and gratitude to God and as a holy and sacred act.[7] According to the Talmud,[8] singing praise to God is actually a law derived directly from the Torah.

The practice of singing songs and playing music in the service of God was an integral part in the history of the Jewish nation. The Rambam (*Eng.* Maimonides, 1135–1204) writes, "When one attains the highest level of his intellect, and achieves as well, a higher state of consciousness, which is the power of 'dimyion'— imagination, then God can, if He wills—reveal Himself to man through a prophetic vision."[9] The prophets would utilize music as a tool to place them in the right mood, that is, to put them into a higher state of consciousness, so that they could then prophesy. Elishah, the prophet, commanded his people, "Now play for me the instruments of music . . . and when the musician will play . . . the hand of God will be affixed upon me."[10] The music plays an important role in the prophet's ability to bring himself to the level of prophecy. Music has the potential to transform the prophet's state of mind from a state of "regular consciousness" to the imaginary state.[11] For example, playing or vocalizing a repetitive melody can turn the tune into a "mantra," and bring the prophet to a higher state of consciousness.

Music has a remarkable propensity for isolation. Rabbi Avraham Ben HaRambam (1186–1237) writes that the prophets would use song to clear their minds and hearts from all thoughts other than God.[12] This is one of the distinctive characteristics of music, the ability to clear the mind of all extraneous thoughts, internal isolation, and to bring one to a higher state of consciousness. Interestingly, sound actually "separates" the brain from the rest of the body. Try if you will to snap your finger around the circumference of your head, at ear level. It should feel as if your brain is detached from the rest of your body. In this way, music isolates.[13]

Music evokes many reactions. One of the most powerful responses is Joy. The Talmud states, "The holy spirit does not rest (upon man) only if one is in a happy mood."[14] The prophets made use of music in this way as well, listening to music that would cause their spirits to be uplifted, and bring them to the happiness necessary to receive the spirit of God.[15] It is said that music is the language of the spiritual worlds,[16] and it is through music that a prophet can communicate with the Divine. Music is the language of the soul, and it is thus, played throughout the entire prophecy.

In the Torah we find that music can be a palliative, if not a cure for depression. King Shaul suffered from chronic depression. It was said to him,[17] "There will be a time, when the evil spirit (the spirit of depression)[18] will rest upon you . . . and he shall play for you music, and you will be comforted." Through song, the air, or aura, surrounding the listener and performer becomes purified, in a manner of speaking. The music filters the air, removing the negativity and leaves a purified and positive atmosphere.[19]

Music's role in Jewish history was not confined by any means to the prophet's utilization of it. In fact, the entire Levite tribe was completely devoted to music; and indeed, it was their sole occupation in the Holy Temple. The Levites would sing songs to God throughout the entire day of service in the Temple.[20]

The Talmud tells a story that illustrates the Levites' complete devotion and dedication to their task, and the degree to which they regarded music in the highest esteem.[21] In the tribe of Levi there was a singer and musician of outstanding talent. He had mastered the art of vocalizing and was able to style his voice to be as clear as crystal. The Levites clamored to be taught by this great master of song; however, he remained unmoved by their sincere requests and refused to teach even one man the secrets of his magnificent voice. The Talmud continues and tells us that the man had good reason, without revealing what that reason was. Nonetheless, the tribe of Levi harbored such ill feelings towards this man, having deprived them of something so important to them that thereafter, at the mere mention of his name, they would curse him as though he were the wickedest of men.

The Torah itself kept the Nation of Israel attuned to music.[22] Not only was the tribe of Levi involved in the art of song, but the entire nation of Israel knew and practiced music. In the times of the Temple, when an individual would be called to the Torah (an "aliyah"), he himself would be the one to read the Torah, with all its musical notes.[23] Everyone was imbued with a musical sense and sensitivity.

The articulation of the written Torah can be divided into two subdivisions, the first being the actual letters, which make up the words of the Torah, and the second being the accentuation, which accompanies the letters and when read, forms the tune of the Torah.[24] Kabbalah sees these two aspects as distinct forms of Divine expression. Let us understand this in the human realm. If one wishes to transmit a rational thought, words would be used to communicate that which one is explaining. However, when the thought that one wishes to share is something beyond the rational, a profound expression of love, for example, the most direct communication is through song. Understanding this in the human realm brings us to an understanding of the Divine realm. When the Torah is read, the expression of Divinity coming through the *melody* of the reading is in fact higher than that of the actual *letters* of the holy Torah.[25]

Until seventy years before the destruction of the second Temple music was an integral part of the Jewish experience. This was the time that the main Jewish court of law was shattered, thus the sages of the Talmud decreed that all music halls should cease to play music.[26] When the final destruction actually occurred in the year 70 C.E., the sages ruled that henceforth no music would be played.[27]

Music did continue, although only for the purpose of a mitzvah, for example, music played at a wedding, or music used in the service of God was permissible.[28] Throughout the ages there were composers of song for the service of God. Many of these compositions were in fact integrated into the prayer books,[29] and are now known as *piyutim*–hymns or poems.[30] Throughout history many of the great Rabbis composed *piyutim*. In the Ashkenaz community, for example, the famed Rabbi of Prague, Rabbi Yehuda Loew (1512–1609), and in the Sefardic communities, Rabbi Yisrael of Norghe[31] (1555–?), were both composers of *piyutim*. Rabbi Yisrael had a group of musicians, assisting him to compose *piyutim*. Rabbi Yitzchak Luria (1534–1572), the great kabbalist of Safed, stressed the importance of greeting the Sabbath Queen with music and song. Thus, from the beginning of the seventeenth century, a custom was established, that of greeting the Sabbath with songs and hymns. In numerous communities, the organ and other instruments were used in the Friday evening services, up until the setting of the sun and the arrival of the Sabbath.

The year 1698 marked the birth of Rabbi Yisrael, the Baal Shem Tov, who began a revolution in Jewish music. The Baal Shem Tov, gave new life, meaning, and significance to song, taking music back to where it began, as a means of serving God in a joyful, and uplifting manner. The lifeblood of the mystical experience that flows through the souls of the *Chassidim* is the teachings of the Baal Shem Tov and the great masters of Mysticism. The mystical experience of music together with other mystical traditions, has for the past few hundred years kept the spirit and vitality of *Chassidim* intact. When one wishes to understand the mystical nature of music, one must turn to the great Chassidic masters, for it is there that the secret of music is preserved.

But first let us delve a bit into the anatomy of music and try, if such a thing is possible, to classify it. Generally we maintain that there are two distinct forms of music; these could be termed Western music and Non-Western music, music of the Far East, Africa, and so on. Western music is generally "goal-oriented" or at least narrative in structure, which is to say that it consists of a series of events that build the listener's expectations. The listener feels that the music is progressing, and he feels the need to sense "where" the music is going. The music is "telling" the listener to move, to go on and progress. Non-Western music, on the other hand, is characterized by the prolongation of one pattern throughout the entire melody, which evokes and arouses a contemplative state in the listener, a sense of timelessness and inner space.

The music of *Chassidim* is diverse in style, it is both "goal-oriented," taking the listener to a specific "destination," and at the same time directed inwards, connecting the listener to his inner being.

In addition, there are no set formulas in Chassidic song. There are no rules, Chassidic song aspires to "set free" the melody from its dogmatic principles; thus, at times, a single note will suffice to express the feelings of the composer, and at times, several movements are needed.

Music has incredible power. It can lead one to rebellion or bring him to remorse, bring tears of joy, or tears of abject sorrow. One melody will awaken its listener, while another will soothe him to sleep. Songs will rouse hate, and songs will arouse love. Every human emotion has its song.[32] *Chassidim* have mastered the art of music in every human situation. Every occasion has its song and every song has its moment.

I do not presume to "explain" or define a song, a pure note, an uplifting musical movement, not even that "simple" thing we call "music."

What distinguishes music from noise is indefinable, and completely individual, unique to each living being, and is truly subjective. While beating with a systematic rhythm on pots and pans is called music in Africa, the Western-minded person may simply call it cacophony. Each civilization, each culture, and even each generation, has its own distinct ways of expressing and defining the idea of music.

Some have called music noise with a rhythm. Listening to my old heater banging away in perfect time compels me to vehemently disagree. But what of harmony, they ask; surely harmony is what defines music. Yet what sounds harmonious to me may be profoundly disturbing to another, and not musical in the least. And thus, I do not seek to make logical that which is above rational. I attempt only to delve deeply into the human reaction to music and the song's profound spiritual effect which resounds deep within all our souls.[33]

The mystics discovered the rainbow of emotions and human possibilities found within a song. On our journey through a mystical song, perhaps we too will find that there is something deep in our soul, long dormant, awaiting that solitary musical note with the power to bring it to life.

NOTES

1. Genesis 4:20–21. See Rabbi David Nitu (1654–1728), *The Second Kuzari*. (Jerusalem: Kamah, 1975), part 4, chapter 249, p. 91.

2. Goethe, quoted in Rudolf Otto, *The Idea of the Holy* (Oxford University Press, 1950), 150–151.

3. Abraham Z. Idelsohn, *Jewish Music in Its Historical Development* (New York: Dover Publication, 1992), chapter 1. Rabbi Yoseph Albo (1380–1435) *Safer Haikkarim* Maamor 3, chapter 8. See also Rabbi Shem Tov Ben Yoseph Ibn Falaquera (1225–1290), *Safer Hamevakesh*. (This text was once printed with the endorsement of the Chida. Rabbi Chayim Yoseph David Azulay.) (Reprinted Jerusalem: Mekorot 1970), p. 86. Midrash Rabbah Lamentations. Introduction 1.

4. Rudolf Otto, *The Idea of the Holy* (Oxford University Press, 1950), 150–151. "Religious worship cannot therefore do without music."

5. Talmud. *Sotah* 30b. *Tosefta*. *Sotah* 6: 2. Jerusalem Talmud. *Sotah*, chapter 5, Halacha 4. For the different opinions of how they sang the *Shirahs Hayam*, if Moshe sang and they all answered; or they sang all together, and so on. In the Jerusalem Talmud. Ibid. The smallest of the Israelites sang with the same inspiration as Moshe.

6. Exodus 15:1–21.

7. One finds, that many times in the Torah, when catastrophe was averted, and salvation appeared, thanks was expressed through song. See, *e.g.*, Exodus 15:1–21, Numbers 21:17, Judges 5, and Psalms 18.

8. The practice of singing in the Temple by the tribe of Levi is a law derived from the Torah. See Talmud. *Erchin* 11a. *Midrash Rabbah Numbers*. Parshah 6. Chapter 10. See also Rabbi Moshe Ben Maimon, *Rambam*. (1135–1204) Hilchot Klei Hamikdash. Chapter 3. Halacha 2.

9. Rambam *The Guide to the Perplexed* Part 2:32. (Jerusalem: Mossad Harav Kook, 1977)

10. 2 Kings 3:15.

11. *Rambam*, Yesodei Hatorah. Chapter 7. Halachah 4. See also Rabbi Yitzchak Aramah. (1420–1494) *Akeidot Yitzchak*. Parshat Shemot. Chapter 35.

12. See *Sefer Hamaspik Leovedei Hashem*. Erech "Hisbodedut". (Jerusalem: Sifrei Rabbanei Bavell, 1984)

13. In addition, when one is in isolation, which is an important ingredient to reach prophesy, one usually sings. Rabbi Moshe Yichiel Elimelech of Levertov, (1895–1941) *Safer Shemirat Hada'at*. Aimrei Tal. Ma'amar Nigun (Bnei Brak Israel: Ginzei MaHaritz, 1986) p. 24.

14. Talmud. *Shabbat*, 30b.

15. *Rambam*. *Yesodei Hatorah*. Chapter 7. Halacha 4. Rabbeinu Bachya. (1263–1340) *Exodus*. Chapter 18. Verse 12. Rabbi Shimon Ben Tzemach Duran. (1361–1444) *Magen Avot*. (Jerusalem: Makor Publishing.) Part 2. Chapter 2, p. 15b. Rabbi Moshe Corodovero. (1522–1570) *Shiur Komah*. (Jerusalem: 1966) Nevuah, p. 60. Rabbi Yakov Emdin. (1697–1776.) *Migdal Oz*. (Israel: Eshkol, 1978) *Even Bochen*, p. 66. Rabbi Avraham Ben HaRambam. *Sefer Hamaspik Leovedei Hashem*. Erech Ha'Prishut. Rabbi Chayim Vital (1543–1620) *Sharei Kedusha*. Part 2. Shar 4. Rabbi Yisrael of Modzitz. (1848–1920) *Divrei Yisrael*. Parshat Mikketz. Maamor Echad M'Remazei Chanukah. Rabbi Meir Ben Gabbai writes, that there were prophets who were perpetually in a prophetic state, while other prophets needed the aid of music to create the appropriate mood. *Avodot Hakodesh*. Cheilek Sitrei Torah. Chapter 23. Rabbi Yonathan Eibechuvetz explains, that when the prophet was joyous there was no need for music. Music was only used to create a joyous atmosphere. See *Tifferet Yonathan*. Parshat Beshalach. Chapter 15. Verse 20.

16. *Zohar*, Part 3: 223b. Rabbi Meir Ben Gabbai (1480–1547), *Avodot Hakodesh*, Cheilek HaTakhlit Chapter 10. Rabbi Nachman of Breslov (1772–1811) *Likutei Moharan*. Part 1. Chapter 3. See also by Reb Nachman: *Likutei Aytzot*. Neginah 3, p. 137.

17. See: *Samuel 1*. Chapter 16.

18. See the commentary by Rabbi Dan Yitzchak *Abarbenal*. (1437–1508)

19. Rabbi Nachman of Breslov. *Likutei Moharan*. Part 1. 54: 6.

20. The poet and philosopher Rabbi Yehudah Halevi (1075–1141) writes, "They—the Levites—did not have any other occupation, solely to play music in the Temple." *The Kuzari* Maamor 2. Chapter 64. See also Rabbi Shimon Ben Tzemach Duran. *Magen Avot*. (Jerusalem: Makor Publishing.) Part 3, p. 56a.

21. See Talmud, *Yuma*, 38a.

22. The Torah itself is called a *Shirah*—song. See *Deuteronomy*. 31:19. There it says that it is a mitzvah to write "The *Shirah*." Although it refers to only one specific part of the Torah, nonetheless, it is from this verse that we know that it is a mitzvah to write the entire Torah. (Talmud *Sanhedrin*. 21b. Rambam. Hilchot Safer Torah. Chapter 7. Halacha 1.) Furthermore, some suggest that since it is not permitted to write one part of the Torah alone, thus the mitzvah of writing The Shirah essentially includes the entire Torah. See *Shagas Aryei*. Chapter 34. *Maharatz Chayot*, on *Nedarim*. 38a. See also *Maharsah*. (Moreinu Harav Shemuel Eliezer Eidels. 1555–1631) On *Nedarim* 38a. *Shenemar*. [See *Psalms*. Chapter 119. Verse 54, in which the Psalmist describes the entire Torah as being a song. Rabbi Eliyohu Ben Moshe Di Vidas. (sixteenth Safad) *Reshit Chochmah*. Shar HaAhavah. Chapter 10. He writes that indeed the entire Torah

is a *Shirah* (song), for it brings happiness to the learner.] Rabbi Moshe Corodovero. *Shiur Komah.* (Jerusalem: 1966) Torah. Chapter 40, p. 45.

23. Rabbi David Ben Yoseph *Avudraham.* (1420–1494) (Jerusalem: 1963) Laws regarding the reading of the Torah, pp. 130–131.

24. The tunes of the Torah are an integral part of Torah; they date back to when the Torah was given. See Talmud. *Nedarim.* 37b. See also Talmud. *Megillah* 3a. *Chagigah* 6a.

25. Rabbi Moshe Cordovero. (1522–1570) *Pardas Rimonim.* Shar 29: Chapter 5. The sixth Chabad Rebbe, Rabbi Yoseph Yitzchak. (1880–1950) *Safer Hamaamorim 5502* (1942) (New York: Kehot Publication Society. 1964), p. 43.

26. See Talmud end of *Sotah.* Midrash Rabbah. Lamentations. Parsha 5:15.

27. Talmud. *Gittin,* 7a.

28. Talmud. *Gittin.* Page 7a. *Tosefot* Titled *Zimmrah.* Talmud *Berachot.* The commentary by the *Rif* Chapter 5. In the beginning. *Rash Berachot* Chapter 5: 1. *Rambam Hilchot Tannit* Chapter 5. Halacah 14. And *Magid Mishnah* (on the Rambam Ad loc.) in the name of the Gaonim. *Shulchan Aruch Orach Chayim.* Chapter 560: 3.

29. There was a great debate over whether or not these piyutim are permitted to be said in the middle of prayers, especially in the middle of the 18 benedictions. See *Beit Yoseph. Shulchan Aruch. Orach Chayim.* Chapter 68 and Chapter 112. *Tur Shulchan Aruch, Orach Chayim.* Chapter 68. See also *Pri Chadash. Orach Chayim.* Chapter 112. Most Halachic opinions permit saying these *Piyutim* even in the middle of prayer. See *Rama Shulchan Aruch. Orach Chayim.* Chapter 68 and Chapter 112. The *Beit Chadash.* Chapter 68. Brings numerous sources dating back to the period of the Gaonim that permit it. See also Talmud *Berachot.* 34a. *Tosefot.* Titled *Al Yishal Rosh Berachot* Chapter 5: 21. *Radvas* in response. Part 3: 532 and 645. Rabbi Yakov of Merve'ge. *Respanso from Heaven.* (Jerusalem: Mossad Harav Kook. 1957), Chapter 58. See also *Safer Chassidim.* Chapters 114 and 607.

30. Perhaps the word *piyutim* originates from the Greek word for poetry. Another name for these hymns is *Keruvetz,* which in Hebrew is an acronym of the verse, "the sound of happiness and salvation in the tents of the righteous." (*Psalms.* Chapter 118. Verse 15.) see *Tur Shulchan Aruch. Orach Chayim. Beit Yoseph.* Chapter 68. *Rama* (Chapter 112. The Rambam opposed *piyutim* because he felt that they were superfluous. See *The Guide to the Perplexed* Part 1 Chapter 59. Nonetheless, he never actually omitted them from the prayer books, in order not to embarrass the composers.

31. Rabbi Chayim Yoseph David Azulay. (1729–1806.) *Shem Hagdalim Marrechess Siforim, Errech. Zimirass Yisrael.* Chapter 27. He writes in the name of the holy Ari Zal, who testified that the songs of Rabbi Yisrael of Norghe are cherished in the worlds above. In the year 1587 Rabbi Yisrael of Norghe published his work titled *Zimiras Yisrael.* A collection of poetic compositions set to well know Arabic and Turkish tunes.

32. Music is used to awake. (See *Rambam, Hilchot Teshuvah.* Chapter 3. Halacha 4. See also Rabbi David ben Yoseph *Avudraham.* Ta'amei HaTekihot. (In the name of Rabbi Saadiah Gaon.) Reason 7.) And music is used to put asleep. (See Talmud. *Eruvin.* 104a. *Shulchan Aruch Orach Chayim.* Chapter 338. *Magen Avraham.*) Music is played at weddings. (See *Radak. Psalms.* Chapter 78. Verse 63.) And music is played at funerals. (See Talmud. *Ketubot.* 46b.) Music is used to cause happiness, and to bring a

person to tears. (Rabbi Yisrael of Modzitz. *Divriei Yisrael*. Parshat Mikketz. Maamor Echad M'Remazei Rosh Hashanah.) Music is played in war. (*Numbers*. Parshat Behaalotecha. Chapter 10. Verse 9. *Deuteronomy*. Chapter 20. Verse 3. *Rashi. Al Yirah*. Talmud *Sotah*. 42a. *Joshua*. Chapter 6.) And music is played in victory. (*Samuel 1*. Chapter 18. Verse 6. *Kings. 1*. Chapter 5. *Psalms*, Chapter 18.) Music is played at momentous moments. (*Genesis*. Parshat Va'yetze. Chapter 31. Verse 27.) And music is played at mundane moments. (See *Jeremiah*. Chapter 48. Verse 33. Talmud *Sotah* 48a.) In sum, music is played at every occasion in the cycle of life.

33. For the mystics, the reason that a person is so moved by music is that music is what the soul is accustomed to hearing before its descent below; music is the language of the upper worlds. Rabbi Meir Ben Gabbai, *Avodot Hakodesh*, Cheilek HaTakhlit Chapter 10. In the name of *Levinat Hasapir*, Parshat Noach. Rabbi Shlomo Alkabatz (1505–1584.) *Manot HaLevi* The Hakdamah. P 36. (Reprinted in Kal Sifrei Rabbi Yoseph Yavetz. Book 2. (Israel: 1990.) Likutim. P 33.) Rabbi Yisrael of Modzitz. *Divrei Yisrael*. Parshat Mikketz. Maamor Echad M'Remazei Chanukah. Rabbi Moshe Yichiel Elimelech of Levertov. *Safer Shemirat Hada'at*. Aimrei Tal. Ma'amar Nigun, (Bnei Brak Israel: Ginzei MaHaritz. 1986.) p. 5. See also *Zohar*. Parshat Vayakel; p. 195b.

2
The Source of Chassidic Melody

"Speech is the Pen of the Heart,[1]
Song is the Pen of the Soul."[2]

"What is a Jew? What defines the Jewish spirit?" The *Tzemach Tzedek*[3] was but a young boy when he asked this profound question of his grandfather, Rabbi Schneur Zalman. Lovingly, the Rebbe answered: "A Jew is a human being in touch with his inner essence and possessed of the ability to unveil it, and bring it forth. How does one connect with one's inner self, one's highest levels of soul, above all, wisdom and comprehension, and then reveal it in a mundane, finite world? This can be accomplished through song."[4]

"AFTER SILENCE, THAT WHICH COMES NEAREST TO EXPRESSING THE INEXPRESSIBLE IS MUSIC."[5]

Sharing an intense, deeply felt emotion with another person, expressing one's innermost feelings, thoughts or desires—these are best done through a song. Words, rather than clarifying the communication, tend to conceal and block the exchange of deep emotion. In the Kabbalah it is explained that words, though they are designed to reveal,[6] are actually a concealment.[7] "Words were invented to hide men's thoughts." To understand this it is necessary to understand that there are different levels of comprehension. Generally, Kabbalah divides them into three parts: *Chochmah*–wisdom, *Binah*–understanding, and *Da'ats*–knowledge. For our immediate purposes, only the first two will be considered. *Chochmah*–wisdom is the initial flash of insight, the intuition of an understanding, a pure, unstructured idea, unlimited by logic or rationale. The idea may not even be completely understood by the one who has thought of it. It is accompanied by a rush of excitement; it overwhelms the one who contains it.[8] *Binah*–understanding is the formulation and communication of this germ of an idea, expanding it to the point where it is understood by the originator of the thought and the one to whom the thought is being communicated. When the thought, or idea, is in the form of *Chochmah*, it has infinite possibility, the thought exists without constrictions or restraints. In order to formulate the thought and communicate it to others, one must put it into words, at first these words are only in the person's mind, and are not actually verbalized (speech within thought), and then words are formed which are actually spoken and which communicate the thought to other people. These words bring down the thought to a state of rational logic, a confined and restricted place, where the idea must be thought through and be contained within mere words. Thus, words actually conceal the essence of the thought while revealing its externality.[9]

When we find ourselves with a pure thought, a deeply felt emotion, and no words which will communicate it without dilution of the original feeling, we sing. A wordless melody from the soul,[10] with the notes becoming a channel from the essence of my soul, to the essence of yours.[11]

Music is a rational element of our feeling, which is penetrated by the irrational.[12] Music has the unique ability to be apprehended by one's rational mind yet at the same time, communicate something which is above logic and human understanding.[13]

Within the extensive repertoire of Chassidic melodies, *Nigunim*, there are various levels, or degrees of holiness. There is a *Nigun Mimula*, a *Nigun Shoteh*, and a *Nigun Michuvan*, the last of which we will explain now. The first two will be explained shortly. A *Nigun Mechuvan* is a melody that the spiritual leader of a Chassidic community, known as the Rebbe, composed himself, or one that was taught by him. As explained above, a melody brings forth the essence of what is within one's soul, and thus the nigun composed by the Rebbe would be a direct expression of the innermost reaches of his elevated soul. Among the early masters of the Chassidic movement, there were many great composers of song. Rabbi Aharon of Karlin, Reb Michal of Zlotchov, Reb Levi Yitzchak of Berdichov, Reb Nachman of Breslov, Reb Schneur Zalman of Liadi and many other Chassidic Rebbes composed truly transcendent compositions. These melodies are the highest forms of Chassidic song, the loftiest expressions of spirituality in a Chassidic group, for they are from the essence of the Rebbe himself.

"Song is the pen of the soul," an expression of the inner depths of the composer's heart and soul. To truly understand the music, one must study the composer himself, his personal life, and his teachings. If one desires true comprehension of a *nigun*, one must study its composer, the Rebbe, his philosophy, his *chassidus*, his virtue. Only then is it possible to have a full appreciation of his composition.

In this light, let us look at the relationship between the Chassidic Rebbe and his followers.

The relationship between a Chassid and the Rebbe is a complex one, involving many different emotions and degrees of connection. These can be expressed in three ways: through actions, speech, and thought.[14] The connection based on action would be considered the most external of the three. This connection consists of the Chassid emulating the Rebbe's ways, doing what the Rebbe would desire of him, and therefore connecting to the Rebbe through actions, namely, the external level of physical action. A somewhat deeper and more profound bond, although still not the most intense, would be one based on speech.[15] The Rebbe would give a Chassidic discourse, and when the Chassid would study it, he would become connected to the Rebbe's speech, which is on a more spiritual and internal, level than that of action. Then there is the most intense, internal, and lofty level of bond between a Chassid and his Rebbe. This is one established upon thought. It is a connection in which one is in sync with the Rebbe's thoughts, to the point at which one has formed a relationship stemming from the Rebbe's innermost thoughts and feelings, so deep that it can actually reach the almost unattainable level of soul called *"yichidah,"* the level of soul which is one with the Oneness of God, a level so intensely concentrated that it could never be expressed in action or even in words. And how does one achieve this spectacular connection? Through the singing of a *nigun* which the Rebbe himself had composed.[16]

Chassidim cherish these *nigunim* above all others, viewing them as the direct route to the Rebbe's essence. In the Talmud it is written, "A disciple should express himself in the same vernacular as his teacher."[17] This statement is interpreted to mean that a student should repeat his teacher's wisdom and teachings in the same style as his teacher, and the interpretation extends not only to his teachings and text, but to his musical compositions as well. The student should sing his teacher's tunes in the same manner and style in which he had observed his teacher singing. In this way the student becomes attached to the teacher in the most intense and internal way.[18]

In addition to the *Nigun Mechuvan*, there is also the *Nigun Mimula* and the *Nigun Shoteh*. The *Nigun Mimula* is defined as a full melody. This is a melody which is composed by the Chassid himself. It is usually composed and sung during a service of God, in prayers and the like.[19] The Chassid becomes so overwhelmed by the melody that it fills him completely; hence the term, full melody. The greatness of the Chassid and the degree of spiritual consciousness he expresses while composing the *nigun*, affect the content of the *nigun* and the spirituality of the tune. There were many great *Chassidim* who never became Rebbes, but whose tunes are much revered by the other *Chassidim*. The *Nigun Shoteh*, the foolish *nigun*, is as it sounds, a *nigun* with no positive nor negative content and has no meaning, serving no purpose.[20]

"EVERYTHING IN EXISTENCE WAS CREATED WITH TWO OPPOSING FORCES."[21]

Every existence is two dimensional, it contains a holy side and an unholy side. This is true of all creations including those of music. Just as music can be composed and sung by holy people for holy intentions, music can also be composed by unholy, unGodly people, who while putting their essence into the composition are actually imbuing it with the lowest levels of their animalistic, selfish souls. And just as a holy melody has the power to connect the listener with the essence of the composer, so too the 'unholy' song has the power to draw its listener down with its lowly essence.

There is a story told of a great Chassidic master. When a devotee once begged to sing a song for the Rebbe, the Rebbe acquiesced, only to rebuke him at the end of the song. In anguish the Rebbe asked of him, "Why did you force me to lower myself to the level of Gehenom?" The Rebbe felt in the tune that the composer was on a low spiritual plane, certainly lower than that of the Rebbe himself, and therefore the Rebbe felt anguish at having been lowered to the level of the composer's essence.[22]

The Talmudic sage, Rav, speaks in very strong language of the negative influence of impure music, that is, music composed through unholy sources.[23] Music is a powerful and ultra-sensitive device which can have tremendous consequences both in a positive and negative sense.[24]

There was once a Torah sage in Talmudic times,[25] who after many years of righteousness, abandoned the ways of the Torah and became an apostate. The Talmud explains that this drastic transformation was caused by profane music.[26] This Torah sage would listen to music composed by non-believers, who had put their heart and soul, their beliefs and convictions into their music. By listening to this music, an upstanding, learned, and holy man was transmogrified into an apostate. The music reached the depths of his soul and steered him astray.[27] It is precisely because music is the most refined and delicate of all physical expressions,[28] that its capacity to carry us to extremes is so potent. Music can open up a person to the greatest spiritual heights, yet it can also lure to the lowest abyss.[29]

The soul of a departed man once appeared before the holy Rebbe of Rapshitz, Rabbi Naphtali Tzvi Horowitz (1760–1826), on the night of Simchas Torah. Tearfully, the soul pleaded with the Rebbe to elevate his debased soul. The man to whom this soul had belonged had passed on many years before, and due to a life of debauchery and sin, his soul was unable to gain admittance to the Garden of Eden, the ultimate paradise for the soul. The Rebbe considered the request, and questioned the soul regarding its life on this earth. However, no matter how deeply the soul searched into its human life, it could not find even one good deed that it had done to merit entrance into paradise. The Rebbe continued to question him and soon discovered that during his stay in this world, the man had been a musician and composer. Simchat Torah arrived and the Rebbe appeared before his *Chassidim* and taught them a new melody. That joyous night of Simchat Torah, the song was sung again and again in complete purity, with all the sincerity of a Chassid serving His Creator. As the sun rose on the new day, the soul joyfully entered the gates of Gan Eden, purified by the very tune he had composed.

The source of a Chassidic melody stems from the essence of its composer. However, the method of transformation from composition to melody to *nigun* is quite varied and takes on many, many forms. There are melodies which are composed over long periods of time, well-planned and formulated, and there are the spontaneous melodies, bursting forth from their creator in a moment of inspiration. There are melodies which are adapted from one's surroundings or adopted from a tune heard and desired.[30] There are *nigunim* that were bought and *nigunim* that were "stolen." Chassidic lore is rich with tales of the birth of a *nigun*, in addition to a great wealth of tunes. And though many Chassidic songs originate from cultures other than their own, once a song was adapted, it gained its own distinct elements, and became a "Chassidic song" with its unique and distinguishable Chassidic nature.

Let us join a Chassidic *farbrengen* and listen in as these tales are told.

Rabbi Moshe Teitelbaum tells of the experience of listening to the holy Rebbe, Reb Shemelkah of Nikulshburg, lead the prayers. He tells of the spontaneous tunes that would spring forth from the holy man's lips, emanating from an unknown source, accompanying his every prayer.[31]

The holy master of Kotzk, Rabbi Mendel (1787–1859), shared a commentary on a famous midrash.[32] The midrash relates[33] that at the time of the Jews' exodus from Egypt, the angels clamored before God in excitement, pleading to be allowed to sing praise to God for this wondrous thing He had done. God did not allow them to sing, however, stating that the Jews must be allowed to sing first, and only then would the angels be permitted to praise God. The Rebbe's explanation of this midrash is based on the essential differences between man and angel. The angel is in a perpetual state of inspiration and holiness, while man is only occasionally inspired and brought to a spiritual high. When a person is inspired and desires to sing, he must utilize the moment, lest the moment pass and the inspiration fade, the song will disappear and never be heard. As the Jews left their exile, they were in a state of great spiritual inspiration and God understood that their song needed expression at that very moment.

Many *nigunim* adapted by *Chassidim*, originated from various cultures and occasionally from the surrounding environment. The early *Chassidim* generally lived in small villages, where the surroundings consisted of farming villages and fields dotted with sheep and those who tended them. The shepherd's task was a lonesome one, lying in the fields, gazing at the sky and scenery, and singing. The shepherd's songs were often quite haunting, emotional, and full of longing. Many Chassidic Rebbes found *nigunim* in these shepherd's melodies.[34]

The Chassidic Rebbe, Rabbi Layb Sares,[35] once heard from the heavenly tribunal above, that in a distant town there lived a young lad with a lofty and holy soul. The Rebbe was intrigued and decided to make the journey to find this child. After much difficulty and effort, he arrived in the town. Immediately he went to the schoolhouse, certain that he would find the lad deep in Torah study; however, the lad was nowhere to be found. Questioning the villagers, he discovered that the boy was a shepherd and at that moment was in the fields tending his flock. The Rebbe hurried to the fields and there he saw a young shepherd. He approached the boy and asked gently, "Who are you?" The boy replied, "I am a Jew and my name is Yitzchak." "And what do you do the entire day while tending your sheep, my boy?" "I sing songs," answered the young shepherd. Thereupon the Rebbe requested that the lad sing him a melody. The young shepherd started singing a common love song much to the Rebbe's surprise, and these were the words of the song, "Forest, O Forest, how vast you are, Rose, O Rose, how distant you are, God in heavens, why have you done this, who can help me, and make the forest small, so that I may be close to my rose . . ." Abruptly the boy switched into his own version of the song, singing, "*Galus Galus Ve Grous Bist Tu.* (Exile, O Exile, how vast you are) *Shechinah Shechinah, Ve Voit Bist Tu.* (God, O God, how far you are . . .)" Upon hearing the great longing and yearning for God coming from deep within this child's soul, the Rebbe realized that indeed this was the very boy of whom the heavens had spoken. He took the lad under his wing, raising him to eventually become the famed and saintly Rebbe of Khaliv, renowned in Chassidic lore for his beautiful and haunting melodies. Years later, as Rebbe, it was his wont to return to the fields and listen to the shepherds' love songs, which he would then transform into *nigunim* of love between man and God.

The first Chabad Rebbe, upon hearing the marching anthem of Napoleon's armies in the year 1812, proclaimed the march a song of victory.[36] From that time on, Napoleon's march became a Chassidic *nigun*, representing the victory of mind over body, spirituality over materialism, the mastery for which every Chassid strives. Today, in Chabad communities around the world, following the final prayer of Yom Kippur, the people sing this song of victory, knowing with complete certainty that they emerged triumphant from their time of judgment, and can be confident of a happy and healthy new year.

Simchat Torah, 1973. A large delegation of French Jews had arrived in New York to spend the high holy days with the Lubavitcher Rebbe. While they were dancing before the Rebbe, the Rebbe unexpectedly began to sing the French national anthem, "La Marseillaise," with the words of prayer that speak of God's glory and tell that all the glory that exists in this world is only for God.[37]

During a Chassidic gathering, a *farbrengen*, many years later, the Rebbe referred to that famous Simchat Torah in which he had sung the French anthem and explained the meaning behind his action.[38] The Rebbe began to delve into the deeper meanings and symbolisms of "La Marseillaise." He explained that the French anthem represents and is the symbol of the French revolution, a revolution of freedom and enlightenment.[39] However, in a negative sense, it also represents freedom *from* religion. It is historically documented that since the era of the French enlightenment, man's perspective of religion has been altered drastically.[40] The Rebbe continued, "In France, this very day, there is a national debate over the anthem, with the vast majority in favor of discontinuing the old anthem and composing a new one. On the surface this seems like a natural progression in a country, but there is an inner, spiritual reason for what is happening in France. When "La Marseillaise" was sung by *Chassidim* with the holy intent of serving God, the tune was transformed to holiness. The anthem that once stood for freedom *from* religion, now symbolizes freedom *of* religion, freedom to practice one's beliefs. Therefore the tune can no longer represent the French enlightenment."[41] Essentially, the Rebbe transformed the anthem from a song of personal glory to a *nigun* which speaks of the glory of God.

This concept of transforming the secular anthem of a nation to holiness is actually much more than a mere metamorphosis of the song itself. Rather, it causes a transformation of the entire nation to which the anthem belongs. In mystical thought it is explained[42] that everything in this world, whether man or beast, has a tune which it sings, a personal melody which arouses its emotions, and inspires it. There are those to whom the tune is a tune of happiness, and there are those that are particularly affected by sorrowful melodies. This is not just found within individual persons; indeed, entire nations share a common tune to which they look for inspiration. Nations as a whole have a personality, and that is reflected in the tunes which they most enjoy and appreciate. The reason that an entire nation of individuals is possessed of a certain defining personality is that they are formed in a way that is beyond simple happenstance. A nation outwardly appears to be a chance meeting between random individuals, who migrated to the same regions at a particular time in history. It goes much deeper than that. Among all these individuals is a shared soul, an energy. In kabbalistic terms it is referred to as a collective soul, which is like a general consciousness that bonds these individuals into a nation. This inner connection between individuals is what draws them to each other and ultimately to form a nation. We find that this spiritual connection also manifests itself in the physical. Nations generally tend to share common goals, values, and ideals. The national anthem of a people translates the epitome of their inner spirit into a composition of music, expressing their personality and essence.[43] Thus, the transformation of the national anthem from an unholy tune to a Godly melody altered the spirit of the nation to whom the tune belonged.

Our forefather Jacob, at a time of famine in the land of Israel, sent his children to Egypt with the following command: "This is what you are to do; take from the best of the land as a present to the king."[44] The word "best" is a loose translation of the Hebrew word, *Mezimras*. The literal translation would be "melody."[45] If the command is translated in this way, then it takes on a new meaning. What Jacob was actually telling his sons was that when they arrived in the land of Egypt, they should sing the tune of the holy land, and that perhaps the holiness of the melody would penetrate the profanity of the Egyptian culture, and soften their selfish hearts so that they would give them the food they were so in need of.[46]

It is a precarious and risky undertaking when one wishes to transform a melody to the holy, especially when the source of the tune is rooted in unholiness; such a responsibility can not be undertaken by just anyone. It takes a master, one who understands music, and possesses spiritual acumen, to initiate this transformation. Rabbi Yehudah Ha-Chassid (1150–1217) said[47] that melodies which were once used or composed by unholy sources, shall not be transformed into holy songs. Furthermore, even tunes which are not necessarily profane, simply secular music, he decreed should not be utilized for Divine service.[48] The Lubavitcher Rebbe received a request from a Jewish composer who wished to transform the words of a rock and roll tune to words of holiness. The Rebbe strongly discouraged him, asking him, "Ultimately, who will truly influence whom? Will the melody be influenced by you or will you be influenced by it?"[49]

It is not to say that this metamorphosis can not be done, only that in order for it to be done, one must be on an elevated spiritual plane, and in addition have a good understanding of music and its delicate nature.

The Kabbalah teaches that within every existence there dwells a soul, a spark of God. The task of man is to locate that spark and elevate it to its original source. This is referred to as *Sh'chinta B'Galutah*, a Divine spark in exile. Such is the case with certain melodies originating from a very lofty source; they descend into exile until they are located and redeemed, and restored to their previous holy state.

A Chassidic Rebbe on one of his frequent excursions into the open meadows came upon a shepherd singing a spellbinding melody. The Rebbe, intensely affected and inspired by the tune, immediately convinced the shepherd to sell him the song. As soon as the Rebbe purchased the tune, the melody left the shepherd's mind and he never remembered it again. The Rebbe then taught the song to his *Chassidim*, explaining his reaction to the tune this way: "This tune of the shepherd was a tune which originally was sung in the holy Temple. For thousands of years the tune has been in exile. Today it is redeemed from its exile, and from now on we will utilize the song solely for the service of the Creator."

There is a similar tale told of a *Chazan*, a cantor.[50] This *Chazan* was the personal cantor for the Rebbe of Tzans, Rabbi Chaim. His custom was that each week he would compose a new tune for the upcoming Shabbat. It once happened that he had not had the time to compose a new melody. Friday arrived and still no tune came to his mind. He decided to take a stroll, thinking that perhaps a tune would come to him while his mind was clear. As he strolled, he grew more and more frustrated as no tune materialized. While he was passing an Austrian military base a beautiful marching tune was being played by the band. Unable to think of his own composition, he decided to use this tune for the Shabbat prayer, which is exactly what he did. After Shabbat ended, he started to feel dishonest about what he had done, and feeling guilty, he decided to confess to the Rebbe. He entered the Rebbe's room, trembling with fear, barely able to speak, because he felt so bad for fooling his Rebbe. Before he was able to say a word, the Rebbe motioned for him to be silent and told him the following story. "Thousands of years ago, in the time of the Holy Temple, there was a sinner who entered the Temple for the purpose of giving a sacrifice. The singers of the Temple, seeing this man, and wishing to change him for the good, began to sing a mournful song to soften his heart.[51] The song so touched the man that it caused him to repent and mend his ways. The Levites, singers of the Temple, rejoiced in his change of heart and transformed the sorrowful tune into a joyful marching melody." The Rebbe looked directly at the *Chazan* and proclaimed, "This is the song which you sang this Shabbat."

Let us look back on these stories. We have heard tales of a *nigun* being born spontaneously, and a *nigun* composed in a moment of inspiration. There were *nigunim* bought and *nigunim* transformed and even a *nigun* redeemed from its exile. There is yet another source for Chassidic melodies: those which spring forth from the heavenly angels above.

This notion of singing angels is deeply ingrained in cultures around the world; it can be found in literature, music, and the arts cross culturally.[52] Let us examine this notion in the light of the kabbalistic view. According to the kabbalah, angels have a real existence, albeit a spiritual one. An angel is the energy, the vitality which is within all of creation.[53] Each heavenly angel is unique, with its own distinct character, spiritual level, and mission which distinguishes them from one another.[54]

In general, angels exist in the world of "Emotions." (This is the inner, "above" world of this physical world. Our world is defined by actions, while the higher world is defined by emotions. I will explain this further in the following chapters.) Therefore, the principal quality and essential character of an angel is defined by its emotions. Each angel has its own identity, its own unique quality, and mission that it must accomplish. Every angel serves as a conduit for the divine energy that flows into this universe. Generally, the manner in which angels serve God is through song; they continuously sing praises.[55] As we find in the morning prayers immediately preceding the *Sh'ma.* "In unison they answer in awe and declare with fear, 'Holy, Holy, Holy, is the Lord; the entire universe is filled with His glory.'" The concept of angels singing does not occur on a physical plane; rather, it exists in a spiritual sense, for the angels are spiritual beings existing on a spiritual level.[56]

"All animals enter and exit with song."[57] *Chassidut* explains that here the word animals refers to spiritual creatures, namely angels.[58] This translates to mean that through song, they both ascend to higher spiritual realms and descend to lower levels, the latter for the purpose of greater ascension in the future. Any ascent or descent they experience is through song. The rhythm and movement of song is the path angels travel on. This is the meaning of the Mishnah, "They (the angels) enter and exit through song."

How does the singing of the angels interact with our lives as humans? Is there a means of tapping into that spiritual energy created by their song and bringing it into our world? Being that the language of the angels is a spiritual one. Is it possible to express that which is inexpressible?

"A prophet is one who lives a life of complete holiness, his mind occupied solely with lofty ideas about God; physical reality plays but a minimal role in his existence. He elevates himself to a higher spiritual reality, then connects himself to the level of angels closest to our world."[59] When the prophet achieves this level, he can then communicate with the angels; furthermore, he can actually hear the spiritual melodies of the angels above.[60]

How does one share such an experience with one who is incapable of reaching such levels? How does one translate the unconventional? This is done through metaphor which relates to life and a level with which we are familiar. In the case of the angels, the metaphor is music. One Friday night, the holy Seer of Lublin[61] (?–1815) entered into a deep meditation. After some hours he emerged from his lofty state and began to sing a beautiful tune, uttering, "This is the tune I heard from the angels above." He had heard the tune the way it existed above, in its spiritual dimension, and as he vocalized the tune, he brought it down into a physical manifestation.

Legend has it that a famous song composed by the holy Rebbe, Rabbi of Koznitz Yisrael , (1733–1814), is a tune he heard from the lips of the angels. One of his disciples argued that it was actually the reverse, that the angels learned the tune from the Rebbe himself. Many years later, the son of that particular disciple retold this story and elaborated. "The angels my father referred to," he said, "are one's own angels, the spiritual extension of each person, that is, angels which man himself creates through his actions." The Kabbalah explains that there are two types of angels: angels that are created by God, and angels created by man. The latter is a direct manifestation of the physical deed of doing a mitzvah. Mitzvot are in fact two dimensional. One is grounded in physical action, and the other, being that it is a direct commandment of

God, has spiritual dimensions and causes an effect in the spiritual realms, creating angels. Man's good deeds create positive angels. The Mishnah states, "He who does a good deed receives an angel,"[62] and negativity breeds negative angels.

We say that song has the power to reveal the inner parts of the soul, to bring out one's innermost emotions. The illustrious son of Maimonides, Reb Avraham, writes[63] that the wise men of the world argue about whether sight or hearing is the sense best capable of affecting one's inner self.[64] Reb Avraham asserts that though sight seems more refined, hearing has greater power than seeing, for when a person hears music, his innermost feelings are aroused and they awaken him to serve his Creator. Music is indeed the key to the soul.[65]

We have come to conclude that music is a powerful tool capable of causing great inspiration. Inspiration is said to be like a candle having a brief life. The challenge is to use it to illuminate, to take the inspiration and internalize it. So now that we have heard the music and are uplifted and inspired, what follows? What is one to do in this awakened state, and how does one channel this arousal to realize the potential within?

In the following chapters, we will explore the possibilities of channeling the inspiration caused by a tune, and see where it could lead us, for each tune is a path with a purpose that each one of us experiences individually, and if traveled with heart the destination is sublime.

NOTES

1. Rabbi Bachya Ibn Pakudah. (1050–1120). *Chovot Halevavot*. Shar Habechinah. Chapter 5. See: *Psalms*. 45:2.

2. A saying by the first Chabad Rebbe, Rabbi Schneur Zalman of Liadi. (1745–1812) See; The sixth Chabad Rebbe. Rabbi Yoseph Yitzchak *Sefer Hasichot 5402* (1942) (New York: Kehot Publication Society. 1986), p. 122.

3. Rabbi Menacham Mendel. (1789–1866) The third Chabad Rebbe.

4. A talk by the sixth Chabad Rebbe. Rabbi Yoseph Yitzchak. On the twelfth of Tammuz 5506. (1946)

5. An expression once heard.

6. In the ancient Kabbalistic text mentioned in the Talmud. (*Sanhedrin*. 65b.) *Sefer Yetzirah*, it speaks about words as being the building blocks of creation. It is through words, utterances, that God creates the world. As it says in the Torah, "And God *said* 'let there be. . . . And there was'. . . ." See also: Rabbi Schneur Zalman of Liadi. *Tanya. Shar Hayichud VaEmunah*. Chapter 11. Rabbi Nachman of Breslov. *Likutei Moharan*. Part 1. Chapter 4: 9. Rabbi Avraham Azulay. (1570–1643.) *Chesed LeAvraham*. (Jerusalem: Yerid HaSefarim.) Part 2. Chapter 11. [It is worth noting that it is believed that the author of Sefer Yitzerah was the patriarch Abraham. See: Rabbi Yehudah HaLevy. *The Kuzari*. Maamor 4. Chapter 25. Rabbi Chasdai Cresces. (1340–1410) *Or Hashem*. Maamor 4. Derush 10. Rabbi Shimon Ben Tzemach Duran. *Magen Avot*. (Jerusalem: Makor Publishing.) In the Hakdamah, p. 1a. Although there are those who attribute it to the teachings of Rabbi Akiva. (12–132 C.E.) See: Rabbi Moshe Cordovero. *Pardas Rimonim*. Shaar 1. Chapter 1. In *Aiotzar Necmad*. On the Kuzari ibid. It is explained, that it is the writings of Rabbi Akiva, as transmitted from one generation to the next, until Abraham. Some argue that there are indeed two different books of Sefer Yetzirah. See: Rabbi Yitzchak De Latters. *Shalhelet HaKabbalah*. Erech Rabbi Akiva.]

7. Rabbi Menachem Mendel of Vitebsk. (?–1788) *Pri Ha'aretz*. (Jerusalem: HeMesorah. 1989.) Parshat Vayigash. Rabbi Schneur Zalman of Liadi. *Likutei Torah*. (New York: Kehot Publication Society. 1996) Parshat Acharei Mot, p. 28d. Rabbi Dovber. The second Chabad Rebbe. *Imrei Binah, (1)* (New York: Kehot Publication Society. 1975.) p. 10c.

8. It was told of the Talmudic sage, Rabbi Yehudah, that when he recognized a new thought in the Torah, his face would literally shine from happiness and excitement. Jerusalem Talmud. *Shabbat* Chapter 8. Halacha 1.

9. Rabbi Schneur Zalman of Liadi. *Likutei Torah*. (New York: Kehot Publication Society. 1996.) Parshat Acharei, p. 28c.

10. Since many Chassidic songs have no words, they are thus sung with vocalized syllables, for example, *bim bam, oy vey*. Different groups of *chassidim* have different syllables.

11. See: Rabbi Moshe Cordovero. *Pardas Rimonim*. Shar 23. Chapter 21, in which he writes that the source of Shir is Chochmah.

12. See: Rudolf Otto. *The Idea of the Holy* (Oxford University Press. 1950) p. 47–48.

13. The sixth Chabad Rebbe. Rabbi Yoseph Yitzchak. *Sefer Hamaamorim 5788* (1928), (New York: Kehot Publication Society. 1986), p. 91.

14. The sixth Chabad Rebbe. Rabbi Yoseph Yitzchak. *Likutei Diburim* vol. 1 (New York: Kehot Publication Society. 1980), p. 206.

15. It is interesting to note that in Jewish thought, humans, who according to Torah are the supreme creatures on earth, aren't called intellectual animals, or rational animals, but a *Medaber*, a creature of speech. Furthermore, the soul of man is his ability to speak. See: *Genesis. Targum Onkulot*. Chapter 2. Verse 7. See also: *Rashi. Ramban. Ad loc*. Rabbi Shem Tov Ben Yoseph Ibn Falaquera. *Safer Hanefesh*. (Jerusalem: Mekorot. 1970) Chapter 14, p. 18. Rabbi Menasha ben Israel. (1604–1657) *Nishmat Chayim*. Maamor 1. Chapter 1.(7) The power of speech is even loftier than the power of intellect, for speech is communication, the ability to connect with someone else,

who has an existence other than your own. The ability to abandon your "Yeshut," your own being, and join with another through speech is an expression of the highest level of spirituality. Therefore the highest expression of soul—spirituality, is the ability to speak. See: The Lubavitcher Rebbe. *Likutei Sichot*. Vol. 6, (New York: Kehot Publication Society. 1972), p. 116.

16. The sixth Chabad Rebbe. Rabbi Yoseph Yitzchak. *Likutei Diburim* vol. 1 (New York: Kehot Publication Society. Brooklyn. 1980), p. 204.

17. Mishnah. *Ediyot*. Chapter 1. Mishnah 3. Talmud *Berachot* 47a.

18. The sixth Chabad Rebbe. Rabbi Yoseph Yitzchak. *Likutei Diburim* vol. 1 (New York: Kehot Publication Society. 1980), p. 102.

19. The sixth Chabad Rebbe. Rabbi Yoseph Yitzchak. *Sefer Hasichot 5702*, (1942) (New York: Kehot Publication Society. 1986), p. 122.

20. See also: Rabbi Yonathan Eibeschuvetz. *Yarot D'vash*. (Jerusalem: Levin-Epshtain.) Part 1, p. 38b. Part 2, p. 6a.

21. See: *Ecclesiastes*. 7:14. "God has made the one as well as the other."

22. *Penimei Kesser*, vol. 2 (Israel: Havad Le'hanatzchat Divrei Yemei HaChassidim. 1987) Chapter on song, p. 221. See also: Rabbi Nachman of Breslov. *Likutei Moharan*. Part 1: Chapter 3.

23. Talmud *Sotah*, 48a.

24. See: Rabbi Yehudah Loew. *Netzach Yisrael*. Chapter 23. Rabbi Loew explains that music has extremely delicate forces; thus it can be utilized for intense spiritual practice, or, if not utilized correctly, can create immeasurable negative reactions.

25. See: Talmud, *Chagigah*. 15b.

26. See: Talmud Ibid. See also: *Midrash Ruth*. Parsha 6. Chapter 4.

27. Rabbi Eliyohu Ben Moshe Di Vidas. *Reshit Chochmah*. Shar HaAhavah. Chapter 10. He writes that the spiritual powers of song are so intense, that if their source is from unholy origin, the listener's soul can be uprooted from its source in holiness. Thus one should be very selective as to which music he plays, even for a small child. See: *Shulchan Aruch Orach Chayim*. Rabbi Yisrael Meir Hakohen (1838–1933) *Mishnah Berurah*. Chapter 560. Shotei HaTziyan 25. Rabbi Nachman of Breslov. *Likutei Aytzot*. (Brooklyn: Moriah. 1976.) Neginah 1, p. 137.

28. As the Ramban writes in *Toraht Ha'adam*. Shar Hagmul, toward the end.

29. See: *Midrash. Rabbah Numbers* Parsha 10. Chapter 4.

30. Adopting music from other cultures has been practiced since the time of antiquity. See: Talmud. *Shabbat*. p. 56b. See also: Rabbi Shimon Ben Tzemach Duran. *Magen Avot*. (Jerusalem: Makor Publishing.) Part 3, p. 55b.

31. Rabbi Shlomo Yosef Zevin. *A Treasury of Chassidic Tales on the Festivals*, (New York: Mesorah Publications Ltd. 1995.) p. 120.

32. Eliezer Shtainman. *Be'er HaChassidut. The Rebbe's of Poland*, (Mochon Kemach. Israel.) p. 281.

33. *Midrash. Rabbah Exodus*. Parsha 23: Chapter 7. (See also Talmud. *Chullin*. 91b.) *Midrash Tanchuma*. Beshalach. Chapter 13.

34. In the Torah, as we quoted in the introduction, the very first mention of shepherds is followed closely by the first mention of musical instruments, allowing us to infer a close affinity between the two.

35. Eliezer Shtainman. *Be'er HaChassidut The first and last of the Rebbe's* (Mochon Kemach. Israel.) p. 77. Rabbi Shlomo Yosef Zevin. *A Treasury of Chassidic Tales on Torah*, (New York: Mesorah Publications Ltd. 1992.) pp. 153–155.

36. The second Chabad Rebbe. Rabbi Dovber (1773–1827.) *Toraht Chayim. Bereishit 2*. (New York: Kehot Publication Society.) P 108: 4. He explains that at times the entire reason for marching tunes in the military is so that it can be elevated later on to holiness. Rabbi Nachman of Breslov, says, that by singing the anthem of a secular nation for divine service, it arouses great mercy above. See: *Likutei Aytzot*. (Brooklyn: Moriah. 1976.) Neginah 5, p. 137.

37. The ancient prayer of 'HaAderet VaHaEmunah' which is said by Ashkenazim on the holiest day of the year Yom Kippur, and by Sefardim on Shabbat, or even daily. The AriZal held this prayer in the greatest esteem. See: *Pri Eitz Chayim*. Shar Hazmirot. Chapter 4. This prayer is an ancient prayer recorded in the first century. See: *The Greater Hekhalot* (Reprinted. New York: Gross Bros. 1966) Chapter 26, p. 12. See also: *Safer HaKana*. (Reprinted Israel: 1973.) Inyon Millah, p. 116. (This kabbalistic Text is attributed to the first century saint Rabbi Nechuniah Ben HaKana. However, most believe it to have been written years later. See: Rabbi Chayim Yoseph David Azulai. *Shem Hagedalim*. Sefarim Kuf, 71. Pai, 86.)

38. At a Chassidic gathering in 5752. (1992) Parshat Vayikra.

39. The tune was actually composed in 1792, later on however it became the anthem of the revolution.

40. The war of 1812 between Napoleon and Alexander the First of Russia sparked a great debate between early Chassidic masters. The masters knew that the victory of Napoleon would lead to the emancipation of the Jews from the oppressive Czarist regime and an almost certain increase in their material comfort and well-being. Most argued that this would be wonderful for the Jews and hoped for Napoleon's victory. However, the first Chabad Rebbe, Rabbi Schneur Zalman of Liadi, felt differently; he argued that although their material well-being would be improved, their spiritual circumstance would suffer greatly. See: Rabbi Schneur Zalman of Liadi. *Igrois Koidesh* (New York: Kehot Publication Society: 1980) Admur Hazaken, pp. 150–151.

41. Although their reasons for debating the issue apparently had nothing to do with the *Chassidim* singing the anthem, it is true that people are sometimes moved by forces higher than their conscious minds. See: Talmud *Megillah* 3A.

42. The second Chabad Rebbe Rabbi Dovber *Shaarei T'shuva*. 2, (New York: Kehot Publication Society. 1983), p. 15.

43. Rabbi Schneur Zalman of Liadi. *Maamorei Admur Hazoken. Inyonim*. (New York: Kehot Publication Society. 1983), p. 106. Rabbi Nachman of Breslov. *Likutei Moharan*. Part 1. 27:8.

44. *Genesis*. 43:11.

45. *Genesis*. 43:11. *Rashi*. Mezimras Ha'aretz.

46. Rabbi Nachman of Breslov. *Likutei Moharan*. Part 2:63. Rabbi Yisrael of Modzitz. *Divrei Yisrael*. Parshat Mikketz. Maamor Echad M'Remazi Rosh Hashanah.

47. *Sefer Chassidim*. Chapter 238. See also: *Shulchan Aruch. Yore De'ah*. Chapter 142:15. Rabbi Tzvi Hirsch of Vilna (?–1733) *Beit Lechem Yehudah*. Ad loc.

48. Rabbi Yoel Sirkes. (Know as the Bach. (1561–1604) Rules, that one may use nonJewish music in the synagogue, with the condition that the adopted music was

never used in any other religious service. See: *Responsa Bach Hayeshanoth*. (Jerusalem: 1980) Teshuvah 127. See also: Rabbi Menachem De Lonzano. (16th and beginning of 17th century.) *Shetei Yadot*, p. 142. Rabbi Nachman of Breslov, says, that a Tzadik possesses the spiritual ability to elevate music of the profane. See: *Likutei Aytzot*. (Brooklyn: Moriah. 1976.) Neginah 10, p. 138.

49. A letter dated the first of Addar. 5741 (1981) printed in *Teshuvat U'Biurim*. (Jerusalem: Kollel Tzemach Tzedek. 1985), p. 255.

50. The root of the word Chazan is from Chaze—to see, for the Chazan must see that all runs smoothly in the synagogue. Especially while reading the Torah. See: Rabbi Nathan Ben Yechiel. (1035–1106) *Ha'aruch*. Chazan. Rabbi David Ben Yoseph, known as the *Avudraham*. On the passage of prayer. *Pitum Ha'ketoret*. (Jerusalem edition. 1963) p. 126. See also: Rabbi Yechiel Michael Epstain. *Aruch Ha'shulchan. Orach Chaim*. At the end of Chapter 53. The root is also the source of the name given to a seer or prophet. Rabbi Nachman of Breslov once said, There is a known saying, "Chazanim are fools." Reb Nachman says that the reason for this is that a Chazan can either derive his tunes from holiness, where a prophet receives his visions, or he can derive his inspiration for music from an unholy source, the foolish. *Likutei Moharan, Part 1:3*.

51. Music softens the heart. Thus, one of the reasons why music was played in the holy Temple, was to soften the hearts of the penitents. See: Rabbi Shem Tov Ben Yoseph Ibn Falaquera. *Safer Hamevakesh*, (Jerusalem: Mekorot. 1970) p. 86.

52. In fact, nothing among the utterances allowed to man is felt to be so divine; "music is well said to be the speech of angels, it brings us near to the infinite." The Scottish essayist, Thomas Carlyle (1795–1881.)

53. See: Rambam. *The Guide To The Perplexed*. Part 2. Chapter 6.

54. Most believe that angels exist only as pure spirit. See *Rambam. Hilchot Yesodei Hatorah*. Chapter 2. Halacha 3–8. Rambam. *The Guide To The Perplexed* Part 1. Chapter 49. Rabbi Yoseph Albo (1380–1435) *Safer Haikkarim*. Maamor 2. Chapter 12. Rabbi Moshe Chayim Luzzatto. (1707–1747) *Derech Hashem*. Part 1. Chapter 5: 1. They are for this reason identified with 'light' for the lack of any other physical term. See: Rabbi Dan Yitzchak *Abarbenal*. (1437–1508) *Genesis*. Chapter 1. Verse 1 (Question 2) by the same author. *Mifalot Elokim*. Maamor 3. Chapter 3. However, there are those who say that angels have the dimension of fire, albeit a more refined fire than what we experience. See *Rambam Hilchot Teshuvah*. Chapter 8. In the commentary *Pirush*. Furthermore some argue that angels have a refined version of the elements of fire and wind. See: *Ramban. Torat Ha'adam. Shar Hagmul*. Rabbi Schneur Zalman of Liadi. *Likutei Torah*. (New York: Kehot Publication Society. 1996) Parshat Vezot Haberachah. p. 98a. By the same author. *Torah Or*. (New York: Kehot Publication Society. 1996) Parshat Bereshit. p. 4b. The fifth Chabad Rebbe. Rabbi Shalom Dovber. *Sefer Hamaamorim—5643–644*, (New York: Kehot Publication Society. 1989) p. 71. (See also: Psalms. 104:4.) There is even the opinion that there are angels of refined fire, refined wind, and even refined water. Rabbi Mattisyohu Delecreta. (Poland sixteenth century) in his commentary to *Shaarei Orah*. By Rabbi Yoseph Gikatalia. (New York: Mariah. 1985), pp. 100–101. Rabbi Shlomo Ephraim Lunshitz (1550–1619) *Kli Yakar*. Genesis. 6:16. [Rabbi Moshe Cordovero (1522–1570) *Pardas Rimonim*. Shar 2. Chapter 7. Writes that angels have refined body of fire. However, in Shar 24. Chapter 11, he writes that they have a refined body, made up of all four elements, Fire, Wind. Water. Earth.] Rabbi

Avraham Azulay. (1570–1643e) *Chesed LAvraham*. Part 1. Chapter 28. Writes that they are pure spirit; however, when they descend to this world, they put on a body of fire and wind, or perhaps even a refined body from all four elements.

55. Rabbi Moshe Corodovero. *Shiur Komah*. (Jerusalem: 1966) Torah. Chapter 21. p. 32.

56. E.g. Talmud. *Chullin*. 91b. *Midrash Rabba*. *Genesis*. Parsha 78. Chapter 1. *Midrash Rabba*. *Exodus*. Parsha 23. Chapter 7. *Zohar*. Part 2. p. 18b.

57. *Shabbat* Chapter 5 Mishnah 1. The question posed in the Mishnah is whether or not animals are permitted to enter public property on Shabbat, with bells around their necks.

58. The sixth Chabad Rebbe. Rabbi Yoseph Yitzchak *Sefer Hasichot 5503 (1943)*. (New York: Kehot Publication Society. 1986), p. 111. The prophet, Ezekiel (*Ezekiel*. Chapter 1.) sees animals as a metaphor for angels, in that both are lower than humans, because only humans have freedom of choice. A human being has the capacity to overcome his surroundings, and to change his own innate nature. Angels do not have this choice; the way they were created is the way they will exist through eternity. In this sense they are like animals, which live their entire lives with the same traits they were created with. Rabbi Schneur Zalman of Liadi. *Tanya*. (New York: Kehot Publication Society. 1965) Chapter 39.

59. *Rambam*. *Yesodei Hatorah*. Chapter 7 halacha 1. See also: Rambam. *The Guide To The Perplexed*. (Jerusalem: Mossad Harav Kook: 1977) Part 2. Chapter 34. Rabbi Avraham Ben HaRambam. In his commentary to *Exodus*. (Jerusalem: Sifrei Rabbanei Bavell. 1984) Chapter 7. Verse 1.

60. Rabbi Schneur Zalman of Liadi. *Likutei Torah*. (New York: Kehot Publication Society. 1996), Parshat Vezot Haberachah. p. 98a. Rabbi Yitzchak Aranah. *Akeidot Yitzchak* Bereishit Shar 6.

61. A. Y. Eisenbach. *Or HaShabbat*. (Jerusalem: 1975.) p. 155.

62. *Avot*. Ethics of our fathers, Chapter 4 Mishnah 11. Rabbi Ovadyah Yarei Bertinora. (1440–1516.) See also: Rabbi Shimon Ben Tzemach Duran. *Magen Avot*. (Jerusalem: Makor Publishing.) Part 2. Chapter 3 p. 22a. Rabbi Yisrael Baal Shem Tov. *Tzavoas Horivash*. (NY: Kehot Publication Society. 1982.) Chapter 17. Rabbi Chayim Vital. *Sharei Kedusha*. Part 3. Shar 7. Rabbi Avraham Azulay. *Chesed LeAvraham*. Part 2. Chapter 19. Rabbi Pinchas Eliyohu Ben Meir of Vilna (1743–1821) *Sefer Habrit*. (Jerusalem: Yerid Hasefarim. 1990.) Part 2. Maamar 11. Chapter 4.

63. *Hamaspik Leovedei Hashem*. Erech, "Kevishas Hakachos Vehamasim."

64. All agree that seeing and hearing are the most refined of all five senses. See: Talmud. *Nedarim*, p. 32b. As explained by the *Maharsah*. (Moreinu Harav Shemuel Eliezer Eidels.) 'Betchilah' There is however debate in medieval thought as to which of these two is the more refined. In Jewish thought, for example, *Rabbi Avraham Eben Ezra* (1089–1164) *Exodus*. Chapter 3, verse 6. Chapter 20, verse 1. *Ral'bag*. Rabbi Levy Ben Gershon (1288–1344). *Exodus*. (Jerusalem: Mossad Harav Kook: 1994) pp. 25–27 and 365. See also the following philosophers: Rabbi Yitzchak Israeli (855–955) *Safer Hayesodot*. (Jerusalem: 1968) Maamor 3, p. 69. Rabbi Shem Tov Ben Yoseph Ibn Falaquera. (1225–1290) *Safer Hanefesh*. (Jerusalem: Mekorot. 1970) Chapter 18, p. 28. Rabbi Meir Eben Aldavie *Shevilei Emunah*. Nosiv 6. p. 304. Rabbi Yoseph Ibn Tzadik. (12th century philosopher.) *Safer Ha'Olam Hakatan*. (Breslau: Schatzky. 1903)

Maamor 2. Shar 4, p. 44. Rabbi Gershon Ben Shlomo. (thirteenth century philosopher. And the father of the *Ralbag*.) *Shar HaShamaim*. (Israel: 1968) Maamor 9, p. 53. Maamor 11, p. 72. Rabbi Shimon Ben Tzemach Duran. *Magen Avot*. (Jerusalem: Makor Publishing.) Part 3, p. 41b. And 52a. Rabbi Yoseph Albo. (1380–1435) *Safer Haikkarim*. Maamor 3. Chapter 10. Argue for the supremacy of 'sight,' while others argue for the supremacy of 'hearing.' See: The Ramban. *Emunah Ubitachon*. Chapter 18. Rabbi Bachya Ibn Pakudah. (1050–1120) *Torat HaNefesh*. (Paris: 1896) At the end of Chapter 13. Rabbienu Yona of Gerondi (1194–1263) *Sharrei Teshuvah*. Shar 2: 12. Rabbienu Bachya. (1263–1340) *Kad Kemach: Zenut Halev V'Ha'ayin*.7. Rabbi Yoseph Yavetz (1434–1507) remarks to *Avot* Chapter 6. Mishnah 2.

65. If you look closely at the personalities who argue, you will see that essentially it is an argument between the philosophers, and the anti-philosophers, the mystics. The Eben Ezra, and the Ral'bag, Rabbi Yitzchak Israeli. Rabbi Shem Tov Ben Yoseph Ibn Falaquera. Rabbi Meir Eben Aldavie. Rabbi Yoseph Ibn Tzadik. Rabbi Gershon Ben Shlomo. Rabbi Shimon Ben Tzemach Duran. Rabbi Yoseph Albo, were all philosophers, while the others were either mystics, or opponents to philosophy. The Ramban was a known mystic. Rabbeinu Yona was not only an opponent to the study of philosophy, he was in fact one of the foremost opponents to Rambam's *Guide To The Perplexed"*, although later on in life he changed his opinion. The same is true of the Rabbi Yospeh Yavetz, who wrote an entire book arguing against the study of philosophy, titled *Or Hachayim*. Also Rabbeinu Bechaya was a known mystic. One can say that the difference between a philosopher and a mystic is that the philosopher says, "Seeing is believing," that is, what one sees is what is indeed real. The physical is the strongest reality. And the father of all philosophers, Aristotle, believed in the supremacy of sight. (See: Rabbi Yehudah Ben Yitzchak Abarbanel. (?–1535) *Vikuach Al Ahavah*. (Israel: 1968) p. 42b. The Greek word *theoria*, theory, is derived from the word *theatria*. Which means to be seen, visualized. A truth is identified only if it can be conceptualized. While others assert that sometimes what you cannot see is in fact more real to you than anything else. For a mystic, spirituality is more real, even though he does not see it physically with his eyes. The apprehending of truth is *Shema Yisrael*. *Hear* o Israel. The sense of hearing. An experience which cannot be conceptualized even in the mind. [See however. Rabbi Eliyohu Ben Moshe Vidas. *Reshit Chacmah. Shar Hayira*. Chapter 8, in which he offers proof from the *Zohar*, that sight is superior then hearing. Rabbi Yisrael the Magid of Koznitz. (1733–1814) *Avodat Yisrael*. (Jerusalem. Mochon Sifrei Tzadikim. 1998.) Parshat Bo, p. 95.]

3

Deveikut/Oneness
Creating Soulular Fusion

The Baal Shem Tov said, "One should constantly be God conscious, and connected with God in every action one does. From the holiest to the most mundane, one should continuously strive to connect and cleave to God."[1]

The code of Jewish law begins with the directive that one should, throughout the entire day, strive to feel God's holy presence in this world. Every single motion and deed that one does is done in front of the King of all Kings, and when this is the modality, one's entire existence becomes holier; even the most mundane of actions becomes a testimony to God's existence and a holy deed.[2]

One of the cardinal teachings of Chassidic philosophy is the concept of *Deveikut*—cleaving to God. This is not a new idea in Jewish thought. Rather, like all the teachings of the Baal Shem Tov, they are in fact a revival of the old, taking on new dimensions and deeper significance. *Deveikut* means to be one with the Divine, to be God conscious throughout one's life. In a sense, *Deveikut* is an extension of one's love. In an attempt to express the meaning of true love for God, the Rambam writes, "When a man is in love, his entire mind is occupied with his beloved, while sitting, while standing, eating, or drinking, his entire being is consumed with this love."³ One's love for God should reach such proportions, as it is written, "I am sick with love for You."⁴ The love which he is experiencing overwhelms him entirely, until the point at which he cannot function properly. This is true *Deveikut*, true love for God.⁵

One of the finest ways for a human being to express love is through a love song.⁶ Kabbalah teaches that the various notes in the octave represent the various levels in a person's love for God. The higher the note, the loftier and deeper is the love being expressed.⁷

Throughout the history of the Jewish nation, when God showed His love and compassion, Jews responded with song and dance, thus expressing their deep love for Him. For example, following the great miracle of crossing the sea of reeds, the newly freed Jews sang the *Shiras Hayam*, the song of the sea.⁸ Furthermore, the higher and loftier the *Deveikut*, the greater the urge to express it through song.

There are many levels of love; there is a calm love and there is a passionate love. The highest level of love, however, is a love which burns like a flaming fire, a love of tremendous proportions, rich with excitement and invigoration. King David experienced such love, as is apparent from his words, "My heart goes out for You."⁹ King David had such an overwhelming love for God that he did not cease to think of Him. All he desired was to be in God's presence. This sort of love was epitomized in the tribe of Levi. Consequently the manner in which they expressed their love was through song.¹⁰

The arrival of the Chassidic movement brought a revival to these expressions of love through song, and *Deveikut* became a hallmark of Chassidus. King David says in Psalms, "I sing praise in the community of *Chassidim*."¹¹ (He referred to righteous men.) However, *Chassidim* fancy to interpret this to mean that wherever one finds a community of *Chassidim*, one will also find song. Song and music play an essential role in the life of a Chassid and without it a Chassid feels spiritually bereft, unable to fully express his love and devotion to God. When it comes to expressing love and *Deveikut*, the most direct road is a song.¹²

A love song begins with feelings, that find expression in words and melody. The tune is accompanied by verbal descriptions of the emotions one feels. This enhances the passion and brings it forth. Once the inner emotions are aroused, the words may be needed to hold the concentration necessary to attain the level of emotion being expressed. The song progresses, and one's entire self becomes involved in the music, as the love is revealed. Soon the words become superfluous, unnecessary, and even a hindrance to the great rush of emotions being experienced. The song becomes a tune, a *nigun*; the music standing alone. There are many Chassidic melodies that begin with words and evolve into a wordless tune. When one is in love, one may experience this phenomenon himself, the feeling of speechlessness, of something infinitely more complex and spiritual than words. This is the elevation reached with a wordless Chassidic melody, a *nigun*.

The love for God can become so overwhelming that at times, one has no way of expressing this love other than calling out to God, "Father, Father."

This manifests itself in the physical realms as well. It is a familiar pleasure to those who have loved intensely, even within a natural love, such as that of a mother for her child, to say the beloved's name—nothing else, only the name of their beloved. What is it about the name of a person that causes a lover to call it out when no other words suffice?

A simple explanation of this phenomenon is as follows: When one speaks of another person and wishes to describe him, one must single out personal traits and describe him using those words. In essence, one is not saying anything about this person as a whole. There is no way to describe a person's entire complex personality in a manner of singular descriptions. However, when calling somebody's name, you are speaking of his all-encompassing being. Therefore lovers experience joy in mentioning the name of their beloved; the name itself awakens them to the entire personality of the one they love.

Chassidut explains a deeper reason for this phenomenon. The name of a person is closely connected with that person's essence of being.[13] The name is actually the vessel and the receptacle through which one's soul permeates and gives life to the physical body. Therefore by the mere mention of a beloved's name, it arouses the greatest of feelings.

For some Chassidic masters at times the only means of expression was to **whistle**. Rabbi Zushe of Hanipoly once stayed at the home of Rabbi Mordechai, the Rebbe of Neshkiv. In the darkest hours of the night, Rabbi Zushe awoke and began to recite the *Tikkun Chatzos*.[14] He lifted his eyes to the heavens and said, "Master of the universe, You know how powerful and intense my love is for You and how close I feel to You. I wish to express my feelings for You, yet I don't know what to do!" Tearfully, he repeated these heartfelt words again and again. Then an idea came to him: he could whistle. And that is exactly what he did. His whistling grew louder and more intense until Rabbi Mordechai and the entire household was awakened by the sound. Rabbi Mordechai instructed his family to leave the house immediately, for he feared the house would catch fire from this holy whistle which emanated from the lips of Reb Zushe.[15]

During Chassidic gatherings, *farbrengens*, the Lubavitcher Rebbe would often ask of the *Chassidim* to whistle in accompaniment to the *nigunim*. The Rebbe referred to this whistling as "the holy whistle."[16] The Rebbe spoke at length regarding whistling.[17] He said that whistling without any purpose is meaningless. When we whistle for the service of God however, this whistling becomes a Holy Whistle, which assists us in the joyful service of the Creator. The Rebbe explained that whistling is also closely connected with the coming of the redemption. As the Talmud quotes[18] the Prophets, "I will whistle to them and I will ingather them."[19] Before the coming of *Moshiach*, there will be a great whistle; according to the Talmud, it is possible that this whistle will emanate from a bird. The Rebbe continued, that if God so desires, this "holy whistle" which we whistle now in exile, could be the ultimate whistle which the prophets predict will herald the redemption.

►┼◄»─0─◄►┼◄

The power of a song is such that it enables the listener to transport himself from his present reality into a new and loftier state of being.

Song uplifts man to a level of perfection, raising him to a state beyond the expressive word, transforming reality, and creating new realities, within the realm of pure *Deveikut*. There is immense power in a melody.

Rabbi Hillel of Poritch,[20] while sitting in a room, deep in study, heard an unusually beautiful tune being sung. He hurried outdoors to determine the source of this exquisite sound. Behind the house there was a field of golden wheat ready for the harvest. To Rabbi Hillel's great surprise, the beautiful music was coming from the middle of the field where a simple Jew labored over the harvesting. The man was singing a Chassidic melody with complete sincerity. Rabbi Hillel was overwhelmed by the scene and exclaimed, "Observe the power of a *Nigun*. This simple man, while involved in mundane and menial work, has uplifted his mind and heart to total Godliness—*Deveikut*."[21]

Song can transform and elevate a person and his deeds to a higher state of consciousness, until the singer becomes oblivious to his surroundings. He enters a state of *Deveikut*, which causes the physical reality of this world to dim and become insignificant. There occurs a complete separation from physical reality and an entering into a new dimension.[22]

What does this mean? We have all listened to music and been moved to a certain extent. Some have even felt themselves transported through song. Yet, what we speak of here is something far beyond the momentary tingle we have all experienced. It is a level of elevation through music which, though difficult to achieve, is attainable by all people, if the determination and concentration is complete.

A renowned master was once in need of a critical surgical procedure. Anesthetics were a new development, and were necessary for this operation. The Rebbe, however, refused to use anesthetics as they were new and largely untested. With great trepidation and apprehension, the doctor conceded to the operation sans anesthesia, certain the Rebbe would beg for it once he was in the process of the painful surgery. Instead the doctor witnessed something spectacular. From the moment he was laid on the operating table, the Rebbe began to compose a melody, and sang throughout the entire surgery. He did not feel the slightest twinge of pain, not even once.[23] This is the power of a song, to distract the mind by elevating it to a higher state of consciousness, and through total concentration make it oblivious to physical reality.[24]

The above mentioned illustrates the ability of song to transport a person from one reality to another. Yet those realities are both existing within the confines of the terrestrial spheres. There are those who have taken music even further, transporting themselves from a state where they are confined to a physical body to a reality where they are one with God.

The holy master, the Baal Shem Tov, while lying on his deathbed, gathered together his disciples, and requested that they sing a song together. As they sang the song, the Baal Shem Tov's soul was slowly drifting from this world. As they neared the end of the tune, the Baal Shem Tov whispered a prayer,[25] and his soul departed his body, entering eternity through song.[26] He lived music; his life reads like a harmonious melody; he ascended through music, and finally, became music.

The same is said of one of the eminent students of the Baal Shem Tov, Rabbi Michal of Zlotchov. Before he died, he began singing a melody with immense concentration, a tune of measureless yearning and *Deveikut*. Suddenly everyone around him saw how with song, he was transcending his physical body, and this world, and how he ascended to the loftier worlds with song. This phenomenon is called *Ratzu Beli Shuve*, a withdrawal without return; it is a transcendent moment when you lift yourself into the sphere of timelessness, and eternity, without ever returning to this earthbound, physical reality.[27] Through melody, one has the potential to reach the highest levels of *Deveikut*, to become "one with the One." When one attains this level, death is simply a transformation from the physical body, and is without any pain, for it is precisely this musical energy that brings about *Kelot HaNefesh*—the ascent of the soul.

We all possess five senses, of which the most mundane is tactile, the ability to feel, to touch physical objects. Above feeling are the senses of taste, smell, hearing, and seeing.[28] Hearing and seeing are considered to be the most refined of all five. Of these two senses, the sense of hearing has a stronger impression on the person. Let's say, for example, that you go to a museum and see a beautiful painting. You see a painting so exquisite that you become completely mesmerized and enchanted by its beauty, to the extent that you feel that you are "losing" yourself, being completely enveloped in the great beauty of the painting. This is the power of sight. With hearing one can literally lose one's existence. One can be so overwhelmed by the beauty of a melody that *Kelot HaNafesh* can occur—a withdrawal of the physical. Music has the potency to enter the person's consciousness and touch the essence of soul.[29] Thus, hearing is regarded as the most important and vital of all senses.[30]

Just as music has the potential to cause *Deveikut* between man and God, it also has the capacity to prompt a *Deveikut* between men. One of the more celebrated Chassidic melodies is one composed by Rabbi Michal of Zlotchov. This Chassid would visit his Rebbe, the Baal Shem Tov, frequently. However, when he was older, and was no longer able to take the trip, he composed a song in its place. The first stanza expressed his deep yearning for his Rebbe; the second, the joy he experienced once he was in the presence of his Rebbe, and the third stanza, the bond and devotion, the *Deveikut*, he felt for his Rebbe.

On the first *Yortzait* (memorial of someone's passing) of the *Magid*, Rabbi Dovber (?–1776), three of his prominent disciples began singing tunes which they had learnt from their master. The three were Rabbi Schneur Zalman of Liadi, Rabbi Avraham of Kalisk, and Rabbi Yisrael of Pilutzk. Each one of these luminaries had a unique way of singing. Reb Schneur Zalman sang with a powerful and deep voice, a voice that when heard would cause one to tremble. Reb Avraham had a very thin and clear voice, full of heart, which, when heard, would make the listener melt with passion and love. Reb Yisrael's voice was sweet and charming, not too strong nor too weak. It was a voice that made one feel at ease, comfortable, and relaxed. As the disciples sang in unison the songs of their holy master, the listeners could feel how they were transcending the limitations of time and space, and connecting, joining their souls with the holy soul of their departed master.[31]

By listening to music, one can glimpse what it may be to exist in eternity.

To attain such a lofty transcendent level, one must be on a high spiritual plane. There is, however, a lower level, where through song, one can remember a previous experience vividly, as though he were once again experiencing it. But beyond reviving memory, a tune can awaken deep hidden feelings that were dormant for many years, feelings of lost love, and the like. Music works wonders on a person's memory; it opens to consciousness previously lost worlds.[32]

Let's say, for example, one visits an art museum and views a magnificent painting which moves him deeply, and at that moment there was music playing in the background. Henceforth each time he will hear that particular song, he will be reminded of this magnificent painting. This is because an experience that one has with one of the five senses will evoke in one's memory the responses of all other senses stimulated at that moment. One may also be reminded of something experienced through a fragrance which was present at the time of the occurrence. The same is true with sounds. When music has accompanied an experience one has had, one may later, through music, be vividly reminded of that experience.

The previous Chabad Rebbe writes of a gathering by *Chassidim* of the *Tzemach Tzedek*, which was held many years after his passing. At first, writes the Rebbe, they started reminiscing about the days gone by, when the *Tzemach Tzedek* was still alive. Then they all stood up and began singing a song which the Rebbe, the *Tzemach Tzedek*, used to sing in prayer. When they reached a certain stanza in the song, in which the Rebbe used to say, "How fortunate is the person who does not forget,"[33] they all spontaneously started to cry with bitter tears. The Rebbe writes that at that moment, one could see the way these *Chassidim* relived their experience, as if it was occurring all over again.[34]

Just as *Chassidim* apply the art of song to cause a *Deveikut* between Rebbe and Chassid, they also utilize its potential to prompt *Deveikut* between themselves. When *Chassidim* assemble for a Chassidic gathering, the protocol is for an elderly, or scholarly Chassid, to speak about what he surmises is important for the other *Chassidim* to hear, while everyone else listens. However, it sometimes occurs that there is more than one Chassid who wants to talk; sometimes the *Chassidim* amongst themselves disagree, so notwithstanding the fact that they are all sitting around the same table, there is still no real *Deveikut* and harmony. However, when they sing together, they experience a genuine *Deveikut*, for song and music by its very nature, draws people closer to each other.[35]

The songs people sing together weave a beautiful tapestry, emanating light and warmth, which encircles them, and warms even the coldest feelings. To paraphrase an old saying, "the spirit of the community is formed by the music it hears"[36] for music unites the many. Since it is music and song that unite and connect people, we encounter many mystical disciplines, whose prime emphasis is to be one unified assembly, for whom music and song play an important role. For instance the practice of the Kabbalistic group in Jerusalem, *Beit Keil* is to sing songs for hours, thus they use music and song to reinforce solidarity and identity in their group.[37]

There are many anthropologists who believe that the concept of music was initially developed by primitive man to strengthen the community and unify the clan.

A chassidic Master once asked, "Why is it that shepherds, men who roam the fields, love singing?"[38] (As noted earlier, the source of many Chassidic melodies is, in fact, melodies of shepherds.) The Master explained that the reason is that music has the power to reveal the essence of man. When a shepherd is alone in the meadows with the animals, without contact with any other human beings, in order for him to stay "sane" and not lose his humanity, he sings. Man essentially is a "social animal"[39] therefore, when a person is alone, he yearns to be among other human beings. The way to express these sentiments is through song, because song reveals the core and essence of man, who is a social animal. Song arouses within the person feelings of wanting to be in the company of other human beings. In addition the hallmark of sound, especially song, is that there is a singer and a listener. When one sings to himself, he creates the illusion of not being alone. Thus, his loneliness subsides.

On a higher and loftier level, song does not only unite two or more people who may retain their separate identities; it has the puissance to create a new existence, to form from the many, a one.[40] Rabbi Pinchas of Koritz (1728–1791) once said, "We notice that if we are alone and attempting to sing a tune that is very high-pitched, we cannot reach this high pitch; but if we sing the same tune with somebody else, who helps us with the singing, then in unison, we are able to reach the highest pitch in the tune."[41] Reb Pinchas explains this phenomenon, saying that when two people sing a song together, the tune creates synergy and fuses the two into a new and more powerful entity. Therefore they are able to reach the higher pitch together.[42] This concept is similar to counterintuitive math where $1+1 = 1$ and the one is more powerful than the sum of the parts.

Another example of this is a wedding. We see that at a wedding (the ultimate unification of two separate human beings, who for many years of their lives might not have even known of each other's existence, and who now are vowing to live together forever) playing music has great value, and has a prominent position at the celebration.[43] In a sense, on the wedding day, the bride and groom metamorphose into a complete and new human being.[44] To attain this lofty level of *Deveikut* or unification, music is played, for music has the power of connection, the ability to unite even opposites.[45]

Dance, like music, has the power of unification. The way *Chassidim* dance is in a circle; they form a circle with an empty space in the middle, that is, with no dancer in the middle. The *Chassidim* face each other. The choreography of the dance is to start with everyone in the circle creating the greatest circumference, they then all move towards the middle, until they are face to face. Then they all move back again towards the outer part of the circle. This continues throughout the entire dance, going back and forth, separating, and reuniting, separating and reuniting. This style of dance represents the idea of *Deveikut* between two or more people. It expresses the idea that although there are times when one cannot be in proximity with others, either in body, or in spirit; nevertheless, we must always come together and reunite in *Deveikut*.[46]

The idea of a circle also represents equality. In a circle there is no head or tail; each link is equally important in completing the entire circle.[47]

The Baal Shem Tov, once commented regarding the dance of *Chassidim* in a circle. He said, "We observe that with people, for example, lovers, who are always together, and never even for the shortest moment of time separated, the excitement and the passion which were originally between the two fade; however, if they separated from one another for a short period of time, and then they reunited, the intensity of feelings and bond between them would become even stronger and more powerful."[48] The *Deveikut* and love after a separation is always stronger, deeper, and more meaningful.[49] So it is when *Chassidim* dance. When one separates from his fellow dancer, he knows that soon they will be reunited in greater love and *Deveikut*.[50]

There is yet another content in which to explain the idea of dance. In mystical thought a question is posed: "Why is it that on the holiday of Simchat Torah, a celebration for the completion of reading of the Torah, which indeed is a momentous spiritual celebration, do we express our joy through dance?"[51] Simchat Torah is really a spiritual celebration, unlike the other holidays, which we celebrate for physical as well as spiritual reasons. Passover, for example, is a holiday that we celebrate not only because God took us out of our spiritual enslavement, but for physical reasons as well, for God took us out of our physical bondage and slavery. However, on Simchat Torah, the holiday is celebrated only for spiritual reasons, since it is the day which we finish reading the Torah. So the question remains, why dancing? Logic would dictate that to sit and learn Torah, is most appropriate. And if overwhelmed by joy, then "dance meditatively" without any external motion. Why is movement so integrated as an expression of this holiday? The explanation is that the ultimate purpose of the soul's descent to this physical and mundane world is not only that our souls, our spiritual dimensions, should attain higher levels of spirituality, rather that the physical should be elevated and transformed to the spiritual. That Godliness should permeate physical existence, and that our bodies should become holy. Therefore, when we dance with our bodies, we are expressing that we do not neglect and forget about our physicality, but rather, work with it and elevate it. The spiritual joy which we experience on the holiday of Simchat Torah permeates our physical reality as well.[52] It is the same with any holy dance one dances. We take the spiritual inspiration which brings us to dance, and allow it to suffuse our entire being.[53]

NOTES

1. Rabbi Yisrael Baal Shem Tov. *Tzavoas Horivash* (New York: Kehot Publications Society. 1982) Chapter 81. See also for earlier sources: Rabbi Bachya Ibn Pakudah. *Chovot Halevavot.* Shar Ahavat Hashem. Chapter 1. *Ramban. Deuteronomy.* 10:20. Rabbienu Yona of Gerondi *Sharrei Teshuvah.* Shar 3:27. Rabbi Eliezer Ezcary (1522–1600) *Safer Cheredim* Chapter 9:10. *Eben Ezra Psalms.* 1:3.

2. *Shulchan Aruch.* Orach Chayim. Chapter 1. See also: *Rambam.* Hilchot De'ot. Chapter 3. Halacha 2–3.

3. *Rambam,* Hilchot Teshuvah. Chapter 10. Halacha 3.

4. *Shir HaShirim.* 2:5 It is known that the entire book of Shir Hashirim is a metaphor for the love between God and man. See: Mishnah *Yodayim* chapter 3. Mishnah 5. *Midrash Rabbah.* Shir Hashirim. Parsah 1. Chapter 11. See *Rambam.* Ibid. At the end of Halacha 3.

5. Rabbienu Bachya. *Kad Kemach.* Kisvie Rabbeinu Bachya. (Jerusalem: Mossad Harav Kook. 1995) *Ahavah*, p. 34. *Ramban. Deuteronomy.* 11:22.

6. As Rabbi Eliezer Ezcary writes, "The finest way for a lover to express his love is through a love song" *Safer Cheredim.* Chapter 10: 6. Indeed he himself composed many beautiful songs, which are today part of the prayers, the most noted being the 'Yidid Nefesh.' See *Safer Cheredim.* Chapter 34. When a person is in love they sing. Rabbi Eliezer of Worms. (c. 1160–c.1238) *Safer Rokeach.* Hilchot Chassidut. Shoresh Ahavat Hashem. See also: Rabbi Yehudah Ha-Chassid. (1150–1217) *Sefer Chassidim.* Chapter 14.

7. The great Chassidic master, Rabbi Levi Yitzchak of Berdichov (1740–1809) *Kedushat Levi.* Likutim. (p. 206.) Rabbi Yisrael of Modzitz. *Divrei Yisrael.* Parshat Mikketz. Maamor Echad M'Remazei. Chanukah.

8. The Talmud says that when God shows His love to man, we must thank and praise him through song. *Sanhedrin* 94a.

9. *Psalms* 63:2.

10. *Zohar* Part 2. p. 19. Rabbi Schneur Zalman of Liadi *Tanya.* Chapter 50.

11. *Psalms* 149:1.

12. The sixth Chabad Rebbe, Rabbi Yoseph Yitzchak, Parshat Noach 1945. (5706) See: Rabbi Moshe Yichiel Elimelech of Levertov *Safer Shemirat Hada'at*, Aimrei Tal. Ma'amar Nigun (Bnei Brak Israel: Ginzei MaHaritz. 1986), p. 18.

13. See at length The Lubavitcher Rebbe, Rabbi Menachem Mendel Schneerson, *Likutei Sichot* (New York: Kehot Publication Society. 1972.) Vol. 6, pp. 8–12.

14. An ancient custom practiced especially by kabbalists. See: *Zohar.* Part 1, pp. 242b and 295b. *Rosh* on *Berachot.* 3b. *Shulchan Aruch.* Orach Chaim. Chapter 1. *Magen Avraham.* Ad loc. King David would awaken at midnight to study Torah. See: Talmud. *Berachot.* 3b. *Midrash Rabbah. Ruth.* Parsha 6. Chapter 1. *Midrash Tanchuma.* Parshat Behaalotecha. Chapter 10.

15. See: *Ohel Elimelech,* (Israel: 1968) p. 134.

16. See: *Sefer Hatoldous. Admur HaZaken* (Israel: Kehot Publication. 1976), p. 216.

17. See: *Sichot Kodesh 5736,* (Brooklyn: 1990) p. 632.

18. See: Talmud, *Chullin,* 63a.

19. *Zechariah* Chapter 10.

20. See: The sixth Chabad Rebbe, Rabbi Yoseph Yitzchak, *Sefer Hasichot 5703,* (New York: Kehot Publication Society. 1986) p. 16.

21. Playing music and singing tunes while doing physical labor, like plowing the land, etc., seems to have been an ancient custom. See: *Jeremiah.* 48:33. Talmud *Sotah.* 48a.

22. Music causes a shift of a person's mundane consciousness to higher realms. See: Rabbi Shem Tov Ben Yoseph Ibn Falaquera. *Safer Hamevakesh,* (Jerusalem: Mekorot. 1970) p. 87.

23. See: The Lubavitcher Rebbe, Rabbi Menacham Mendel Schneerson, *Hisvaduyot 5744.* (1984), (New York: Vaad Hanachot B'lehak. 1985), Vol. 2, p. 1373.

24. Rabbi Eliyohu Ben Moshe Di Vidas writes that Shir (song) brings a person to true Deveikut. *Reshit Chochmah.* Shar HaAhavah, Chapter 10.

25. Oh Lord, please do not bring me to the foot of conceit. See *Psalms* 36:12.

26. The Talmud speaks of dying with 'a kiss of God.' (Talmud. *Berachot*. 8a. *Moed Katan*. 28a. *Baba Batra*. 17a. *Midrash Rabba*. *Deuteronomy*. Parsah 11. Chapter 10.) Which is regarded as the easiest death. (Talmud. *Berachot*. 8a.) The Rambam writes that when the great saints of Israel saw that their time was nearing, they would meditate extensively, until they would reach a level of ecstasy, where their souls would exit their bodies with pleasure. With a 'kiss of God.' Rambam. *The Guide To The Perplexed*. Part 3, end of Chapter 51. Rabbeinu Bachya. *Kad Kemach*. Kisvei Rabbeinu Bachya, (Jerusalem: Mossad Harav Kook. 1995) *Ahavah*, p. 35. The highest level of Deveikut is manifested when a person ascends to heaven without any pain, through a 'kiss of God.' See also: *Ma'arechet Elokut*. Chapter 8. Attributed to Rabbi Todros HaLevi Abulafia. (1220–1298) Rabbi Menachem Azaryah De Fano. (1548–1620) *Maamor Hanefesh*. Part 6. Chapter 7. Rabbi Yehudah Ben Yitzchak Abarbanel. (?–1535) *Vikuach Al Ahavah*, (Israel: 1968.) p. 41a.

27. The second Chabad Rebbe Rabbi Dovber, *Pirush Hamilot*, (New York: Kehot Publication Society. 1980) p. 84. He explains that song serves a purpose only when there is not complete 'deveikut'. When you reach a higher level of *deveikut*, that you are one with the One, you cannot even sing.

28. Rabbi Meir Eben Aldavie, (fourteenth century) *Shevilei Emunah*, (Jerusalem Edition. 1990) Nosiv 4, pp. 206–207. Man has five fingers, each finger corresponding to each one of these senses. The thumb corresponds to taste; therefore, children suck their thumbs. The ring finger corresponds to smell; therefore, if one cleans his nose, he does so with this finger. The middle finger is for touch; therefore, it is the longest finger, in order to be able to touch other things. The index finger is for sight; therefore, one cleans his eyes with this finger. The pinky is for hearing; thus one cleans his ears with this finger.

29. The sixth Chabad Rebbe, Rabbi Yoseph Yitzchak. *Sefer HaMaamarim 5699*, (1939) (New York: Kehot Publication Society. 1986). Eivdu Ess Hashem. See also same author *Sefer HaMaamarim 5709*. (1949) (New York: Kehot Publication Society. 1986)

30. In Jewish law, the capacity to hear is the most significant of all senses. Thus, if a person harms another and makes them deaf, the financial punishment is substantially greater than if harm is done to any other organ. See: Talmud. *Baba Kamma*. 85b. *Rashi* titled Chirsho. See also: *Rambam. Hilchot Chovel Umazik*. Chapter 2. Halacha 12. *Shulchan Aruch, Choshen Mishpat*, 420:25.

31. The sixth Chabad Rebbe, Rabbi Yoseph Yitzchak. *Likutei Diburim*. (New York: Kehot Publication Society. 1980) Vol. 2, p. 552.

32. Rabbi Moshe Yichiel Elimelech of Levertov *Safer Shemirat Hada'at*. Aimrei Tal. Ma'amar Nigun, (Bnei Brak Israel: Ginzei MaHaritz. 1986) p. 17. See also: Rabbi Nachman of Breslov *Likutei Aytzot*. (Brooklyn: Moriah. 1976.) Neginah 8, p. 138.

33. In brief, this verse is speaking about the soul's descent. The process of the soul's descending into the physical world is a process of forgetting; we forget the spirituality and Godliness that we experienced when we were in the worlds above, before our souls descend. However, the purpose of the descent is that we should, in this physical and temporal world, remember our previous existence, and hence act accordingly, the way our real selves, our inner soul, the Godly soul, want us to act.

34. The sixth Chabad Rebbe, Rabbi Yoseph Yitzchak. *Likutei Diburim*. (New York: Kehot Publication Society. 1980) Vol. 1, p. 236.

35. Rabbi Moshe Yichiel Elimelech of Levertov. *Safer Shemirat Hada'at*. Aimrei Tal. Ma'amar Nigun, (Bnei Brak Israel: Ginzei MaHaritz. 1986) p. 9.

36. As the Chinese say, in the name of Confucius, "The spirit of the community is formed by the music it hears; hence a government must encourage one kind of music, and forbid another."

37. See: Louis Jacobs *The Jewish Mystics* (Keter Publishing House. Jerusalem Ltd. 1976), Chapter 14: p. 156. See also: Abraham. Z. Idelshon. *Jewish Music. In Its Historical Development*. (New York: Dover Publication. 1992) Notes to Chapter xix. Note 2, p. 518.

38. Rabbi Moshe Yichiel Elimelech of Levertov. *Safer Shemirat Hada'at*. Aimrei Tal. Ma'amar Nigun, (Bnei Brak Israel: Ginzei MaHaritz. 1986) p. 3. See also the footnote.

39. See: *Rambam. The Guide to the Perplexed*. Part 2. Chapter 40. Part 1. Chapter 72. 'Man can not survive alone.' See also: *Rambam Hilchot De'ot*. Chapter 6. Halacha 1.) Rabbi Shimon Ben Tzemach Duran. *Magen Avot*. (Jerusalem: Makor Publishing) Part 2. Chapter 1, p. 8b. Thus it is understood why a *Metzora*, a leper, is considered as dead. (Talmud. *Nedarim*. 64b.) because since a *Metzora* must be alone, (*Leviticus*. Chapter 13. Verse 46.) and can not have any contact with other human beings, he is considered as though dead. See the famous adage, "Friends or death." Talmud. *Taanit*. 23a.

40. The sixth Chabad Rebbe, Rabbi Yoseph Yitzchak. *Likutei Diburim*. (New York: Kehot Publication Society. 1980) Vol. 2, p. 334.

41. *Midrash Pinchas*. p. 28: Chapter 36. See also: *Aimrei Pinchos*, (Benei Brak: Mishor. 1988.) p. 105.

42. See: Talmud *Sotah*. 34A.

43. The custom of playing music at weddings seems to date back to Biblical times. See *Radak. Psalms*. 78:63. (See: Rabbi Gavriel Tziner. *Nitei Gavriel*. Hilchot Nesuein part 1, p. 249, for early sources of music at weddings.)

44. As it is explained, that up until marriage one is considered as only having a half of body, with a half of soul, and at marriage, one becomes reunited with the second half, of body and soul, and together become a new human being. (See: Talmud *Yevamot* 63a. *Zohar* Part 1:85b and 91b.) Therefore it says, (See: the Jerusalem Talmud. *Bikurim*. Chapter 3. Halacha 3. *Rashi Genesis* Chapter 36, verse 3.) On the day of your wedding, God forgives you for all your sins which you have done up until this day, because the person that did the sins yesterday, meaning you, does not exist anymore, since you are now a new and different person. Accordingly, there is great importance in the type of music played at such a special occasion. See: *Igroth Moshe. Evven HaEzer*. Teshuvah 96.

45. Rabbi Nachman of Breslov. *Likutei Moharan* Part 1: 237. Eliezer Shtainman. *Be'er HaChassidut. Kisavay Reb Nachman*, (Mochon Kemach. Israel.) p. 167. See also: Rabbi Moshe Yichiel Elimelech of Levertov *Safer Shemirat Hada'at*. Aimrei Tal. Ma'amar Nigun, (Bnei Brak Israel: Ginzei MaHaritz. 1986.) p. 10.

46. Rabbi Schneur Zalman of Liadi. *Likutei Torah* (New York: Kehot Publication Society 1996), Shaminee Atzeret. Bayom Hashenei. See also: Rabbi Pinchas of Koritz. *Midrash Pinchas*, (Jerusalem: 1971.) p. 28. (Chapter. 34)

47. Rabbi Tzvi Elimelech of Dinav. (1785–1841) *Bnei Yissochar*. Maamorei Chodesh

Tammuz Av. Maamor 4. Rabbi Tzadok HaKohen of Lublin. (1823–1900) *Machshevet Charutz*. Chapter 19.

48. *Kesser Shem Tov* Chapter 40 (New York: Kehot Publication Society. 1987) *Jeremiah*.

49. Parenthetically, this is one of the reasons why the Torah says that a husband and wife should continually separate and reunite. They should refrain from physical intimacy for a period of time in every month, so that their passion and love for one another should always be like new and exciting, as on the day of their marriage. (See: Talmud, *Niddah*, 31b.)

50. The second Chabad Rebbe, Rabbi Dovber. *Torath Chayim Shemot*. (New York: Kehot Publication Society. 1975), p. 496. See also: The fifth Chabad Rebbe. Rabbi Sholom Dovber *Yom Tov Shel Rosh Hashono. 5666*, (New York: Kehot Publication Society. 1984) p. 296.

51. The fifth Chabad Rebbe, Rabbi Sholem Dovber, *Samach Tisamach 5657*, (New York: Kehot Publication Society. 1965), p. 102.

52. Rabbi Yisrael Dov Ber of Vilednick, writes that through dancing we elevate our feet, with all that 'feet' represent to God. *Shearith Yisrael*, (Israel: M'Chon Ohr Yisroel. 1998) p. 132b.

53. This notion of transforming our physical bodies into holiness will be ultimately achieved in the time of the redemption, at the time of the resurrection of the dead. As the Ramban, the great Jewish mystic and codifier of law (1194–1270) writes, (*Ramban Torat Ha.Adam. Sharr Hagmul*) the ultimate reward for our souls, (for all the *mitzvot*, and good deeds done throughout our existence on this world,) will not be in a time when our soul are departed from our bodies, in the world of souls, the world of "Gan Eden"—Paradise, but in a time when our bodies and souls are joined together in this physical world. (See: *Targum Yonoton. Isaiah*. Chapter 58 verse 11.) In that time we will have already totally transformed our physicality. Our physical bodies will have been transformed into spiritual identities, and therefore our physical bodies will be able to live forever just as anything that is spiritual—beyond time and space—lives forever. This is the highest level of "Deveikut" that man can achieve. This sort of transformation, from the physical to the spiritual, was achieved by the prophet Elijah; therefore the Bible says that the prophet's body did not experience death, that his physical body did not die, but was transformed into a spiritual being. His body went to heaven, (*Kings 2*. 2:11.) that is, his physical body was transformed into a peace of heaven; it became a spiritual entity.

4
Simchah/Happiness
Evoking and Expressing Joy

Rabbi Nachman of Breslov says, "It is a great mitzvah to live life in a constant state of joy."[1] life in a constant state of joy."[1]

One of the fundamental teachings of the holy master, the Baal Shem Tov, and of the essential teachings of Chassidic mysticism, is that man should always serve God with joy and happiness.

If we are to discuss chassidism, let us begin by defining what a Chassid is. Today the term refers to the followers of the Baal Shem Tov. However, the term Chassid is not a new concept; it is actually a very old and ancient term,[2] used to define those who are devotees to Torah, people whose religious performance exceeds that which the literal law demands.[3] There is also a more specific meaning of the word Chassid; throughout history the name Chassid came to mean different things.

In the times of the Talmud, a Chassid was someone who meditated, one who sat for nine hours of the day in meditation.[4] The Talmud tells that the *Chassidim* of those times would pray and meditate, for nine hours each day, three hours for every prayer; one hour for meditation before prayer, one hour for the actual prayer, and one hour for meditation after prayer.[5] There are those who explain that a human being cannot, under normal circum-

stances, be in continuous meditation, in a higher state of consciousness (what the Kabbalah calls *Mochen D'Gadlut*—expanded consciousness)[6] for more than three hours at a time.[7] This extensive,
prolonged meditation was what those *Chassidim*, in the times of
the Talmud, excelled in.

Later on in history, the term Chassid was given to the Chassidei
Ashkenaz, devotees in medieval Germany, who flourished from
the twelfth century onwards. They were known to be ascetics,
people who served God with—and through—denial and rejection.
They disregarded and even punished their physicality. They chas-
tised their bodies through fasting and inflicting pain on themselves. One of the great Chassidei Ashkenaz, Rabbi Yehudah Ha-
Chassid wrote that if a person wanted to do appropriate *Teshuva*
(repentance), they should attempt to fast as often as possible. Furthermore, they should go during the winter months to a body of
frozen water, crack the ice, and sit in the freezing water. While
during the summer months, they should go to a cave full of in-
sects and sit among them.[8] The idea was that the physical morti-
fication of the flesh, one becomes indifferent to the physical and
thus closer to the spiritual.

A great light was revealed upon this world, when in the year
1698, the Baal Shem Tov was born. He taught that it was time for
man to make peace with himself and his body, and peace with
the physical world around him. (The prevalent religious practice throughout the entire Western world was fighting the physical.) He said that a human being should attempt to serve God with
body and soul in unity, a person should be happily disposed and
serve God with joy and gladness in his heart.[9] As a philosopher
once observed, the ultimate experience of religion is for a person
to be *converted* from being a sickly soul, a soul where evil and negativity reside, to a person where positiveness and happiness are
his essential being, a person who says yes to life.[10] One finds these
ideas expressed in Jewish thought even prior to the Baal Shem
Tov;[11] however, as is with all ideas of *Chassidut*, with the Baal
Shem Tov's teachings, these ideas took on a newer and deeper
meaning.

How does one get to feel this way? How can a human being maintain always being happy and joyous? This can be accomplished by meditating on the lofty idea, that everything that exists was created by God, who is the ultimate good. Therefore, everything which is created has a purpose—a positive design.[12] By contemplating on the mystical idea that all of creation is filled with God's glory, whether a blade of grass, or a speck of sand, it contains within it a divine energy which gives it its life and vitality, one becomes internally happy. It was precisely for this reason that in the early stages of Chassidism, even before they were known as *Chassidim*, they were called the *Freileche*, the happy ones, for they were always happy and cheerful.

Scholars, social critics, and historians have frequently discussed and attempted to discern the Chassidic response to the 'outside', secular, modern world, which I will henceforth refer to as modernity. The issue of modernity began a few hundred years ago. The gates of the Jewish shtetels were coming down, and the era of the 'enlightment' started. For the first time since the Jews were exiled, some 2,000 years previously, a Jew could be a free man. This opened up a new world to the Jewish people, a secular world, a 'modern' world, and with it, the dilemma of dealing with the blandishments of modernity. The *Haskalah* movement was of the opinion that the Jews should embrace modernity in its entirety. They felt that it was time to rethink the "old" ways; this eventually gave birth to the progressive movements within Judaism. There was another faction, the "Torah *Im Derech Eretz*," led by Rabbi Shamson Refoel Hirsh (1808–1888), which was of the opinion that there is good to be found within modernity, and that one can lead a modern life, yet still remain under the precepts of the Torah, i.e., Modern Orthodoxy. Yet another movement, led by the *Chatam Sofer*[13] (1762–1839) claimed that the prohibition of *Chadash* (new grains), which is found in the Torah, can be interpreted to mean a prohibition against anything new, that is, modern, and that therefore the response to modernity is the complete rejection of it. What is the Chassidic response to modernity? How has it maintained and cultivated Judaism in this modern world?

The primary teachings of the Baal Shem Tov, as just mentioned, is the concept of joy. Herein lies the strength of *Chassidim* in dealing with the influences of modernism. A person who is dissatisfied with himself or his situation, tends to allow himself to be affected by outside influences and opinions, which he naturally feels are better than what he has. While a person with a strong self-esteem, one who is happy with himself and his lot, and feels accomplished and satisfied, does not feel the need for anything that others have to offer. He feels that what he has is best and therefore, he can say, "Why look elsewhere?" This is, perhaps, one of the objectives the Baal Shem Tov set out to achieve through his teachings of Joy. He brought Jews to the realization that they are wonderful, the Torah they inherited is glorious, and that they are possessed of the greatest treasures imaginable. With this attitude, outside, modern influences have no bearing on a Chassid's life. There is no need to look outside because what is inside is superior. Such is the Chassidic response to modernity.[14]

Regarding happiness, it is worth mentioning that it is *not* one of the 613 commandments of the Torah,[15] nonetheless, as a Chassidic Rebbe once phrased it, "Although *Simcha*–happiness, is not a positive commandment,[16] and depression is not a sin, *Simchah* can bring a person to such great heights, as no mitzvah can; and depression can bring a person, to such depths, as no sin can."

The idea of happiness and its necessity for serving God is best illustrated with a metaphor of war.[17] It is well-known that in war, it is not necessarily the physically stronger nation that wins. It is possible for the weaker one to win, if its fighting is with more "happiness," more conviction, hence, they are motivated. If one nation feels happy to do its duty, while the other is just fighting because the soldiers were forceably drafted, the nation fighting with excitement may win.

The same is true with man's inner struggle, the internal strife and duality, the struggle between the animalistic and Godly souls. On one hand, there is the animal soul, which says that man's ultimate objective is to serve himself. This is the soul that views the world with the thought, "How will I gain? Its perspective is always its own aggrandizement?" (This can be on a physical level, with reference to obtaining wealth, on a mental level, referring to obtaining knowledge, or even on a spiritual level, in reference to acquiring a spiritual experience.) On the other side, you have your Godly soul, which says, "How can I become transcendental? How can I do a good deed, not for my own personal gain, and with no ulterior, selfish motives?" The nature of this Godly soul is altruistic, while the nature of the animal soul is egotistic. A person can observe for himself the battle of the souls when it comes to an act of charity. A person can give charity with two diametrically opposed intentions, a Godly intention and an animalistic intention. If you give charity because you feel the other person's pain, if it disturbs you to see someone else's suffering, you are doing it out of empathy. You are doing a holy, transcendental act that comes from your Godly soul. If, however, one gives charity because one feels that by giving to the poor, he can boost his own ego, then it is an animalistic, selfish act (albeit, still an act of charity, for now the poor person has what to eat). A person may give charity for social reasons, to become an important person in his society. Or, perhaps, a person may see a poor beggar on the street and hand him a dollar, knowing that the reason that he gave the dollar was not so much because he felt the other person's pain, but because the act would allow him to feel good about himself. He feels proud of himself for doing the right and proper thing. Some may even give charity so that they can feel superior to other people, so that they can feel that they are the "givers" of society, while the others, less fortunate, are the "receivers." (Perhaps this is not a conscious thought; it may lurk in one's subconscious.) Hence, charity can be given as an expression of compassion, which then ennobles the donor and the world, or it can be self-serving in motivation, which demeans the giver and the 'energy.' Ultimately an act is only an act. Its value and meaning is formed by where the act comes from.

Internally the issue is to create a context of joy. This will not guarantee that no problems will arise, rather this enables one to handle the problem without being the problem. Therefore, being happy is the path along which we cope with the vicissitudes of life.[18]

Knowing that life is lived in strife and struggle (and only through joy can a person persevere), may cause a person to become depressed. The very notion that a human being must live such a life of continuous strife may cause depression! If this occurs, have in mind that the ultimate objective, and the purpose of the descent of man's soul upon this earth, is to bring God's radiance to the world and to ourselves. This is accomplished by enhancing the role of the Godly soul and minimizing that of the animalistic one. This is a lifelong task that is more difficult for some than for others, yet it is a task we can not desist from.

Life is a journey. Although there is the ultimate goal and aim to aspire to, that is, to become a Godly human being, it may be that the purpose is in the struggle itself.[19] Most people cannot control their subconscious animalistic instincts; temptations arise unintentionally and without thought. However, the purpose of the journey is to master the conscious self, so that it will not consciously surrender to the animalistic soul. Once a temptation arises from the subconscious, and forcefully enters the mind, one must push it aside and not give it any thought. The alternative to mastery is to be hostage to one's passions. The satisfactions in this modality are temporary and over time ever more difficult to maintain. Yet despite the mastery one cannot fully conquer the subconscious. It is only a *Tzadik* who can actually master his subconscious, instinctive, animalistic soul, and transform himself into a Godly human being, at which point there are no more temptations. (Even at the lofty level of *Tzadik*, struggles continue, although not between doing good and evil, but rather in the choice of which good to do.[20] The journey remains continuous.)

If, however, one feels that he is a *Tzadik*, and that there should not be those tedious struggles between good and evil, if one envisions himself as having a much loftier challenge, then he is most probably fooling himself, talking himself into being someone that he really is not.

The source of someone's depression is his thinking that he is something or someone that he is really not.[21] "Either Caesar or nothing." This type of statement encourages depression, because one talks himself into thinking that he should be another Caesar, or spiritually, another Moses, when in essence the reason he is looking elsewhere is that he can not face his real self. He is afraid of himself.[22] Thus the first step in overcoming depression is knowing who you are and what you want of life, on both an emotional level and a spiritual one.

Hence, an important ingredient for happiness and for the free flow of energy is to be completely in touch with oneself, to the extent that you know your strong points as well as your weak ones. You then feel completely comfortable with your shortcomings as well as your greatness, for indeed they all make up this unique person which is you. There remains no part of your character unexamined that might cause you to be embarrassed and ashamed of its existence. You are completely in touch and proud of yourself.[23] The beauty and charm of a human being, is that, unlike the angels, they have imperfections.

I employed earlier the metaphor of war. A Chassidic Rebbe once pointed out that in war, a leading motivator for fighters to be victorious, is music.[24] There are specific songs composed especially for combat. When the men in the field hear these tunes, they awaken within them the courage to overcome the enemy. Even the weak are aroused to great strength. The same holds true with one's inner battles, one's own "war." When one feels that his own enemy, the foe within him, is gaining force, one should sing a tune of victory, and thus persevere.

Happiness and joy pave the way to great spiritual heights.[25] Joy is a constant in terms of our discussion and not occasioned by performing *mitzvot* or otherwise.[26] The holy Seer of Lublin, Reb Yitzchak, befriended a well-known thief in town; his disciples were very much disturbed by this. When they finally mustered up enough courage to ask the Rebbe how he could befriend such a sinner, he answered that since this man was perpetually happy and joyous, the question was really, "How can you not like such a person?"

All the above was written to bring out one crucial point: the importance of serving God with joy. Indeed, one of the finest ways to bring yourself to be joyous is through singing happy tunes. One master writes that the easiest way to counter depression is through singing happy tunes.[27]

A melody can change a person's mood, even to the extent of changing his emotions from one extreme to the other, so that he can go from despair to happiness. How is it done? Kabbalah teaches that an appropriate melody reaches the listener's essence of soul, the level of *Yichidah*—Oneness,[28] which is also called in the Kabbalah, *Makif*, all-encompassing and transcendent, which is higher than the person's external and manifested emotions.

The explanation is as follows: Every human being possesses a soul, which in turn is made up of many internal as well as external parts. The most external part of a human being is his ability to act. [We notice that when someone does a certain action, constructing a house, for example, that it is imaginable that no one will ever know that he is the one who made it. This shows that actions being the most external part of one's being, it makes it possible that after the action is done, it will not show connection with the builder any longer.[29]] At a deeper and higher level of soul is one's ability to speak. Consequently it is much more closely identified with the person. [If you know someone well, and you hear someone else repeating a thought that he had heard from that person, you can easily identify the one who originated the thought.] In an even deeper part of one's soul are emotions and intellect, the mental capacities of man, which are closer to the essence. Thus it can happen that you experience such overwhelming emotions, or such deep thought, that you cannot reveal them to anyone except yourself. You cannot express them to anyone who has an existence other than your own. This phenomenon occurs because the emotions are so deeply rooted in your heart that you cannot express them externally.

Nevertheless, these emotions are still not the essence of your being, of your soul; they are still considered something external which is imposed unto your essence. "Essence precedes existence." Emotions are experiences which are imposed on the essence of your soul. Philosophers have argued that man is born with a mind like a "blank sheet of paper upon which experience writes."[30] The core of the soul, that is, the essence of one's being, is the level of the soul which is above any form of external expressions. It is too deep and internal to be expressed externally, even to one's self. Therefore, when you sing a melody, which as discussed earlier, has the power to reach the essence of soul (the level of *Makif*), your mood can change easily. All the emotions you may experience now, for example, depression, are only "external emotions"; they are not the essence of your being. When a joyous melody comes along, and touches the essence of your being, it can affect you and change your mood from one extreme, of being depressed, to the other, of being happy and joyous.[31]

We notice, writes a Chassidic master,[32] that if a melody is composed skillfully and is beautifully written, it is clear how each stanza leads to the next; there seems to be one continuous flow of the tune. The music moves.[33] In addition, if the tune is really exquisite and graceful, the end of the tune and the beginning of the tune will be beautifully connected. It feels as if there is one continuous cycle, as if the tune never began and never ends. This is where the real charm of a tune is expressed. The reason for this phenomenon is that an inspiring, thoughtful tune emanates from the part of the composer's soul that is called *Makif*. *Makif* can also be translated as a circle, something that encircles something else. Thus, the tune is formed like a circle, and appropriately, the melody also reaches the inner depths of the listener's soul, the listener's *Makif*. This is the level of the soul that on one hand is less palpable and less consciously felt because it transcends being and intellect, and on the other hand, resonates in the deepest parts of consciousness, because it is all-encompassing. Unlike the intellect, which resides in the brain, or the power to see, in the eyes,

Makif exists in no one place in the body more than in another. This level of soul exists everywhere. It encompasses our entire existence. This, indeed, is the power of song: the ability to reach the highest levels of soul, the level of *Makif*.

Interestingly enough, the custom of *Chassidim* is to dance in one continuous circle, again recalling the continuity of *Makif*. Similarly, the Hebrew word for song is *Nigun* (ניגון) which is the same when read backwards and forwards. A song, then, is a continuous circle.

A Chabad Rebbe once said[34] that by definition Chabad means intellect, for the word Chabad is an acronym for *chochmah*—wisdom, *binah*—understanding and *da'at*—knowledge, the three main intellectual capacities of man. Therefore the Chabad philosophy is to take the highest levels of inspiration one can have and to internalize them, to bring them down to the level of human understanding. The aspirations of a Chabad Chassid is to internalize every experience possible. When a Chabad Chassid dances, he takes the *Makif*, which the idea of a circle represents, and draws it down to his own level; he internalizes the *Makif* (the experience) into his own level.[35]

All of the above refers to a person who is not necessarily in a joyous mood, and who, through song, can change his mood and become happy. There is yet another truth in song, and that is that through song, one can transcend the moment, the power of song being such that it can transform the singer or listener into another reality. It is perhaps for this reason we find that often the most enchanting Chassidic melodies were inspired and composed at the darkest moments of time.

Chassidim throughout their history sang tunes, even joyful tunes in the most devastating times. Even while they were being physically beaten, they had the escape agent called song. I once heard from an older Chassid an experience that occurred when he was sent away to Siberia, for spreading Judaism in Stalin's Russia. Once while he was working in the labor camp, and was in midst of doing hard physical labor, he began singing a Chassidic melody. The fellow working along side of him, asked him, "How can you in such terrible times sing such happy tunes? From where do you procure such strength?" The Chassid explained to him that the difference between them was that when the man was sent away to Siberia, away from his environment and culture, away from his occupation, he felt down and depressed because he was completely out of place. "However," said the Chassid, "my true vocation has no boundaries, has no specific place; it can be done anytime and in any place. My preoccupation is to serve the creator of the universe. Therefore I am joyous everywhere and anywhere I go."

A cheerful tune evokes and brings forth a person's happiness, and conversely when a person is happy (which a person should always be), the way to express and display his joy is through singing happy tunes. When the Jews left Egypt and experienced the splitting of the red sea, they all sang the *Shirahs Hayam* together. Traditionally, the melody they sang was a joyful tune.[36]

In truth, every single human being has reason to be happy; one can be happy from the mere fact that he is alive and can experience the sensation called happiness. Happiness is truly a matter of perspective and attitude, and whether or not one is willing to be happy. There is a parable told of two people walking along the road. One of them happened to be deaf. Suddenly a beautiful tune was heard; it was so enchanting that the one who could hear started dancing to the music. His friend who was deaf thought the other was simply out of his mind. The same is true of the beautiful music of the Creator and His creation.[37] If you are a person who can hear the music, then you sing along and dance; if, you are spiritually deaf, and not in tune with the music of the universe, then you wonder why it is that there are people who are perpetually joyful.[38]

Moreover, when a person is happy, he will express his feelings by dancing. The joy that he experiences will not only affect him emotionally, in his heart, but will overwhelm him so completely that his entire existence shares in that ecstasy, and his feet will be filled with joy, and will start dancing on their own. *Chassidim* believe that when the Torah says, "And it shall come to pass because ye hearken,"[39] it is telling us that a person should be so involved and absorbed with the commandments of God, that even his heels (the lowest physical parts of the body, which also represent the lowest parts of the soul), shall be permeated with Godliness. And this type of involvement with God, one can accomplish through dancing with one's feet.

There is another concept of dance that is connected with the idea of joy. We notice that when someone experiences joy in its highest form, he automatically forgets about his own ego, his own self-pride. He experiences a true level of *Bittul*—self-nullification. He loses himself in a positive way. People will even change their very nature at times of immense joy. For example, if someone is by nature very calm and collected, an individual whom you will never find acting wild, or even showing enthusiasm, it can be seen that at a personal moment of intense joy, for instance, the marriage of a child, this same ordinarily calm person can start dancing wildly with rapid movement. At a moment of extreme joy, one may lose himself completely. The proof that one is truly in joy is that he loses his ego, and goes out of his "own world." The joy which he is experiencing means a great deal, and the rapture overwhelms him completely.[40]

Taking leave of one's ego in a moment of rapture is expressed in Chassidic dance as well. As mentioned earlier, *Chassidim* dance in a circle, signifying the equality of the participants. There is no better or worse dancer in a circle, and all dance in the same manner and direction. This represents the concept of equality. No single individual should ever feel superior to his fellow man, everyone in a sense is equal; each person with his unique and significant course in life. No two people are exactly alike, and each individual has something positive to contribute.

When people are happy, the social boundaries between them, boundaries between the rich and poor, or between the intelligent and the foolish, cease to exist. At a moment of true joy a person does not care much about the superficial boundaries and distinctions that are essentially invented by society. Happiness equals *Bittul*. Where there is happiness, there is *Bittul*.

Moreover, in order for a person to experience true happiness, he must practice and possess *Bittul*. Namely, his own personal existence, his necessities, must not take up too much space.[41] A humble person feels that all his physical and spiritual gratification are a gift from above, and that he does not deserve such goodness. In his humility, he believes that it is only out of God's benevolence that he receives anything at all. Therefore, if he does not receive, he does not become distressed.

When a person lowers his expectations of life in this way, and tries to differentiate between that which he really needs, and those needs dictated by social pressure, or the like, he will realize a happier and more fulfilling life experience. *Bittul* is a primary ingredient in the recipe for happiness. As the Psalmist says: "See you humble people and rejoice."[42] When one is humble, he can then rejoice. When *Chassidim* dance in a circle, they hope that they will eventually achieve this intense and lasting level of happiness through *Bittul*.

NOTES

1. Rabbi Nachman of Breslov. *Likutei Moharan.* Part 2: 24. See also: *Kesser Shem Tov.* (New York: Kehot Publication Society. 1987) *Hosofot* Chapter 169. "In the eyes of *Chassidim*, joy is considered a biblical commandment, a mitzvah."

2. See: The book of *Maccabees 1.* Chapter 2. Verses 42–44. Chapter 7. Verses 8–18.

3. *The Guide To The Perplexed.* Chapter 3; 53. The Rambam explains that Chassid means a person who does more than he has to; he excels. See also: *Rambam Hilchot Deot.* Chapter 1. Halacha 5. *Rambam Shemonah Perakim.* Chapter 4. Talmud. *Shabbat,* p. 122b.

4. In the Talmud these *Chassidim* are known for numerous acts of piety. Eg; Talmud. *Baba Kamma.* 30a. *Nedarim.* 10a. *Niddah.* 38a. And known as *Tzadikim,* righteous men. See: *Midrash Rabbah. Bereishit.* Parsha 62. Chapter 2. In the commentary by Rabbi David Luria (1798–1855) Radal (2).

5. Talmud *Berachot* 32b.

6. This means to hold two opposing thoughts simultaneously. There is a story told how once when the second Chabad Rebbe, Reb Dovber, was a young man, and he was baby-sitting his child, he engrossed himself deeply in thought. Suddenly his baby started crying; however, since he was so involved in thought, he did not hear the child. Reb Dovber's father, Reb Sheneur Zalman, who lived on the lower floor,

when hearing the child, rushed upstairs and picked up the child. Later he rebuked Reb Dovber, saying, "no matter how deep one is in thought, one must hear a child's cry." Expanded consciousness means to be in touch with two realities simultaneously. However, for most of us, who operate on a lower level of consciousness, when we want to study, we must put ourselves in a situation which is conducive to study, in a quiet room, for we are very one-dimensional, and we can only focus completely on one thing at a time. The Rebbe wanted his son to be able to exist simultaneously in two realities (meditating on) the spiritual and the physical (hearing the baby cry). (See: The third Chabad Rebbe. The Tzemach Tzedek. *Derech Mitvosecho.* (New York: Kehot Publication Society. 1986.) p. 81. (See Chapter 7, p. 129)

7. Rabbi Yakov Emdin (1697–1776.): *Siddur Yahvatz.* The section following the morning prayers.

8. See: *Sefer Chassidim.* Chapter 167. With regards to a particular sin. (For a general overview on the Chassidei Ashkenaz. See: Gershan Scholem *Major trends in Jewish Mysticism* (New York: Schocken Books Inc. 1946.) The third lecture. p. 80.

9. Generally in Jewish thought, the idea of paining the body is not a way of serving God. The Talmud (*Tannit* 11a). says that if a person inflicts pain upon his body, which he cannot bear, he is sinning. (See also: *Shulchan Aruch Orach Chaim.* Chapter 571: 1) Furthermore, one must view his body not as his own possession, but as the property of God, a holy commodity. See: *Radvas. On the Rambam. Hilchot Sanhedrin* Chapter 18. Halacah 6. *Shulchan Aruch Harav. Chashen Mishpat. Hilchot Nezkei Guf VaNefesh.* Chapter 3. Rabbi Shlomo Yoseph Zevin. In *Leor Ha'Halacah.* (Jerusalem: Beit Hillel.) p. 310–328. He poses an interesting question: he asks, "If Shylock in 'The Merchant of Venice' were to take his contract (which demands a pound of flesh) (The pound of flesh which I demand of him I dearly bought, is mine, and I will have it.") to a Rabbinical court, what would have happened? He answers that without question it would be null. One can not sell his own flesh; it is not his to sell. Chassidic masters spoke harshly against any paining of the body whatsoever, and strongly suggested to work with the body. See: *Kesser Shem Tov.* (New York: Kehot Publication Society. 1987.) Chapter 231 and *Hosofot* p. 92. *Hayom Yom.* 28th of Sh'vat. See also: *Rambam Hilchot De'ot.* Chapter 4. Halacha 1. *Rambam Shemonah Perakim.* Chapter 4. *Kitzur Shulchan Aruch.* Chapter 32. Rabbi Moshe Chayim Luzzato. *Mesilat Yesharim* Hakdamah. Chapter 26.

10. William James. *The Varieties Of Religious Experience* (Penguin Classics) Lecture ix. Titled 'Conversion.'

11. Rabbi Chaim Vital, explains, that a Chassid is a person who serves God with happiness. See: *Sharei Kedusha.* Part 1. Shar 3. The Second Chabad Rebbe. Rabbi DovBer writes, that although the term Chassid has come to represent throughout history, various styles in Divine service, nonetheless, there is a common denominator between all *Chassidim,* and that is, that they all aspire to transcend the physical, and cleave to God. See: *Migdal Oz,* (Israel: Machon Lubavitch. 1980) p. 345.

12. A major contribution to Jewish thought which the Baal Shem Tov revealed is the idea of "Hashgacha Pratiout" (Divine Providence). He taught that every single incident that occurs in this universe, even a tiny leaf being turned over by a blowing wind, has a purpose in the master plan of the universe. When one contemplates on this, they will surely be happier human beings, knowing that life is not meaningless,

but does indeed have a purpose. See also: Rabbi Eliyohu Ben Moshe Di Vidas *Reshit Chochmah*. Shar HaAhavah. Chapter 10. Where he writes that the belief in divine providence causes happiness.

13. It is interesting to note, as I heard from a grandson of the Chatom Sofer, that there exists a manuscript from this Rabbi on music. In it, he speaks of all the seven musical notes and explains each one, and what it represents, and why each note awakens different feelings in the listener. A Chassidic Rebbe who was also known as a great composer of song, Rabbi Yisrael of Modzitz, writes that there are essentially seven notes in each octave, which arouse seven different feelings, whose source is the seven Sefirot of emotions. These seven correspond to the seven days of creation. He also writes that when the Psalmist enumerates in Psalms, Chapter 29, seven sounds, he is alluding to the seven notes in an octave. See: Rabbi Yisroel of Modzitz. *Divrei Yisrael*. Parshat Mikketz. Maamor Echad M'Remazei Chanukah. See also: Rabbi Schneur Zalman of Liadi. *Likutei Torah*. (New York: Kehot Publication Society, 1996) Parshat Naso, p. 29b.

14. Perhaps a similar situation in history would be at the time of the golden age of Spain, when many Jews were assimilating. It was perhaps for this reason that Rabbi Yehudah HaLevy wrote *The Kuzari*, in which he is in a sense telling his Jewish brethren not to look elsewhere, but to look into themselves. "You are," he writes, "the heart of all people; you are special, and your homeland, Israel, is the heart of the universe." The books goal perhaps was to boost the self-esteem of the Jewish people.

15. Albeit that the holy Ari-Zal. Rabbi Yitzchak Luria, (1534–1572) writes in regards to the verse. "For you have not served me with joy" (*Deuteronomy*. Chapter 28. Verse 47.) The Torah is telling that even if you will do all the *mitzvot*, but you will not serve God with joy you will still deserve . . . , (Rabbi Yeshayah Halevi Horowitz. (1560–1630) *Shalah HaKodesh*. Shenei Luchot Habrit. Introduction to Mitzvas. 10 discourses. Discourse 3:4. See also: Rabbi Yoseph Albo. *Safer Haikkarim*. Maamor 3. Chapter 33.) And the Rambam as well, also writes of the importance of joy. (See: *Hilchot Lullove*. towards the end.) Nonetheless, according to all opinions *Simcha* is not one of 613 *mitzvot*.

16. Rabbi Chayim Yoseph David Azulay writes in *Avodat Hakodesh. Tziparon Shamir* Chapter 11: 161, that the word, Simcha, is an acronym for "Simchas mitzvah Chiyuv Hu," Happiness while performing a mitzvah is an obligation. Furthermore, Rabbi Yoseph Albo writes in *Safer Haikkarim*, Maamor 3. Chapter 33, that doing a mitzvah with Simcha completes the mitzvah.

17. Rabbi Schneur Zalman of Liadi. *Tanya*. Chapter 26. See also: Rabbi Moshe Chayim Luzzatto. *Mesilat Yesharim*. Chapter 9, in which life as a struggle is compared to war.

18. Rabbi Chayim Yoseph David Azulay writes in *Avodat Hakodesh. Morah Be'etzbah*. Chapter 10: 320, that the lack of happiness in serving God weakens one's potential to persevere in life. Furthermore in *Orchot Tzadikim*. (Jerusalem: Orot Chayim. 1986). (Author unknown, although some attribute this classic to the teacher of the Rambam. Shar Hasimcha p. 80), it is written that Simcha causes mental as well as physical health, which is a prerequisite for serving God.

19. Rabbi Schneur Zalman of Liadi. *Tanya*. Chapter 27.

20. Talmud. *Gittin.* 56a. Here it shows how a Tzadik must make choices within good.

21. Rabbi Schneur Zalman of Liadi. *Tanya.* Chapter 27.

22. In the words of an existentialist, Søren Kierkegaard, "If the self does not become itself, it is despair." *The Sickness Unto Death* Søren Kierkegaard, (New Jersey: Princeton University Press. 1983) p. 60.

23. See also: Rabbi Schneur Zalman of Liadi. *Maamorei Admur Hazoken. Maarezal.* (New York: Kehot Publication Society. 1984.) p. 29. Happiness is achieved when the essence of one's g-dly soul is completely revealed. Rabbi Schneur Zalman of Liadi. *Maamorei Admur Hazoken. Haktzorim,* (New York: Kehot Publications Society. 1986) p. 553.

24. Rabbi Moshe Yichiel Elimelech of Levertov. *Safer Shemirat Hada'at.* Aimrei Tal. Ma'amar Nigun, (Bnei Brak Israel: Ginzei MaHaritz. 1986) p. 20–21.

25. Perhaps the greatest master of Kabbalah in the past five hundred years, the holy Arizal once said that the reason he received these great insights of Kabbalah was that he served God with joy. Rabbi Eliezer Ezcary *Safer Cheredim.* Hakdamah LeMitzvot. 4. (The fourth condition.) Rabbi Chayim Yoseph David Azulay. *Avodat Hakodesh. Morah Be'etzba.* Chapter 10: 327. By the same author. *Lev David.* Chapter 14: 3. Rabbi Schneur Zalman of Liadi. *Torah Or.* (New York: Kehot Publication Society. 1996.) Parshat Toledot. p. 20b. Rabbi Pinchas Eliyohu Ben Meir of Vilna *Sefer Habrit.* (Jerusalem: Yerid Hasefarim. 1990.) Part 2. Maamar 12. Chapter 4.(4). Part 2. Maamor 14. Chapter 9. Rabbi Yisrael Meir HaKohen. *Shulchan Aruch Orach Chaim Mishnah Berurah.* Chapter 669:11. Rabbi Yakov of Polonnoye. *Toldot, Yakov Yoseph.* Parshat Reveh.

26. The prophet Elijah once told a sage that a jester, a person who brings joy to the depressed and lonely, deserves a portion in the world to come. See Talmud *Tannit* 22a. Rabbi Eliyohu Ben Moshe Di Vidas writes in *Reshit Chochmah.* Shar HaAhavah. Chapter 10, that every exercise a person does, they shall do it with *Simcha,* joy.

27. Rabbi Schneur Zalman of Liadi. *Maamorei Admur Hazoken. Inyonim.* (New York: Kehot Publication Society. 1983) p. 403. See also: Rabbi Nachman of Breslov *Likutei Aytzot.* (Brooklyn: Moriah. 1976.) Neginah 8, p. 138. Rabbi Pinchas of Koritz. *Midrash Pinchas,* (Jerusalem: 1971.) p. 89. (Chapter 14)

28. The second Chabad Rebbe Rabbi Dovber. *Shaarei T'shuva.* 2, (New York: Kehot Publication Society. 1983.) p. 15.

29. However, an architect will always be identified with a house he has designed because he has put a deeper part of himself, his artistic skills, into the action.

30. The British philosopher John Locke (1632–1704) argues that man has no essence or innate ideas to begin with. However, according to Jewish thought, there is indeed an essence to man. The soul-mind is a "Colored sheet of paper which experience writes upon." The emotions are imposed on the essence, which existed previously with a distinct nature.

31. Rabbi Moshe Yichiel Elimelech of Levertov. *Safer Shemirat Hada'at.* Aimrei Tal. Ma'amar Nigun, (Bnei Brak Israel: Ginzei MaHaritz. 1986.) p. 5. Through song, the essence of soul is revealed, the part of soul that is pure and above all negative

traits. When revealed, the depression ceases to exist. Therefore a prophet, when angry and depressed, would use song to transcend those feelings. (*Kings 2*. Chapter 3. Verse 15.)

32. The sixth Chabad Rebbe. Rabbi Yoseph Yitzchak. *Safer Hamaamorim 5702.*— 1941. (New York: Kehot Publication Society, 1964) p. 48. See also: Rabbi Schneur Zalman of Liadi. *Maamorei Admur Hazoken Haktzorim*, (New York: Kehot Publication Society. 1986) p. 511.

33. See: Roger Scruton. *An Intelligent Person's Guide To Philosophy*. (Allen Lane The Penguin Press. 1996. USA.) Chapter 11, for an interesting view of what exactly moves in music.

34. The sixth Chabad Rebbe. Rabbi Yoseph Yitzchak *Likutei Diburim*, (New York: Kehot Publication Society. 1980) Vol. 1: p. 47.

35. It appears that there is perhaps another reason that *Chassidim* dance in a circle. The Talmud says (*Taanit*, 31a.) that at the time of redemption, God will form a great circle with the righteous people, and together they will dance. Thus *Chassidim* dance in a circle to be reminded of that day. A Chassid once said that by dancing in a circle, a person can learn a few things about life: A) Even if the weak who cannot keep up with the dance, retire, the dance goes on, that is, each person is essentially on his own in the dance of life, and B) Man is never completely alone; for even if an individual decides to leave the dance, the collective whole dances on. See: Eliezer Shtainman. *Be'er HaChassidut*. Vol. 2 of *Chabad Chassidim*, (Mochon Kemach. Israel) p. 73.

36. From the talks of the sixth Chabad Rebbe, Rabbi Yoseph Yitzchak, on the night of the seventh day of Passover, 5698 (1938).

37. See: Chapter 9 footnotes 3–5.

38. See: Rabbi Moshe Chayim Ephraim of Sudylkov. (?–1880) (A Grandson of the Baal Shem Tov.) *Degel Machanah Ephraim*. Parshat Yitro, p. 35a.

39. *Deuteronomy* 7:12 (The origin of this thought is that the word that the Torah uses for "because" is *ekev*, which means "heel" in Hebrew.)

40. The fifth Chabad Rebbe Reb Shalom Dovber, *Samach Tisamach 5657* (New York: Kehot Publication Society. 1965), p. 50. See also: Rabbi Schneur Zalman of Liadi, *Siddur Im Dach*. (New York: Kehot Publication Society. 1965) The intentions of Mikvah, in the beginning.

41. The sixth Chabad Rebbe. Rabbi Yoseph Yitzchak. *Sefer Hamaamorim 5710 (1950)* (New York: Kehot Publication Society. 1986), p. 237.

42. *Psalms*. 69:33.

5
Marirrut/Sadness
Medicating the Soul through Music

The wisest of men said, "There is a time for everything; there is a time to weep, and a time to laugh; a time to wail, and a time to dance."[1]

There is room for expression of countless emotions in the service of God.

There are times when a person should be joyous and cheerful, which by extension means feeling close to God, experiencing God's imminence. There are also times when one should serve God out of awe and reverence, with feelings of distance from the all powerful Creator, a humble feeling of our own limitations. As the Psalmist says, "Serve God out of fear with unveiled trembling,"[2] which translates to serving God with a sense of awe.

Generally, a person should serve God through happiness. Nonetheless, the dilemma of Godly service exclusively through joy is that it may eventually lead to spiritual complacency.[3] One who is perpetually happy begins to feel comfortable with his situation. This, however, may lead to two undesired eventualities: The first being that one who is always happy and comfortable may start to feel that he has done enough, that he has matured spiritually, and there is no more room for spiritual growth. This idea is completely antithetical to the Torah. God is infinite; therefore, if one wishes to connect with Him, one must aspire to be as He is—infinite. A person must continuously grow spiritually. If one is content with the his accomplishments of yesterday, what then is the purpose of today? A person who is perpetually content becomes like the sponges of the sea, which though initially mobile become immobile. It is endemic for a human being to work and to grow. As it is written, "Man was created to toil."[4] Thus, it is understood that the danger of happiness is that it may breed contentment, which in turn cultivates and nurtures spiritual death.

In the second circumstance, complacency may at times prompt man to sin. People who are always happy have a tendency to feel virtuous about themselves. They may, because of their contentment, become pompous and even egotistic, all which lead man to iniquity, and spiritual carelessness. Because of man's fragile nature in the area of consciousness, there exists a fine line between what we may call true happiness and what is simple frivolity and callousness.[5]

For these, as well as other reasons, a person should serve God with humility, through fear and awe, in addition to happiness.[6] The easiest way to accomplish this is through proper meditation. When a person contemplates how far he is from the truth, and how separate, alone, and alienated he is in this world, and from God, he becomes frightened, bitter, and down on himself. This experience is what is called *Marirrut*.

There is however, a vast difference between being bitter about yourself and your situation, and being in despair.

In Hebrew, the word for bitter, is *Marirrut* and the word for despair, is *Atzvut*.[7] The difference between the two is that when a person is in despair, and feels depressed, this usually means that he stops having any feelings whatsoever. He may even believe that there is no purpose in life. Even people he loves and cares for may start to lose their meaning to him. A depressed person's heart, metaphorically speaking, stops working. His heart hardens, and he becomes unresponsive to all that is around him. These feelings are the complete antithesis of everything holy and Godly, which is synonymous with life and fluidity. Life is growth and movement. *Marirrut* has a different dynamic than *Atzvut*. When someone is bitter about his situation, and examines his spiritual life, he realizes that he has distanced himself from the path and alienated himself from Godliness. His heart does not stop, does not stiffen; on the contrary, he is overwhelmed with longing for Godliness and holiness. It is indeed because of the lack that he has become bitter. The bitterness is a signal that it is time for him to advance spiritually. He is no longer complacent with the status quo, and he is motivated to begin a new cycle of growth.[8] Thus, the proof that what one is experiencing is *Marirrut* and not *Atzvut* is from the fact that one takes action and does something about these feelings. These feelings provoke movement, and growth.

The Mishnah states, "Who is wealthy? One who is happy with his lot."[9] This is confined to the material domain only. Spiritually, however, we are encouraged to feel discontented, lest we become complacent. It is even good occasionally to be bitter with, and about, oneself. Bitterness as we have shown can be an incentive for movement. But as with so much else, bitterness should not be a way of life; rather a catalyst that breaks one's complacency, to reach happiness, and serve God through joy.[10]

Marirrut may be likened to the concept of pain. One can examine the issue of pain from two perspectives: the obvious reaction to pain is that it hurts; it is uncomfortable and irritating. However, if one reflects upon it, one realizes the positive aspect of pain as well, and that is that without pain, one would not know if he were suffering from an ailment. Pain is the way the body tells the mind that danger looms. When one cuts himself, for instance, and does not experience pain, it is possible to not notice the wound and thus endanger one's self. Hence, pain serves as an indicator of injury, as a protector to the body. The purpose of pain is to cause a positive reaction, so that the person will go to seek help. The same is true of *Marirrut*. A person can be spiritually unwell and not even notice it. However, when one is feeling down for whatever reason, and he evaluates these feelings in a spiritual sense, he is utilizing his bitterness for a higher purpose and therefore creating a positive effect. This means that instead of just being down, he can utilize his feeling of bitterness as an incentive for spiritual growth. These feelings can assist him as pain does, because these feelings of *Marirrut* compel the person to become a better human being. These feelings cause awareness to the person that he is spiritually out of alignment and must do some spiritual healing. However, if one experiences too much of it, one may become slowly immune to it. In this same way, *Marirrut* is only good in small dosages.

A group of people once came to a Chassidic Rebbe, and said that they would like to become his *Chassidim*, but that first they had a question to ask. They complained that they had seen a Chassid crying on Simchat Torah, a happy day on the calendar, and singing joyous tunes on the Ninth of Av, a day of mourning commemorating the destruction of the holy Temples. Their question was obvious, "How can someone cry on such a happy day, and rejoice on such a sad day?" The Rebbe answered them, "The Chassid you saw was happy because he was a man with a vision of the future. When he saw the destruction, he saw God's words of the destruction, as foretold by the prophets, being fulfilled. When the Chassid realized this, he knew for certain that God's promise that there will be a time of rebuilding will surely come true as well, and the thought itself made him happy.[11] And as for the crying, the Rebbe told them that crying does not necessarily come from being depressed or sad; it can also come from *Marirrut*, which is bitterness. When Simchat Torah came along, the Chassid was stirred to thinking about himself and how distant he was from the holiness of the Torah, how great the day was, and how alienated he was. He was so moved by these thoughts that he started crying, and this was indeed positive *Marirrut*.[12]

The most basic way for one to become bitter about his spiritual state of mind, *Marirrut*, is through the appropriate examination of his situation, *cheshbon hanefesh*. When one thinks seriously about his situation, what he has actually accomplished in life, and what he aspires to; where he thinks he should be spiritually at this moment in time, and where he actually is, his heart will be opened and emotionally moved, and these 'bitter' feelings will stimulate him to become a better human being. The *Marirrut*, though bitter and painful, acts as an irritant to open to new possibilities.

In mystical thought, a bridge or conduit is said to exist between the mind and the heart; this enables the heart to feel what the mind is thinking about, and for the mind to understand and articulate what the heart is feeling.[13] There are times when this connection is impaired or broken, so that the capacity to feel life is absent. This is a huge handicap, and creates a deficit in one's interaction with life and living, as well as his growth. In order to bridge this rift and repair the passageway, he may need a melody, a song, which can restore the harmony and balance, and hence the connection.

"Voice arouses intention."[14] We are perpetually expressing ourselves through song. Speaking is singing only in a narrower range. Communication is a function of intention, which in Hebrew translates as *Kavanah*. But *Kavanah* can also mean a window.[15] We can infer that with the appropriate tune, or voice, one can open a window from the mind to the heart.[16] To communicate powerfully one mobilizes not only the words which appeal to the intellect, but also song which resonates in the heart. It is the latter that opens the listener to the feeling tones in the message.

A Chassidic master once observed that there are perhaps three reasons why at times a tale would not arouse feelings. Either the story is told to a person who does not fully understand it, because he simply does not have the intellectual capacity to grasp its plot. Or, the person does have the capability to understand, but he is simply not interested in understanding. He does not want to understand, intentionally closing his mind to such thoughts. Or finally, perhaps the story is told to a person who cannot really understand, because he is so far removed from the moral of the story that it makes no sense at all to him. When a story with a spiritual moral is told, and the person hearing the story is completely removed spiritually from anything the story is saying, the story cannot and will not penetrate or arouse him spiritually. Therefore, if there is a person for whom intellectual persuasions and stories do not work, to arouse him spiritually, the best method would probably be to sing a melody. When one sings a song full of heart, the melody can serve as a conduit through which the story and its theme can penetrate and pierce the soul.[17]

Often, one does not need anything else but the melody. One does not need a thought, nor even a story behind the melody, for the melody itself can penetrate the heart and arouse the greatest spiritual feelings. A great Chassidic Rebbe was able to remove all evil from within man with song.[18] A song that is slow and thoughtful can bring a person to real *Marirrut* which is a prerequisite and a prime factor in doing *Teshuvah*—returning to one's spiritual source.[19] The first Chabad Rebbe composed ten Chassidic melodies. His *Chassidim* say that if you sing any one of those melodies, you will do *Teshuvah*, because within these songs have been implanted intensely deep and holy emotions from the composer's soul. These songs are imbued and permeated with emotions of a soul yearning to be close to God; thus, if one sings it and understands it, he will also be moved to become closer to God.[20]

Many Chassidic Rebbes would use song to bring people closer to God. One of these outstanding masters was the Modzitzer Rebbe, Rabbi Yisroel Taub. When he passed away, a famed Chassidic Rebbe, Rabbi Meir of Austravitze, said to his own disciples, "I am envious of Reb Yisroel, for he left such a vast collection of melodies for the world to appreciate and be inspired by."[21] His disciples asked him, "And your teachings are worth nothing? They too, are something to be proud of." The Rebbe answered them, "Through the study of my teachings, very few will actually change their lives for the better; however, his tunes will bring many to *Teshuvah* for countless generations to come."

Here is a short story about this great Chassidic Rebbe, Rabbi Yisroel Taub, showing the effect that music has on the listener.[22] It is told that in the town of Modzitz where the Rebbe lived, there was a large Russian military base. (In those days Modzitz was under the Russian government; the Russian name of this town was Ivanogrod.) The routine of the Rebbe was that on Shabbat he would sing songs throughout the entire day. Once as he was singing his Chassidic melodies, a Russian officer, who happened to be the conductor of the military orchestra, was strolling by his house. When he heard these beautiful melodies being sung, he decided to make it a habit to walk past the Rebbe's house to hear the wonderful tunes. One day, he worked up the courage and entered the Rebbe's house. Once inside, he asked if he could please speak with the Rebbe in private. When he was finally alone with the Rebbe, he broke down and cried bitter tears. This is what he told the Rebbe, "The truth is that I am a Jew. When I was but a small boy, the army kidnapped me, together with many other Jewish children, and for many years now, I had totally forgotten that I was Jewish. However, since I started hearing the Rebbe's songs, I began to remember my youth, and I want to return to my source. I must know," he pleaded of the Rebbe, "what to do." The Rebbe instructed him on how he should proceed in accomplishing his goal; however, the Rebbe warned him to do all he instructed with complete secrecy. When the holiday of Passover came along, he told the Rebbe that he wanted to make a Kosher Passover, and the only way he could do it was if he told his commanding officer. The Rebbe told him to tell his superiors, and that they would not trouble him at all, and so it was, that he became an observant Jew in the Russian army. Moreover, not only did the melodies of the Rebbe change his own life for the better, but when his superior heard about the Rebbe, he also wanted to meet him. After a while, the commanding officer and the Rebbe became close friends, and when the Rebbe's daughter got married, the officer gave permission for the official army orchestra to play at the wedding.

A song, as explained earlier, has the potential to bridge the gap between the heart and mind. However, there are those for whom this is not a problem; their heart—mind connection operates proficiently. They feel what they think, and can articulate their feelings quite well. Their failing is in not actualizing the feelings. They do not take action. People of this ilk too can be helped by a slow meditative tune that permeates their being. As one Chassidic Rebbe said, "Song opens the heart and allows the feelings to penetrate the entire being."[23] And from the heart, it imbues the entire body.[24]

A human being may find himself in extreme emotional situations. As an example, a wedding, a cause for rejoicing, or a funeral, which brings one to sadness. In both these instances, music is played,[25] because it is the best vehicle for expressing emotions that defy words. When the emotion is too overwhelming to express with the conventional tools of speech, one may find that it can then be best expressed in song.

In life there is comedy and there is drama; one causes you to be joyous and laugh, while the other provokes you to be sad and cry. In truth, there exists but a fine line between the two. What makes one person laugh may cause the other to cry and vice versa. If one sits down on a chair and it suddenly collapses, it may seem comical to the people sitting next to him, however, he feels the pain. Sometimes one may feel so happy that one begins crying, and one may sometimes start laughing upon hearing terrible news. The cause is that our minds think linearly, processing information one step at a time. First we think A, then B, and so on. We expect life to follow this same logic; we assume that life will be lived linearly, with a natural progression of sequences, and when faced with a challenge, an unexpected obstacle, we try immediately to process it with the standard tools. So we make up reasons for occurrences and happenstance. For example, you are planning to meet your spouse at the restaurant at eight o'clock, and you are unexpectedly late, simply because you did not realize the time. When you arrive late, you don't say that there was "no reason," and that you just forgot the time. You make an excuse, so that it makes sense, and fits within the pattern of things that are expected. You create a reason to make "sense" of the issue, yet the reason may not be factual.

Tragedy is perhaps sad because it shatters all form and pattern, while comedy is joyous, because it is a release, and transcends form. Through comedy you transcend your inflexible and paradigmatic frame of mind. The heart of comedy is contradiction, which is contrary to linear thinking.

When there arise in life situations which are not in the pattern of things, a tragedy, death, or, on a happier note, falling in love unexpectedly, since one's rational mind is not equipped to process these experiences, one either starts laughing hysterically, or crying bitterly.[26] Both of these outbursts are expressions of emotions which are not expected. Music is played at both such moments, to enhance the feelings and more importantly, to help and assist in expressing these overwhelming feelings.

In conclusion, although the idea of *Marirrut* may at times spur growth, and can be a means and an incentive to compel one to do *Teshuvah*, nonetheless, a human should strive to have the precise equilibrium, the appropriate balance in life. The Zohar asks, when one is doing *Teshuvah* and is sorrowful, from where does his happiness come?[27] The Zohar answers that in the time of the Temple, the joy was aroused from the singing and the jubilant atmosphere in the Temple.[28] This means that in today's day and age when there is no Temple, to create the joy a person's *Teshuvah* on its own must be permeated with a sense of joy, in order to stabilize and properly balance the emotional scale. A human being must never feel *Marirrut* to such an extreme that there is no happiness in his life. One must strive to have a balance between happiness, without becoming complacent, and *Marirrut*, without being depressed.[29] And ultimately happiness must prevail.

NOTES

1. *Ecclesiastes*. 3:4.

2. *Psalms*. 2:11.

3. Rabbi Schneur Zalman of Liadi. *Tanya*. Chapter 1.

4. *Job* 5:7. See: Talmud. *Sanhedrin*. 99b.

5. Rabbi Yisrael Dov Ber of Vilednick. *Shearith Yisrael*. (Israel: M'Chon Ohr Yisroel. 1998), p. 152b.

6. The Lubavitcher Rebbe. *Sefer Hamaamorim Meluket*. Vol. 2, (New York: Kehot Publication Society. 1988) p. 148. *Sefer Hamaamorim Meluket*. Vol. 5, (New York: Kehot Publication Society. 1994) p. 59.

7. Mystical thought generally condemns Atzvut, depression, very strongly. See: Rabbi Chaim Vital. *Sharei Kedusha.* Part 1. Shar 2 and Shar 5; Part 2. Shar 4. Rabbi Pinchas Eliyohu Ben Meir of Vilna *Sefer Habrit.* (Jerusalem: Yerid Hasefarim. 1990), Part 2. Maamor 2. Chapter 2. And especially Chassidic mysticism See: Rabbi Schneur Zalman of Liadi. *Tanya.* Chapter 1. *Igeret Hakodesh.* Letter 11. *Tzavoas Harivash.* (New York: Kehot Publication Society. 1982), Chapter 15. Rabbi Nachman of Breslov. *Likutei Moharan.* Part 1 23: 1. Rabbi Menachem Mendel of Vitebsk (?–1788.) *Pri Ha'aretz.* Parshat Mattot—Massei. Rabbi Moshe Chayim Ephraim of Sudylkov. (?–1800.) *Degel Machanah Ephraim.* Parshat Vayichi. Rabbi Michal of Zlotchov. (1731–1786.) *Malchei BaKodesh,* (Israel: Mechon Zechut Avut. 1998) p. 79. Rabbi Yisrael Dov Ber of Vilednick. *Shearith Yisrael.* (Israel: M'Chon Ohr Yisroel. 1998), p. 25a. Rabbi Nachum of Chernobyl. (1730–1787) *Meor Einayim* (Brooklyn: 1975) *Hanhagot Yesharot.*

8. Rabbi Schneur Zalman of Liadi. *Tanya.* Chapter 26.

9. *Avot.—Ethics of our fathers.* Chapter 4. Mishnah 1.

10. Rabbi Schneur Zalman of Liadi. *Tanya.* Chapter 26.

11. The Talmud relays a similar story about the great sage, Rabbi Akiva, who upon seeing the Temple Mount in a ravaged state burst out laughing. He explained that if the somber words of the prophets could be fulfilled, how much more can we be certain that the prophets' words of condolences will surely also be fulfilled soon. Thus, Rabbi Akiva was a person who saw the future, the hope of the rebuilding, overwhelming the present, that is, destruction. He saw things in their entire historical perspective. *Makkot,* p. 24b. Rabbi Avraham Eliyohu Platkin. *Birrurei Halachot,* (Brooklyn, New York. 1973) p. 158. The Lubavitcher Rebbe. *Likutei Sichot.* (New York: Kehot Publication Society. 1982), Vol. 19, p. 67.

12. The sixth Chabad Rebbe. Rabbi Yoseph Yitzchak. *Sefer Hasichot 5703* (1903) (New York. Kehot Publication Society. 1986), p. 41.

13. The fifth Chabad Rebbe, Rabbi Shalom Dovber. *Sefer Hamaamorim 5679* (New York: Kehot Publication Society. 1988), p. 347.

14. *Shulchan Aruch, Orach Chayim.* Rabbi Dovid ben Shmuel (1586–1667) *Taz.* 101: 3. Rabbi Eliyohu Ben Moshe Di Vidas *Reshit Chochmah.* Shar HaKedushah Chapter 15. The fifth Chabad Rebbe. Rabbi Shalom Dovber. *Sefer Hamamorim Ranat (5659)* (New York: Kehot Publication Society. 1984), p. 6. See also: *Sefer Hachinuch.* Mitzvah 384.

15. In the book of *Daniel,* 6:11, it says the word "vichivin," which is the root of the word Kavanah, and there it refers to windows.

16. The previous Chabad Rebbe, Rabbi Yoseph Yitzchak, on the twelfth day of the month of Tammuz 5692. (1932)

17. The previous Chabad Rebbe, Rabbi Yoseph Yitzchak, on the night of the seventh day of Passover 5706 (1946).

18. Told by the previous Chabad Rebbe, Rabbi Yoseph Yitzchak, on Simchat Torah 5689 (1928) about Rabbi Schneur Zalman of Liadi.

19. See: *Rambam.* Hilchot Teshuvah. Chapter 1. Halacha 1. And chapter 2. Halacha 2–4. Rabbeinu Yona *Sharei Teshuvah.* Shar 1. Chapters 12–13. Rabbi Yehudah Loew. *Nesivot Olam. Nosiv HaTeshuvah* Chapter 5. See also Rabbi Schneur Zalman of Liadi. *Tanya.* Chapter 26. See also: *Igeret Hateshuvah* Chapter 7.

20. The previous Chabad Rebbe, Rabbi Yoseph Yitzchak. on the 19th day of the month of Kislev 5691. (1931).

21. Eliezer Shtainman. *Be'er HaChassidut.—The Rebbes of Poland,* (Israel. Mechon Kemach) p. 207.

22. See: *La Chassidim Mizmor* (5696.–1936 Jerusalem), the article by M. Kipnis.

23. The previous Chabad Rebbe, Rabbi Yoseph Yitzchak, on the twelfth day of the month of Tammuz 5692 (1932).

24. See: *Zohar.* Part 3, p. 161b.

25. Music at a wedding dates back to Biblical times. See: *Radak. Psalms.* 78:63. And at a funeral, dates back at least to Talmudic times. See: Talmud. *Ketubot.* 46b.

26. Crying demonstrates the mind being overwhelmed. Rabbi Schneur Zalman of Liadi. *Or HaTorah.* (New York: Kehot Publication Society. 1996) Parshat Vayishlach. p. 26a. Rabbi DovBer. The second Chabad Rebbe. *Ner Mitzvah Vetorah Or.* (New York: Kehot Publication Society. 1979) *Shar Hayichud,* p. 6. In addition to tears of sorrow, there are tears of joy. See: *Zohar.* Part 1, p. 98b. *Shulchan Aruch. Orach Chaim.* Chapter 288. *Taz.* 2.

27. *Zohar.* Parshat Vayikrah. p. 8a. See also: Rabbi Eliyohu Ben Moshe Di Vidas. *Reshit Chochmah.* Shar HaAhavah. Chapter 10. Rabbi Yisrael Dov Ber of Vilednick. *Shearith Yisrael,* (Israel: M'Chon Ohr Yisroel. 1998) pp. 170–171.

28. One of the reasons that there was music played in the Temple, was, so that the high priest would be in the right mood to prophecise. See: Rabbi Shimon Ben Tzemach Duran. *Magen Avot.* (Jerusalem: Makor Publishing.) Part 3, p. 52b.

29. See: *Zohar* Part 3. p. 75a. Rabbi Schneur Zalman of Liadi. *Tanya.* Chapter 34. Rabbi Yisrael Dov Ber of Vilednick. *Shearith Yisrael,* (Israel: M'Chon Ohr Yisroel. 1998.) p. 25b.

6
Tefilah/Prayer
Moving Towards the Infinite

While in prayer, the Talmudic sage, Rabbi Meir, would sing various melodies.[1]

In order for the reader to fully understand how song assists one who is praying, he must first comprehend the meaning of prayer in general, and especially, how it is presented in mystical thought.

The purpose of prayer is to create a connection and union between man and God, the finite and the infinite. The root of the Hebrew word for prayer, *Tefilah*, is *tofel*, which means to adjoin, to connect.[2] Prayer is likened, say the kabbalists, to the ladder in the dream of Jacob, which stands on the ground, and reaches into the sky.[3] Thus, the course of prayer is to connect ourselves to God one step at a time, climbing the ladder of perfection. At the outset of prayer one starts off on the lowest rung, and eventually one climbs until he is joined and becomes 'one with One.' Prayer is a service, a devotion of the heart;[4] and with complete heart and soul one unites with God.

The root for the word mitzvah is *Tzavta* meaning connection.[5] Through every mitzvah a human being performs, he enters into a relationship with the Infinite, a relationship similar to that which exists between two human beings. Prayer is the foundation and backbone of this relationship.[6] As in any relationship that we experience in life, the most important ingredient is the foundation. There must be a sacred foundation of trust, honor, and respect upon which the relationship is built; the same is true with man's relationship with God: there must be a strong foundation, and that is prayer.

Another crucial component in any thriving relationship is communication, the ability to talk and exchange ideas. Once communication breaks down, there is no hope for the relationship.[7] This indeed is the basis of prayer, man's verbal communication with God. Prayer is the foundation of the relationship, and through every action, every mitzvah, that one performs thereafter, one reinforces and strengthens this connection.

Just as in any relationship between two human beings, one has to give of himself, in order to draw closer to the person he wants to enter into a relationship with, so it is with one's relationship with God. Every relationship is a give and take, each person relinquishing something in order to unite with another whom he loves. The giving or giving up is primarily an acceptance of the other. As we covered earlier, being heard is a way of feeling one's existence, thus being a listener and allowing another person to be heard, is the greatest gift one can give another. In order for man, a physical being, to connect himself with Godliness, spirituality, he must first relinquish his attachment to the way he thinks life should be (the human mind is a reifying machine) and surrender to the spiritual.

There is a parable for this concept in science. Let us say, for example, that an object is moving towards light. In order for it to unite with the light, it must give up something of itself, and therefore, it shrinks away slowly as it moves closer. Science says that the greater the speed of movement, the greater the contraction will be. For instance, a yard stick moving with ninety percent of the velocity of light would shrink to about half its length; thereafter, the rate of contraction becomes more rapid, and if the stick could attain the velocity of light, it would shrink away to nothing at all.[8]

To know what we are giving up in the physical realm, it would be appropriate to understand the physical makeup of the world. The material make-up of this physical world comprises four basic elements,[9] the highest being Fire, then Wind, Water, and Earth.[10] Everything in the physical world has within it these four elements, which are the building stones of creation.

Just as in every physical entity there exist these four elements, the same is true within the world at large: there are four basic types. There is the inanimate, the vegetative, the animal kingdom, and humans. These four distinctions correspond to the four basic elements.[11] The **inanimate** is equated with **earth**, because like the earth, the inanimate does not move. The **vegetative** is analogous to **water**, for the life of the vegetative comes from water, and it has natural, instinctive tendencies. In addition, it grows in quality (it bears fruit), and in quantity (it grows from youth to old age), but it does not have any individualistic will. The **animal kingdom**, which is composed of living beings, moving creatures, is likened to **wind**, which is the symbol of movement. Wind moves freely around the world, and it is not concentrated nor connected to one particular place; it is therefore akin to an animal who can roam the world freely, and is not bound like the vegetative to one single place alone. **Humans** are likened to **fire**,[12] the epitome of movement and rapid motion. And like fire which faces upwards, so does man stand erect, facing above, not like all other animals, who face downwards.[13]

Hence, humans, as the rest of creation, have contained within them these basic four elements, albeit the primary one in humans is fire. Therefore, when a human being wants to connect with the divine, he must "give up" something from himself, give up from all his four elements. What does losing one's four elements mean exactly? This one may understand through analyzing an experience by the prophet, Ezekiel. The reason I chose prophesy as an example is that it is the highest and loftiest connection a human being can aspire to have with the Divine.

In the prophesy of Ezekiel,[14] the first experience he had to overcome before being able to conjoin with the level prophecy, was 'A stormy wind (wind), a great cloud (water), and a blistering fire (fire).[15] These elements are what the prophet encounters in the earliest stages of prophecy.[16]

The notion of the prophet's encountering and enduring these three elements, represents the negation of his physical existence prior to connecting with the Divine.[17] In the case of prophesy, this means to negate one's physical, conventional, and rational mind, and to open oneself to a higher and loftier knowledge. And since the prophet's objective is to experience the Divine on the level of intellect, to fuse his mind with the Divine Wisdom, the enduring of the three elements, represented in 'a stormy wind, a great cloud, and a blistering fire' also represents the three elements as they exist in the intellect.

The first level that the prophet must confront is a "stormy wind." When a prophet reaches a higher meditative state,[18] the mind then becomes highly sensitized and every small sound it hears, even the slightest of extraneous thought, will agitate the mind immensely. This state is what is called a "stormy wind." Thus, the first objective for the prophet is to clear the mind totally, so that no inappropriate thoughts arise.

The next step he must encounter is the "great cloud," which represents the prophet's experiencing of opaqueness, nothingness, a sense of void. A thick cloud hovers over any sort of thought he may want to experience; his mind blanks out. This is the next level that the prophet must overcome: he must master a total sense of emptiness.

Following this, the prophet ascends to a higher level, and experiences a "blistering fire," which symbolizes awe and dread, the feeling of being overwhelmed by Godliness, astounded by His holiness; this is a sensation that causes him to feel that perhaps he should retreat, and not go any further. It is only after the prophet goes through these three levels, integrates these elements, and annihilates his ego that he experiences a true union with the Divine.[19] This is how these elements mentioned above exist within the mind of man.

The aforementioned formula applies to anyone who wishes to connect himself with the Divine. The first step one must take is to relinquish and transcend his physicality, the four elements from which all human beings are assembled. Every human being like everything else in the creation, is made up of these four basic elements. His material body has these four elements, and so do his mental capacities and his soul.[20] They are all assembled from these basic four elements: earth, wind, water, fire.[21] Thus far we have seen how these four elements reside within the mind of man. But we must delve deeper on how they exist in every human being's physical, mental, and soulular realities.[22]

Earth represents action within man, and his capacity to take action. Action is likened to earth, because actions in and of themselves are dry; they can be done without emotion. Water, however, represents man's emotions; these are fluid; they contain signs of life, vitality, and movement. Emotions flow within a person like waves of water.[23] Wind is likened to man's intellect, which like wind is intangible. It is removed, aloof. It is for this reason that intellect can operate in a detached way. At times one may think intellectually with one's mind, yet remain mentally uninvolved from the issue one is thinking about. Fire represents man's will. Will is the idea of connection: When a person wants something he feels connected with it and a spark is ignited. The greater the desire for the object or person, the greater the passion or flame. The nature of fire is that it consumes itself if not fed. It can destroy if not contained, or it can warm and create light if channeled properly. But on a higher level as flames leap upward, the will of the soul is to connect and be consumed, to 'lose itself' in the will of God.[24]

There are four parts and four names to each person's soul, one's Godly as well as one's animalistic soul.[25] The lowest level is *Nefesh*—soul, the next, *Ruach*—spirit, then *Neshama*—breath, and lastly *Chaiyah*—living essence. These four correspond to the four basic elements. The lowest level, **Nefesh**, is **earth**, the capacity to do **action**, a functional consciousness. **Ruach** is water or **emotions**, an emotional consciousness. **Neshama** is **wind**, the power of **intellect**, a cognitive consciousness. And **Chaiyah** is **fire**, man's **will**, which is a transcendental consciousness.

In order for a human being to enter into a relationship with the divine, that is, to pray, he must strive to release the four basic elements, relinquish his entire physical reality. Thus, the person's body is actually sacrificed as it were through praying. A person (a physical body) who takes the time to pray, rather than spending time accomplishing things for his own materialistic benefit, such as eating, drinking, sleeping, and the like, is at that moment of prayer, offering his entire body, with all its basic four elements, to God.[26] More specifically, the nullification of the animalistic soul, with its four elements, is accomplished through the four divisions of prayer.

In order to fully understand these divisions of prayer, it should be articulated that the four elements are not only a phenomenon that exist in the physical world, but are also manifested in the spiritual worlds above.[27]

Kabbalah speaks of **four** general worlds.[28] The lowest in the chain is our physical world, with its spiritual counterpart, the world of *Asiyah*—completion, the world of action. This is where the physical in concept and action are predominant. A higher, loftier world is the world of *Yitzirah*—formation, the world of pure emotions. A higher world yet is the world of *Beriah*—creation, the world of intelligence. The highest of the worlds is the world of *Atziluth*—emanation, nearness, a world which is one with Godliness.[29]

These four worlds correspond to the four names of soul, whether the Godly soul or the animal soul. They in turn correspond to the four elements, *Nefesh*—soul, corresponds to *Asiyah*; *Ruach*—spirit, corresponds to *Yitzirah*; *Neshama*—breath, corresponds to *Beriah*; and *Chaiyah*—living essence, corresponds to *Atziluth*. Therefore, with every rung one climbs in prayer, every step one takes to elevate himself, he elevates another element of his animalistic soul. Every step takes one higher and to a more profound level in his godly soul, because with each level that one elevates the animal soul, he connects with the corresponding level of the Godly soul. Furthermore, through every ascent of prayer, one enters the corresponding spiritual world. It is precisely for this reason that the morning prayer was divided into four sections. With each section of prayer, one enters a loftier level of consciousness, a higher level of soul, into a higher realm of worlds.[30]

Name of God—*Yud*	*Hei*	*Vov*	*Hei*
Worlds—*Atziluth*	*Beriah*	*Yitzirah*	*Asiyah*
Soul—*Chaiyah*	*Neshama*	*Ruach*	*Nefesh*
Capacities—Will	Intellect	Emotions	Actions
Consciousness—Transcendental	Cognitive	Emotional	Functional
Elements—Fire	Wind	Water	Earth
Types—Human	Animal	Vegetative	Inanimate
Prayer—*Shmone Esrei*	*Keriat Shema*	*Pisukei D'zimrah*	*Birchot Hasachar*

The first section of the morning prayer is the morning blessings (*Birchot hasachar*). These prayers are a combination of two concepts. In the first part of these prayers, a person offers thanks to God, for providing for all his physical needs. He offers thanks for God's giving strength to the tired, for dressing the unclothed, and the like; then he recites the procedure of the offerings in the holy Temple, and how and where the sacrifices would be offered. In both of these prayers, the content of the prayer is analogous to the lowest parts of one's soul, the action aspect. And indeed it is also analogous to the lowest level of worlds, the world of action.

In the first part of these prayers, in which a person offers thanks and acknowledges God for providing for all necessities, a person is proclaiming that everything comes from God. Thus, everything that is form or action on the level of *Nefesh* belongs to God, and thanks to him they are manifest in our life. The same is true with the second part of the prayer, the offerings. The idea of sacrifice is to take a physical entity, such as an animal or wheat, and transform it into holiness. This is achieved by having it be consumed by the Godly fire on the altar. This mirrors the expression of man's relinquishing, or surrendering his world of actions, his *Nefesh*, to God. Thus, the first part of prayer gives causality to all that exists in the physical universe and one gives up his ego and attachment of all physical necessities.

In ascending the ladder of prayer, having elevated *Nefesh*, one enters the world of *Yitzirah*—the "world of emotions," the state of *Ruach*-consciousness. In this stage of prayer, one enters one's own personal world of emotions. The objective at this level is to "give up" and surrender one's emotions. This is the second rung of prayer, the section which is called the "passages of praise." In this segment of prayer, one's emotions are aroused by continuously praising God for the miracles of creation, and the wonders that God has done throughout history. This is the idea of a person sacrificing and elevating his emotions to God. It is saying that regardless of subjective feelings about how it ought to be, one subsumes these egotistical emotions to a love and devotion to God. All feelings are now redirected, channeled, and dedicated to God. Hence, the only emotions he experiences are holy.[31]

Having dedicated all emotions, one ascends the ladder of holiness, the ladder of prayer, and enters the world of intelligence. This is the world of *Beriah*, corresponding to the level of *Neshama*. This section of prayer, is called the "recital of the *Shemah*." In this segment, one prays sitting down[32] (contrary to the end of the previous prayer, where one was standing.) The difference between standing and sitting is that standing indicates movement, excitement, and emotions, while sitting down shows that the person is calm, sedate, and collected, using his intellect. All the preceding excitement and inspiration that had been experienced, all the previous emotions, which by now have been transformed completely to Godly emotions, are now intellectualized. All the previous feelings are internalized and become a true reality, not just a passing emotion.

The word *shemah* in Hebrew means "hear," or "listen;" therefore, it implies that one should take all the inspiration experienced until then, and listen to it. These awesome feelings should not be left in the emotional state alone; when the initial excitement dies down, so may the entire inspiration, but listening, hearing, internalizing these emotions makes them part of existence, part of experience. Think about it and then think about it again, until it becomes part of your consciousness. This is the level of *shemah* the world of intelligence.[33]

It is after the reading of the *Shemah*, when one has already "sacrificed" the three previous levels (of actions, emotions, and intelligence), that one can enter God's private chambers. That is when one is ready to pray the final and loftiest of the prayers, the *Shemone Esrei*.[34] Of this prayer it is said[35] that when one recites it, one should envision himself standing in front of the master of the universe, in God's private chamber. During the prayer, one stands with both feet together, implying that no further movement is needed, for at this time one has reached the apex of the spiritual ladder.[36] And although swaying during prayer is generally encouraged,[37] nonetheless during the *Shemone Esrei*, it is strongly discouraged,[38] for at this stage of prayer there is no self-expression.[39] When one arrives at this level of prayer, one is completely nullified as a separate entity in the presence of God. One has in this stage of prayer pierced God's innermost chamber.[40] Here one is in the world of *Atziluth*, where the soul is one with its creator, and separation is nullified. In this world, one declares that even the will, which is the nearest and closest thing to one, is now "sacrificed" to God. (Will runs deeper in one's soul than intellect does; thus, if a person wills something strongly, even the greatest intellectual persuasions will not change his will.) At this state, after elevating one's actions, emotions, intelligence, and will, one desires and yearns to be consumed entirely in the greater existence of God.[41] A Chassidic Rebbe once said; The world assumes that prayer occurs in the presence of God, when in truth prayer is Godliness itself.[42]

At this lofty stage of prayer, one has relinquished his concept of existence—one's ego. One loses himself completely in the unity of God. Yet at this momentous state of intense prayer, one is instructed to ask for physical nourishment, for health, and the like, which seems to be an obvious paradox. If one has reached non-existence, with no ego, how can one request personal, materialistic necessities? It is as if one suddenly regained his existence—his ego. The answer is that indeed at this plateau of prayer, one has completely relinquished his existence as ego, but now finds himself again, and regains his existence within the greater existence of God. One's existence, *Yesh*—ego, unites and is fused with the ultimate existence: God, the true *Yesh*. Therefore, when one prays at this level for what may seem as to be personal, material necessities, the truth is that one is reciting these prayers only because that is the ultimate will of God. God, in a way, "wants" every human being to have all their physical necessities, so that they can take all that is physical and transform it to holiness. At this level of prayer, one's personal will is an extension of the will of God. The *Yesh* of the individual unites with the true *Yesh*.[43]

All the above was offered to explain the possibilities of prayer according to mystical thought and now, one can progress to understand the utility of song in this domain. We will examine tunes used to introduce prayer, to assist in praying, and the types of songs used for those purposes.

When we speak of music and its connection with prayer, one is immediately reminded of the time when the holy temple in Jerusalem was standing. Instead of having set times for prayer, one brought an offering, and music was played as an important part of the temple's service. The tribe of Levi was in charge of the music, and when an offering was being served, the Levites would sing and play music.

There are perhaps three reasons for playing music in the Temple. The rational reason, is that just as music is played in the courtyard of a king, in order to enhance the ambiance and splendor of the court, so it is in the courtyard of the king of all kings. In God's temple, music was played to add to the grandeur.[44] The spiritual reason, is to awaken the person who is offering the sacrifice, to do *Teshuvah*, to return.[45] As we have seen music can soften one's heart, and that is a prerequisite for doing *Teshuvah*. The mystical reason, is that music, or song, serves as a conduit for elevation. A requisite for the elevation from the physical to the spiritual to occur, music and song has to accompany the offering. As with any elevation to transpire, it requires the inspiration of song to assist the elevation.[46]

Since the destruction of the "great temple", in its stead the 'small temples',[47] the synagogues serve as places to congregate and offer. Instead of physical offerings, we pray,[48] and to assist prayer (offerings), as in olden times, we use music and song.

To prepare oneself for such a noble endeavor as prayer, it is the custom among the mystically inclined to immerse themselves in a *mikvah* (a ritual bath). The idea of immersing oneself completely in water symbolizes being totally covered and enveloped in Godliness. This is because one who immerses himself in a *mikvah* is actually being surrounded and completely enclosed by a mitzvah. Hence, *Mikvah* represents the idea of man's being totally nullified by Godliness, which is precisely the objective of prayer, that is, to reach the higher levels of *Bittul*—self-nullification. In the highest state of prayer, one's entire existence is relinquished to God; all four elements of the physical body, as well as the four traits of the animal soul, are wholly nullified.

The word in Hebrew for immersing is *Tovel* (טובל) which is composed of the four letters, *Tet* (ט), *Vav* (ו), *Beth* (ב), and *Lamad* (ל). These letters are the same four letters with a different format, used for the word nullify, in Hebrew, *Bittul* (בטול) *Beth* (ב), *Tet* (ט), *Vav* (ו), *Lamad* (ל).[49]

The concept of *mikvah* can be achieved, without an actual *mikvah* being available, through song.[50] When a person sings a melody prior to prayer, with concentration and intensity, until his entire body is covered with perspiration, then we say that the water of his sweat becomes like the waters of the *mikvah*: They transform into holy water,[51] since it is sourced by an act of preparation for prayer. There is a story told about the holy Rebbe, Rabbi Yisrael of Rushin (1796–1850),[52] it happened that one of his *chassidim* came to the Rebbe to complain about his son-in-law wasting precious time before prayer, and that he neither meditated nor went to the *mikvah*. The Rebbe asked him, "So what does he do?" The answer was that "He wanders about singing songs that you have composed." The Rebbe told him not to worry. By singing holy tunes with great energy, until one actually begins to sweat, one has accomplished as great a preparation for prayer as is possible.

There is another way that song can assist one to prepare for prayer. It puts one in the correct frame of mind, the proper mood, which is both happy and meditative.[53] When one sings a slow and meditative melody, the tune slowly permeates his being, and helps his mind and heart to be thoroughly focused on what he is about to undertake. Thus, a meditative tune can serve as a preparation for prayer, as well as being an integral part of the prayer itself. "Song helps to eradicate any extraneous thoughts during prayer."[54]

Song has the capacity to clear the mind, and empty it of extraneous thoughts during prayer. One of the words in the Hebrew language for song is *Zimrah*, which has two connotations. One is to sing, while the other is to cut off or to uproot.[55] These meanings are actually interconnected. When one sings, during or prior to prayer, an authentic and meaningful tune, and comprehends what the song represents, this automatically cuts off and negates all external thoughts. Therefore, if one wishes to pray, and wants his mind to be clear and pure of any unholy thoughts, then one should sing a slow, meditative tune. In this way, singing serves as a suitable preparation for prayer.

There are particular groups of *Chassidim* who not only sing before prayer, but also clap with their hands. Reb Nachman of Breslov says[56] that when a person claps his hands in the air, it is not a frivolous act, but that through this action, one is purifying the immediate space, until it becomes as pure and holy as the holy land of Israel. And when the air around you is immaculate, you are more susceptible to experiencing purity of thought.

Some *Chassidim* even dance before prayer; the dance is used as a form of meditation. This type of meditation is "externally directed," which means that it is practiced by concentrating one's mind on an external object of movement. Concentrating and meditating on a continuous motion like the rush of water can assist one to reach a higher state of consciousness.[57] This technique is also plausible in a kinesthetic sense, by concentrating on repetitive and continuous body movement. When you meditate on your own body movement, you can through the meditation reach an expanded awareness, a higher state of consciousness.[58] Or, you can use the body movement for itself, even without concentrating on what you are doing. By the mere fact of doing something over and over again, like a mantra, you can reach a higher state of consciousness.[59]

Just as there are tunes utilized as an introduction to prayer, which are the meditative and slower tunes, there are also in Chassidic circles tunes that accompany the prayer itself.

There is, however, a vast distinction between tunes which are sung as an introduction to prayer, and tunes which accompany prayer itself. Usually introductory tunes are specifically calculated tunes. These are tunes meant to inspire and to soften one's heart, so that one can be ready for prayer. However, tunes that are sung during prayer are spontaneous expressions from the heart. These tunes are sung almost automatically. There are songs to the heart (introductory tunes), and songs from the heart (spontaneous expressions). It was once asked of the first Chabad Rebbe, Rabbi Schneur Zalman of Liadi, "Why do *Chassidim* sing during prayer?" The Rebbe answered, "It is only natural for someone who is truly inspired and overwhelmed to spontaneously sing and dance.[60] It isn't that *Chassidim* intentionally plan to sing during prayer. It is just a spontaneous and reflexive expression which emanates from a person's inner essence, the inner depths of his soul."[61]

Ordinarily, at the onset of prayer, one begins with initial feelings of *marirrut*—bitterness. One feels his own separateness and alienation from anything Godly.[62] One may even feel forlorn, when meditating on the fact that one's lofty soul has descended into this lowly world; reflecting on how much of one's time is spent on maintaining the physical (e.g.: making a living), which distracts one from focusing on *shlemut* both internally and eternally. To accompany these feelings, one sings songs of yearning, of wanting to be close. These are songs of penetration, which enter the soul and arouse it; these initial slow tunes are inspired by *marirrut*. However, once one commences praying and ascending the ladder of prayer, the progression of holiness, one begins to realize and align with the ultimate purpose of God's creation (and the purpose of the descent of the lofty soul). It is for the soul to become more spiritual, not through withdrawal and resignation of all that is physical, but rather to be in this physical world, in the here and the now, to work with it and to elevate it. When one comes to this realization, one begins to experience joy. When one possesses the knowledge that one is in harmony with God's design and with the Divine song, one can then experience bliss. Consequently one's prayer is housed in happiness and the melodies are songs of joy.[63]

Thus, prayer, and the melodies which accompany the prayer, are a synthesis between the two extreme emotions, between *marirrut*—bitterness, emptiness, and *simchah*—happiness, closeness.[64]

There is a story told about the prayers of Rabbi Levi Yitzchak of Barditsheve.[65] It once happened that when he began praying, he sang a slow and somber melody, as a preparation for prayer, the tune expressing a deep bitterness. All of a sudden, he started singing a happy and joyous tune, with great excitement and fervor. Soon after, when he recited the prayer, "God have mercy," he once again sang a slow tune. After awhile, he recited the next paragraph, "God help us," and once again sang a happy and joyous melody; this lasted throughout the entire prayer. Prayer is a continuous balancing act between two states of consciousness, a state of happiness—of feeling close, and a state of feeling distant. For at the outset of prayer, in the very inception of prayer, one may feel apart and removed; and may therefore sing a more somber, meditative tune, a tune expressing one's lowliness, one's distance and yearning. However, as one progresses up the ladder of prayer the tunes may change to tunes of wanting to be close, and finally to joyous songs.

The Kabbalah teaches that there are four types of song, one level above the other.[66] The first and most simple of melodies is a *Shir Stam*, literally a plain, ordinary melody, a tune expressing how the composer was feeling at the time it was composed. It can be a melody expressing happiness, or it can be a slow, somber melody, expressing bitterness. A *Shir Stam* is a *nigun* that expresses a single feeling. At times a *Shir Stam* can be of a happy nature, and at times, it can be full of bitterness, yet never more than one emotion is expressed.

Above this is a *Shir Mirubah*, literally, a quartet.[67] In these types of melodies, there are usually two or more stanzas; one stanza, a joyous one, may express the composer's happiness, while another expresses his bitterness. A *Shir Mirubah* is a melody that contains the expression of more than one emotion.[68]

The third level of song is the *Shir Kaful*, which literally means a twofold melody, a melody that combines two contrary feelings simultaneously. It can communicate a feeling of happiness, which is a feeling of man's closeness, one's love for God,[69] while concurrently expressing a person's feelings of distance, *marirrut*—bitterness. In one stanza, one can hear two opposing feelings being expressed, feelings of being close and feelings of being distant.

The highest level in song is called a *Shir Pashut*, a simple melody. This type of melody is one that emanates from the inner depths of the composer's being. In these melodies, there is a fusion of many emotions. Therefore, the hearer can sense two contrasting sentiments being expressed. On one hand, the melody seems very simplistic, as if it is not expressing anything at all. Yet, if one really listens attentively, one can sense how despite its simplicity, it is expressing the deepest and purest feelings of its composer. Within this seemingly simplistic tune, there exists a myriad of emotions.[70]

During prayer, one can utilize all these types of song to assist in his *Kavanah*—intention. At the outset of prayer, when one's emotions are still one-dimensional, and one feels either bitterness or happiness, a *Shir Stam* expressing one of these feelings can be

most apropos. As one enters the higher chambers, one may experience ambivalent feelings. One may feel very close, and therefore, happy; yet, what occurs frequently is that the closer one gets,
the more he realizes how far and distant he really is. Thus, he may
feel *marirrut* or bitterness. He may then require a tune that expresses both these feelings simultaneously, a *Shir Kaful*, to assist
in his prayer.

When Chassidic prayer is discussed, it is appropriate to clarify
that in fact there are two philosophic perspectives within the
Chassidic movement about how one should pray. One is "Chabad"
Chassidim, the intellectual branch of *Chassidim*. (As mentioned
earlier, Chabad is the acronym for the three intellectual capacities of man.) The Chabad *Chassidim* serve God through their intellect. Every emotion, every feeling must filter through their
intellect before they can be expressed. The others, generally, are
the *Chagas Chassidim*, the emotional *Chassidim*. (*Chagas* is the
acronym for *Chesed*—kindness, benevolence, *Givurah*—severity,
strength, and *Tiferes*—compassion.) They serve God through their
emotions.

The difference between these groups of *Chassidim* manifests
itself also in the way they pray. *Chagas*, the emotional *Chassidim*,
maintain that a person should pray with displayed emotions, with
excitement and vigor. Furthermore they say that one should
allow his inner emotions, his inner feelings, to flow, until even
his external existence, his physical body can also participate in
the ecstasy. For example, if a person prays with such intensely
felt emotion that while in prayer, he feels a desire to sing, then he
should sing. And if he feels that he wants to dance, then he should
dance. In general, one should surrender to his emotions. This
notion was taken to the extreme by the *Chassidim* of Reb Abraham
of Kalisk; it is well-known, within Chassidic circles, how these
Chassidim would be so full with emotions during prayer that they
would actually swirl in somersaults from great ecstasy.[71]

Body movement can be also used, as a Chassidic master once
said, to ignite and set one's emotions on fire. "If you desire to set
your soul on fire, do so through body motion, for motion gener-

ates warmth."[72] External body motions during prayer can arouse emotions.[73]

The melodies which these emotional *Chagas Chassidim* sing while in prayer are fast-paced and rapturous melodies, ecstatic tunes flowing with a bounty of emotions. They are melodies that electrify and excite the heart.

Chabad, the intellectual branch of *Chassidim*, asserts that one's mind should at all times control the heart. Emotions generally should be harnessed by the mind; they should be intellectualized emotions, "composed emotions," without any external manifestations. Contrary to the *Chagas* master, who suggested igniting one's soul through "external bodily" movement, the Chabad masters say that the movement of the melody itself generates warmth.[74]

In Chabad thought, it is taught that emotions that arise directly from the heart, have external manifestations, so it is possible, that the source of the emotion may not be from a holy origin, but simply from the frivolity of the heart. The manner of knowing if the source is from holiness or not is to ascertain from whence the emotions stem, and how they are expressed. If, before he began praying, one prepared himself with utmost seriousness and meditated, and when one actually started praying, the thoughts of the mind aroused feelings and penetrated the heart, then it is known that the source of the emotions was holy. However, if the emotions are not rooted in the intellect, then one can never really be certain if it is a holy or unholy emotion. Therefore, in order for the emotions aroused during prayer to be holy emotions, they must originate in the intellect, according to Chabad philosophy.

Consequently, the melodies which Chabad *Chassidim* sing during prayer are slower and more meditative. They are melodies that assist in concentration and in meditation. They are reflective and mystical tunes that promote introspection and self-evaluation.

Once a Chabad Chassid's emotions are aroused, they are intellectual emotions, emotions which remain in the heart, without any external expression. The second Chabad Rebbe, Rabbi Dovber,[75] writes about this in one of his more celebrated Chassidic discourses, "The Tract on Ecstasy."[76] The proof that most emotions (especially those with external manifestations) experienced during prayer are not holy, is that even while being all emotional during the prayer, to the extent of dancing and clapping in excitement and ecstasy, until it seems as if the entire body is involved in the experience of prayer, the person's mind, which should be the source of all of the excitement, is empty. It is void of any Godly thoughts.

Hence, when a Chabad Chassid begins meditating prior to prayer, he begins with his mind, his intellect, with the aspiration that from his mind, his thoughts will trickle down into the heart, and arouse his emotions. Once these emotions are aroused, they are manifested in a calm and collected manner.

Once, a Chabad Chassid walked into one of the *Chagas Chassidim* synagogues. The custom of these *Chassidim* was to scream and shout, and to run about during prayer. At the end of the prayer, the Chabad Chassid went up to the podium, and said in jest, "My dear friends, have you ever attempted this with goodness? Have you tried to beseech God 'nicely' without shouting?" This statement is characteristic of a Chabad Chassid, for a Chabad Chassid maintains that one should always remain composed and collected, and never lose one's self; even one's emotions should be calm, especially during prayer.[77]

The model Chabad melody, sung during prayer, is of a slow meditative makeup, which assists the Chassid in meditating on the prayer. It helps the Chassid understand the meaning of the prayer, what he wants to achieve with the prayer, and the like. Moreover, after he engages his emotions through contemplating, he can meditate on the emotions themselves. To use colors as an analogy, each color represents a different emotion. The color white, as an example, represents the attribute of *Chesed*—kindness. White expresses the idea of purity, cleanliness, while the color red represents the attribute of *Givurah*—strength,[78] being the color of blood, battle, etc. The same is true with melodies. There are different types of melodies, some of which evoke and represent the attributes of kindness. These are more peaceful, mellow tunes.

Then there are tunes that elicit and represent the attributes of strength. These tend to be more forceful, and vigorous. Therefore, when one sings a melody that corresponds to the prayer he is with at that moment, the tune can assist him to connect better to the prayer and to concentrate on the emotion.[79] This would be a true Chabad prayer, a prayer overflowing with intellectual emotions, without any of the external manifestations, and without any dancing or jumping.

However, it must be noted that the same Rebbe, Reb Dovber (who was quoted above as speaking against any external body movement) writes that there are, in general, two methods with which to serve God.[80] One is the Chabad or intellectual way, which is to reach God through the intellect, one level at a time. In this method, one moves from one level of understanding to another, higher level of understanding, from one level of holiness to the next.[81] The other path which can get you there is called *Rikidah*, to jump. Just as it is in the physical sense that when someone jumps up, his head shifts a step higher, a step above its normal position. So it is in the spiritual plane; to jump spiritually, means to go beyond "your head," above the intellect, above the rational. One reaches God, not incrementally, but by skipping and jumping many levels instantly. In this case, one's connection with God is not through one's intellect, but above one's intellect. Therefore, a person can reach numerous levels at one time.[82] The Rebbe recognizes that there are moments when the person is spiritually in such a state of ecstasy, the pitch of the energy being so high, that he is experiencing difficulty containing it. Here room is made to express and discharge the energy by physical means, for they are now experiencing emotions without, and above, their intellect.

Thus, in normal circumstances, the only external emotions a Chabad Chassid shows is giving voice to a Chassidic melody. He sings a melody expressing feelings of being close to God, happy tunes, or he may choose an intellectual tune, which is slow and meditative. As the celebrated mystic, Rabbi Yehudah Ha-Chassid, writes, "If one wishes to pray with the right intentions, let him sing melodies that correspond to the intentions he is seeking to acquire, for instance, happy tunes to arouse happiness," or, a meditative tune to evoke a meditative mood, and so on.[83]

At times, a melody can actually substitute for prayer. The Talmud states, "Delighted is one who can pray the entire day."[84] For most working people to take this statement at face value, and pray the entire day, is unreasonable. However, there is a way in which one can accomplish this and that is by employing a wordless melody that is associated with or has been utilized during prayers.[85] Consequently when one sings these tunes, it is as if one is in fact praying.[86] Therefore, it is possible for one to pray through song the entire day. Even while one is working and doing the most mundane things, one can by means of song connect with God, as through the loftiest levels of prayer.

There is a parable which is told in the name of a great Chassidic master[87] that once upon a time, there lived a wealthy king, whose child was exceptionally gifted. He was brilliant, very handsome, talented, and so on. Once, while the king was contemplating his child's future, he thought that for the further development of the boy, it would be advantageous if the boy were sent away to a distant land, not under the king's rule, where no one knew the king nor the kingdom. There he thought, the boy would grow to be independent and self-sufficient. However, before the king sent the boy away, he told him, "My child, I want you to always remember who you are, and where you come from! I want you to always keep in touch with your family by writing letters home, and after a few years, when I feel that you are ready, and the objective has been accomplished, I will send for you to come home." So off the boy went on his journey to a far away land, to a place where no one knew him nor his father's kingdom. At first, the boy was very lonely, as he missed his father and his home. He had no friends, no money and, indeed, he made certain to keep in touch with his household. However, as time passed, he fell in with the dregs of society, and went on to become a successful thief. The more successful he became, the more he forgot of his father and his father's kingdom. At first, he stopped writing home; then slowly, over much time he even forgot the language which was spoken in his homeland. Ultimately he forgot everything, even his own identity, and that he was a scion of royalty.

Many years went by, his good fortune changed, and he lost his wealth and 'notoriety.' He became a pauper, living in the gutters. One day, he heard that a certain king from a distant land was coming to visit, and that whoever wanted to, could approach the king, and make any request of him. So he decided that he would also go to greet the king. As he approached the king's throne, he started recollecting how once he had lived with a king; then he remembered that his very own father was a king, and that he was an only child to a mighty king. As he neared the king, it occurred to him that the king very much resembled his father. The more he thought, the more certain he became that this king indeed was his father. However, he doubted that he would be acknowledged as the king's son, as his appearance had changed, and what is more, he no longer spoke the language of the king. Feeling his abandonment he began crying, for he wanted to be with his father. The next day he again went on the line to greet the king. When he was in the presence of the king, he began motioning towards his father, the king, trying to show that he was his long lost child; however, no one understood what he was trying to do or say. They simply thought him crazy. The guards began pushing him aside, but when he saw that he was losing his chance, he lost his composure and began crying bitter tears. When the king heard his crying, his voice, he remembered his child, who used to cry with a very similar voice. And as he looked at this poor man crying, he realized that this indeed was his long lost child. They embraced and lived happily ever after.

This parable symbolizes the descent of the soul into this lowly world. When a soul comes down to this physical world, to inhabit a body, it leaves its spiritual home, and the presence of God. The reason for the descent is so that man can overcome the challenge of serving God even in this mundane and physical world. Prior to the soul's descent, the soul swears not to forget its true identity, and to remember from whence it came.[88] However, it happens more often than not, that as time goes by and we assert our independence, we become indifferent to spirituality, and slowly begin forgetting the true source from which we come, and to which we belong. Finally, at times we even forget the "language of God." We forget the skills needed to approach God. There is, however, a 'last resort', that which we may draw upon when all else fails, and that is to "voice" our songs. A person is always capable of reaching out to God simply by singing with a voice from the heart. As it says in the prayers of penitence, *Shemah Koleinu*, heed our voices. One beseeches God, pleading; please just hear who it is that is praying. It is I, your lost child, who after so many years of distance yearns to return home.[89]

To illustrate this point further, I would like to relate a story about the Baal Shem Tov, of blessed memory. Once, he was praying on Rosh Hashanah, marking the new year, with his disciple. One can well imagine the great intensity with which they prayed. A young ignorant villager was walking past the synagogue, when he heard the sound of the 'shofar' being blown.[90] The sound reminded him that he was also a Jew, and that the day was a holiday for the Jewish people, so he entered the synagogue. When he picked up a prayer book, he realized that he did not know the language in which the book was written. This made him very sad, and as he was contemplating his misfortune, it occurred to him, that God surely understands any language. Therefore he thought he could pray in any language, and since he was a farm boy, the first sound to come to mind was the sound of the rooster. So he lifted his voice and started crowing like a rooster in a whispering way. As he got into it, he slowly began forgetting where he was, until he was crowing on top of his lungs. When the disciples of the Baal Shem Tov heard these dissonant sounds from the back of the synagogue, they turned and saw a young child dressed as a peasant, repeatedly screaming on the top of his lungs, "Kukariku! Kukariku!" They walked over to the child, thinking him to be mentally disturbed, and asked him kindly to leave the synagogue. However, the child was stubborn, protesting that he was also praying, and therefore he would not leave. A great commotion broke out drawing the Baal Shem Tov's attention and prompting him to ask what was going on. Hearing the explanation, the Rebbe said, "You should know that during the prayer, I felt a tremendous level of holiness present in the synagogue, a holiness that I have not felt in a very long time, and I wondered where this holiness was coming from. Now I know. It came from the prayers of this simple child, who with all sincerity prayed to God with a simple, pure heart. These prayers were more cherished than all our prayers with all the intentions we had."[91]

Up until this point, we have discussed how through prayer one unites and connects with God, and how song can assist a person on this spiritual and lofty voyage.

⊢⊷⊶○⊷⊶⊣

"There are chambers in heaven that can only be opened through song."[92]

There is another concept of prayer. The Talmud says,[93] "One should always sing God's praises before requesting something." It is for this reason that the first division of "the prayer" (the *Shemone Esrei*) consists of praising God.[94]

The obvious questions are, why praise, what exactly is the purpose of praising? What is the objective of a human, finite, mortal praising an almighty powerful God? Does God really need a human being to praise Him? If not, why praise?

The simple answer is that praising God is not for God's aggrandizement, rather for the benefit of man. It is so that a human being can realize the omnipresence of God. It is so that humans recognize that He alone is the master of the universe. Therefore, when one sings God's praises, one is telling himself of God's greatness.[95]

However, Kabbalah teaches that there must be some inner and deeper meaning in praising God; there must be an intrinsic purpose to praise besides the refinement of man.

An analogy can be drawn to the praising that occurs between two human beings.[96] Why is it that people praise each other? What is there to be achieved by praising? Let's say, for example, that parents praise their children, telling them how smart they are, how nicely they behaved, and so on. What do parents accomplish by saying these things?

We will explain praise from two perspectives, one is the common everyday way we interact, coming from our egos. And the second is spiritual, in which the praiser through a creative act of praise, ennobles the listener. The common use is to manipulate certain desired and desirable behavior by the listener. Praise can be applied in personal relationships, whether amongst friends, or to children. Parents may feel that by telling their children how smart they are, they will actually become, or at least act, smart and intelligent. (Perhaps, the same manipulative technique has worked on the parents.)

However, according to this theory, the idea of praising has only a superficial impact, for one does not really change someone by praising. It is just that when you praise someone, encouraging him to be something that possibly he is really not, he will act as if he is really such a person. If that would be the reason for praise, then the person who is receiving the praise must be one who is fooling himself, or at the very least, someone who is out of touch with himself, for an honest person would not behave differently because of other people's perception of how he should act. We know, however, that this is not the case, for even honest people are affected by praise. The *Zohar*[97] speaks of two great sages, Rabbi Yehudah and Rabbi Shimon Bar Yochai. Rabbi Yehudah would praise Rabbi Shimon, telling him how holy he was, and that he was as holy as the holy day of Shabbat. The reason that he praised Rabbi Shimon was not to induce him to act as holy as the Shabbat. Either he was that holy already, and thus the praise meant nothing to him, or, if he was not, then praising him would not make any difference. Thus the question is, why did Rabbi Yehudah praise Rabbi Shimon?

The spiritual reason for praise is that, many times, people do not really know themselves. They have never had the opportunity to articulate or to reveal their hidden talents. For instance, when people who are by nature smart or talented, it does not necessarily translate into the actualization of that potential. A lot of very talented people go through life without ever realizing their potential and the tremendous abilities they have contained within them. For many, this may be because they lack self-esteem, and that is perhaps because of their childhood. They might have shown their creative talent as young children, but their parents misinterpreted the signs, and therefore discouraged them from being what they truly wanted to be. Instead their parents told them to be like them, and to like their peers in school, that is, "normal." Therefore, when such children grow older, they lack the proper self-esteem and self-confidence; they are too shy and timid with who they really are. They may be what we may call humble in a negative sense; they may feel that they really are not talented, as their parents had always told them.[98]

On the other hand, for some, it is not that they do not realize their "greatness," but that they keep their greatness to themselves. In the case of Rabbi Shimon, it was not that he did not know of his holiness; rather he was simply being that way, not needing to prove it or demonstrate it. What he did or did not do emanated from his state. He was a master who used his energy appropriately and efficiently. He did not need, like most human beings, to be or do a certain way for the sake of approval. He danced his own tune, without "connecting" with others.[99]

Now one can perhaps understand the idea of praise. Praise is a revealing agent: It is instructive by nature. There are those who may be ignorant of some talent or trait they possess. When praise comes, then with it certain knowledge or insight may be triggered. Consequently, more of the person receiving the praise may be available to himself, and the world. Sometimes we need another to remind us of who we really are. In the case of Rabbi Shimon, the praise caused him to "lower" himself and not to keep it all contained inside.

Earlier in the book we discussed how communication occurs, both on a verbal and musical level. It could be said that when two people are in harmony they are like sympathetic tuning forks resonating to each other. Should there be disharmony then there is no resonance. So when we praise, through speech or music, we are attempting to evoke a feeling tone in the other, a response that is aligned with our desires. A master communicator causes a recreation of the message within the listener, by making sympathetic distinctions that become the shared reality. It is a creation and recreation.

The same is true with regards to a mortal's praising of God.[100] It is self-evident that God as He exists for Himself is above and beyond any compliments and praise that man can possibly utter. However, in order for God to manifest his greatness to man, to reveal his strength, and to sustain the world; to show his compassion, to heal the sick, and so on, man praises Him, and through that awakens, attracts, and makes real, the "attributes of God." When man praises God as the sustainer of life, he reveals this attribute within God (figuratively speaking), and thus it is drawn down to this world.[101]

Once[102] the Baal Shem Tov visited a town where there lived in the synagogue, an old Jew, a *parush*. (A *parush* is one who disregards all physical and materialistic pleasures (an ascetic).) The *parush*'s custom was that he would eat only once a day, and even then only a small piece of hard bread. The rest of the day was spent in holy service. Upon his arrival the Baal Shem Tov walked straight into the *parush*'s room, and asked him how he was feeling, and how his physical needs were being taken care of. The old Jew, however, did not deign to look at him. The Baal Shem Tov then asked, "Why do you not support and sustain God?" When the *parush* heard these seemingly condemnatory words, he became angry, and signaled for the Baal Shem Tov to leave the synagogue at once. It was then that the Baal Shem Tov began to explain what he meant. We all know, he said, that man receives his sustenance from God; the question, however, is, where does God receive his nourishment? The answer, said the Baal Shem Tov, is as the Psalmist sings.[103] "You are holy, enthroned upon the praises of Israel." You are holy, God, as you are for Yourself, transcending all.[104] However, the manner through which God lowers Himself (so to speak) to the level of creation, enthroned,[105] is through the praise of Israel.[106] When a human being praises God, he provides God "his nourishment," for through praise, man reveals Godliness throughout the entire universe. Therefore, the Baal Shem Tov told the *parush* that he must say God's praise, and thank God for all.

Indeed it may be true that in order for there to be the revelation of Godliness into this lowly world, the idea of praise is needed. But why is it that when the Baal Shem Tov wanted the *parush* to praise God, he asked him how he was feeling physically? Why was it not sufficient to praise God for sustaining him with all his spiritual necessities? The Baal Shem Tov should have asked him how his prayers were progressing, how his studies were, and the like.

The Baal Shem Tov asked about mundane issues, and not spiritual matters, because the ultimate purpose of creation is to imbue even the most physical of objects with Godliness, and man joins in that endeavor. Thus, in praising God for the physical, and for providing for all one's mundane necessities, one is essentially recognizing that all comes from God. This is how man draws down and reveals Godliness in this world. Therefore, the Baal Shem Tov purposely asked him how he was feeling physically, in order to focus him to praise God for all the physical benefits that God provides. In this way Godliness is revealed in this physical world.[107]

This is generally the idea of praising God, and particularly praising God during prayer. In prayer, man praises and sings to God for sustaining him with all his physical necessities. The Chassidic Rebbe Rabbi Pinchas of Koretz, would continually speak in high praise of music and song. He once said, "Lord of the universe, if I were able to sing, I would not allow You to remain above. I would charm you with my songs, until You would descend here below, and remain with us forever."[108]

Consequently, it is well understood that the notion of singing God's praises throughout the day, and especially during prayer, a time when one beseeches God to reveal Himself, is so profoundly valued.

We have explained that prayer is an expression of the soul's yearning to be close to God, to unite with the 'One.' Through prayer one redefines his definition of *Yesh*, which is one's existence, one's ego, and becomes part of the greater existence of God. One completely loses his *Yeshut*—existence in God. Prayer is a monumental, individualistic, spiritual journey, where one ultimately finds himself existing in a higher spiritual reality, which means that the experience one has during prayer is a personal, intimate, and subjective metamorphosis. Now, one may ask, why is it that when one wishes to sing God's praises (in a formal setting of prayer), one must sing songs composed thousands of years ago, by Moses, King David, the Prophets, and so on. Why, one may ask, shouldn't a person be able to sing their own songs, in their own language? Why use "old, pre-existing, tunes"?[109]

The holy Rebbe of Peasetzna, Rabbi Klunmus Kalmish (Shapiro) (1889–1943), writes that in times gone by, when the Prophets and the saintly men of Israel saw Godliness, they perceived spirituality as if seeing it with their physical eyes, with proximity and closeness. They were able to sing new songs, new tunes imbued with great spiritual insight.[110] Today, however, when one is out of proximity in time and geography (in *galut*—exile), when we desire to sing to God songs of praise, we use their lyrics. However, the Rebbe writes, when we sing these tunes today, they take on a new dimension, a new life. A parallel would be of a short person looking from a distance and seeing vaguely a white object surrounded by green, having no idea of what he is seeing. Then someone possessed of greater height happens along and tells him: the white you are seeing is the king's palace, the green is his gardens, and so on. Once the shorter man is told what it is that he is seeing, he then says, 'yes, I also see it now.' However, the taller man's vision can only assist the shorter, if the shorter man with less visibility sees at least something. But if he sees nothing . . . the same is true today; we are like the short man; at moments we may indeed see something, and we may even experience exalted, lofty feelings, yet the experience is without clarity. The experience is only complete when we stand on our ancestors' shoulders, and say, Oh, now I understand what you have been seeing all along. And when we do stand on their shoulders, we can perceive even more.[111] Thus, we give new life, fresh insight to an old and well-trodden road; we shed our own light, our unique experiences on a path that has been traveled for thousands of years.[112] Each generation, each person, sings the same tune on a different octave.

NOTES

1. *Zohar. Rayah Mehemnah*, Mishpatim, p. 114. See: The second Chabad Rebbe Rabbi Dovber. *Shaarei T'shuva*. 2, (New York: Kehot Publication Society. 1983.) p. 15, where the Rebbe explains this passage of Zohar at length.

2. See: *Genesis*. 30:8. *Targum Onkelot. Rahsi. Seforno.* Ad loc. Rabbi Schneur Zalman of Liadi: *Torah Or.* (New York: Kehot Publication Society. 1996) Parshat Terumah. p. 79d. Rabbi Yoseph Yitzchak. The sixth Chabad Rebbe. *Sefer Hamaamorim 5709*, (New York: Kehot Publication Society. 1986) p. 79. Rabbi Menachem Mendel of Vitebsk. *Pri Ha'aretz.* (Jerusalem: HeMesorah. 1989.) Parshat Vayigash.

3. See: *Genesis*. 28:12. See: *Zohar.* Part 1, p. 266b. Part 3, p. 306b. *Tikunei Zohar.* Tikkun 45. See also: Rabbi Schneur Zalman of Liadi. *Likutei Torah.* (New York: Kehot Publication Society. 1996) Parshat Beshalach, p. 2b.

4. Talmud. *Taanit* 2a. *Sifre.* Parshat Ekev. 41. *Midrash Tehillim.* 66: 1.

5. In Hebrew the word for commandment is mitzvah, which can also mean "connecting." See: Rabbi Schneur Zalman of Liadi *Likutei Torah.* Parshat Bechukotai. p. 45c. See also: Rabbi Eliezer Ezcary, *Safer Cheredim.* Chapter 70. Rabbi Yehudah Loew. *Tifferet Yisrael.* Chapter 9.

6. There is an argument among the codifiers of the law, as to whether or not prayer every day is a commandment, one of the 248 positive commandments. In Hilchot Tefilah, 1: 1, the Rambam says it is indeed a mitzvah of the Torah to pray each day. However, most authorities hold differently. (See: *Chinuch.* mitzvah. 433 Rambam. *Safer Hamitzvah* 5.) The question asked is how can prayer, which is such an important part of man's relationship with God, not be a mitzvah? Chassidut explains in *Likutei Torah.* Parshat Balak. p. 70b. that the reason is not that they hold that it is not important, but on the contrary, that its significance is far beyond that of all the 248 other *mitzvot*, which depend on prayer as their foundation. Tellingly, when the Talmud states the number of limbs in the body as 248, (*Bechorot.* 45a.) corresponding to the 248 positive commandments, [Talmud. *Makkot.* 22b.] the vertebrae of the spine are included, but the spinal cord itself is not (Mishnah *Oholot.* Chapter 1. Mishnah 8.) Again not because it is not important, but conversely, because it is the strength and the foundation of the body; thus it is in a sense higher than any limb. Prayer is to momentous to our relationship with God, which is the objective of all *mitzvot*, that it stands above any commandment. It is the very foundation of the relationship. (See: Talmud *Berachot*, 28b, in which the main part of prayer is likened to the backbone—the spinal column of man.)

7. See: Talmud *Sanhedrin*, 27b, where the Talmud defines an enemy as one to whom you haven't spoken, because of anger, in three days.

8. For the unscientific mind, an easy read on this concept would be Lincoln Barnett. *The Universe and Dr. Einstein* (New York: Bantam. 1979), especially Chapter 7.

9. *Midrash Rabba. Numbers.* Parsha 14: 12. *Safer Yetzirah.* 1: 9–12. See also: *Rambam,* Hilchot Yisodei Hatorah. Chapter 3: Halacha 10. Rabbi Moshe ben Nachman. (1194–1270) *Ramban. Genesis.* Chapter 1. Verse 1. Rabbeinu Bachya. (1263–1340) *Genesis.* Chapter 1. Verse 1. Rabbi Nisan Ben Reuven. (1290–1380) *Derashot HaRan* (Jerusalem: Machon Shalom. 1977.) Derush 1. Page 1. Rabbi Gershon Ben Shlomo. (Thirteenth century) *Shar HaShamaim.* (Israel: 1968) Maamor 1. Shar 1, p. 5. Rabbi Shimon Ben Tzemach Duran. *Magen Avot.* (Jerusalem: Makor Publishing.) Part 2. Chapter 1. p. 9a. Although there are many theories in philosophy, in regards to the amount of elements there exist in nature. (See: Rabbi Yitzchak Israeli (855–955) *Safer Hayesodot.* (Jerusalem: 1968) Part 2. Maamor 3, pp. 62–77. Rabbi Yitzchak Israeli *Yesod Olam.* Maamor 2. Chapter 1. Rabbi Dan Yitzchak Abarbanel. (1437–1508) *Genesis* Chapter 1. Verse 14.) Nonetheless, in arguments such as these, one assumes the opinion of the Kabbalists over the opinion of the philosophers. And since the Kabbalah speaks of there being four basic elements, thus, it is the prevailing opinion. See: Rabbi Eliyahu Ben Meir of Vilna. (1743–1821) *Safer Habrit.* (Jerusalem: Yerid HaSefarim. 1990) Part 1. Maamor 5. Chapter 5.

10. *Emunot Vedeyot.* Maamor 1. Chapter 3. Rabbi Saddiah Gaon speaks of the four elements as being Hot (fire), Cold (water), Moist (wind), and Dry (earth). Rabbi Shimon Ben Tzemach Duran. *Magen Avot.* (Jerusalem: Makor Publishing.) Part 2. Chapter 4. p. 35b. The Lubavitcher Rebbe, *Igrot Kodesh.* (New York: Kehot Publication Society. 1990), Vol. 19. p. 239. Rabbi M. M. Schneerson writes that these four elements should not be confused with what science calls elements, (Scientists believe there are 96.) because these four elements are the four basic general ingredients of creation, which can themselves be broken down to 96, or even more, specific elements.

11. Fire is the loftiest of all four. *Midrash Rabbah Numbers.* Parsha 14: 12. *Rambam.* Hilchot Yesodei Hatorah. Chapter 3. Halacha 10. Rabbi Pinchas Eliyohu Ben Meir of Vilna *Sefer Habrit.* (Jerusalem: Yerid Hasefarim. 1990.) Part one. Maamar 11. See also: The fifth Chabad Rebbe. Rabbi Sholom Dovber *Yom Tov Shel Rosh Hashono.* 5666. (New York: Kehot Publication Society. 1984), p. 111. Here they explain fire as the highest element; thus, it is equated to man. However, Rabbi Schneur Zalman of Liadi, in *Likutei Torah,* Parshat Pinchot, p. 75d, explains that the element of fire is lower than Ruach, wind, and thus animals correspond to fire. Ruach is the highest—Man. This also seems to be the opinion of the Ramban, Rabbi Moshe ben Nachman. (*Ramban Genesis.* 1: 2.) However, see *Rabbienu Bachyah. Genesis.* Chapter 1: 2, where he explains that the Ramban's opinion is also that fire is the highest, and thus symbolic of man.

12. See: Rabbi DovBer. The second Chabad Rebbe. *Berchat Chasanim,* (New York: Kehot Publication Society. 1976.) p. 32.

13. In Jewish thought it is explained that the reason that human beings stand erect in contrast to all other animals, who face downwards, is that each creature is facing his own source. Man faces above, to the worlds "above," while animals face their source, the earth. See: *Safer Hayashar.* (Bnei Brak: Mishar. 1989.) Shar 1, p. 14. And Shar 5, pp. 62–63. (The author of this classic is unknown. See: Rabbi Chayim Yoseph David Azulay. *Shem Hagdalim Marrechess Siforim. Zayin.*) Rabbi Yoseph Yavatz, in his commentary to *Avot.* Chapter 3. Mishnah 18. Rabbi Moshe Metrani. (1500–1580) *Beit Elokim* Shar Hatefila. (Jerusalem: Otzer Hasefarim. 1985) Chapter 7. Shar Hayesodot. Chapter 42. See also: Rabbi Yoseph Ibn Tzadik. (Twelfth century philosopher) *Safer*

Ha'Olam Hakatan. (Breslau: Schatzky. 1903) Maamor 2. Shar 1, p. 26. Rabbi Menasha Ben Israel *Nishmat Chayim.* Maamor 4. Chapter 3.

14. See: *Ezekiel.* Chapter 1.

15. *Ezekiel.* Chapter 1 verse 4. See also: *Kings 1.* Chapter 19. Verse 11–12. *Job.* Chapter 38. Verse 1.

16. In this verse it mentions only three of the elements. (fire, water, and wind) The same is true in other books of Kabbalah, where it also mentions (only) three. (See: *Sefer Yitzerah* 1: 9–12. 3: 4. See also: Rabbi Yehudah HaLevy. *The Kuzari.* Maamor 4. Chapter 25.) The reason for that is that the fourth element, earth, is at times considered to be part of the other three. Rabbi Moshe Cordovero. *Pardas Rimonim.* Shar 9. Chapter 3. It is from these three elements fire, water, and wind, that the element of earth emerges. See: By the same author. *Or Neerav.* (Israel: Kal Yehudah. 1965.) Part 6. Chapter 2, p. 46. *Ma'arechet Elokut.* (Jerusalem: 1963) Chapter 12. [The author of this ancient text is unknown. There are those who attribute this text to Rabbi Todros Halevi Abulafia. (1220–1298) See: Rabbi Moshe Corodovero. *Pardess Rimonim* Shar 6. Chapter 2. While others attribute this text to Rabbi Peretz Hacohen. See: The Lubavitcher Rebbe. *Likutei Sichot.* Vol. 16. (New York: Kehot Publication Society. 1980) p. 491.] Rabbi Shalom Dovber. The fifth Chabad Rebbe. *Sefer Hamaamorim.* 5655, (New York: Kehot Publication Society. 1983) p. 11.

17. The three primary Kelipot, Rabbi Yoseph Gikatalia. (1248–1323) *Shaarey Orah.* (New York: Mariah. 1985.) Shar 5, p. 100. Rabbi Moshe Cordovero. *Pardas Rimonim.* Shar 25. Chapter 7. Rabbi Pinchas Eliyohu Ben Meir of Vilna *Sefer Habrit.* (Jerusalem: Yerid Hasefarim. 1990.) Part 2. Maamor 10. Chapter 3. (See also: Rabbi Schneur Zalman of Liadi *Tanya*, Chapter 6) See: Rabbi Eliyohu Ben Moshe Vidas. *Reshit Chacmah.* Shar HaYirah. Chapter 4, where he explains these three elements as being A) Pride, B) Stubbornness, and C) Anger, the source of all of them being egotism.

18. This is the first step in prophecy. *Rambam.* Yisodei Hatorah. 7: 4.

19. The reason that these elements are not found mentioned by all prophets. See, for example: *Isaiah.* 6:1), is that since these prophets experienced their prophesies in the holy land of Israel, their vision were not clouded. Rabbi Avraham Azulay. *Chesed Le'Avraham.* Part 1. Chapter 25.

20. A person's animal soul, as well as his Godly soul, has these four elements. See: *Likutei Torah.* (New York: Kehot Publication Society. 1996.) Parshat Emor, p. 32b.

21. In the first stages of modern medicine, in the times of Hippocrates, physicians believed (see: Rabbi Mayor Eben Aldavie. *Shivilei Emunah.* Nosiv 4. Rabbi Moshe Chayim Ephraim of Sudylkov. *Degel Machanah Ephraim.* Parshat Bereishit). that since there are four basic natures in man, dry—earth, moist—wind, cold—water, and hot—fire, therefore, in order for one to be healthy, it is appropriate for there to always be the correct balance among the four. Interestingly enough, in China, even today, they still practice this sort of medicine. However, they believe in five basic elements. The element of air is omitted in Chinese thought. According to them the five elements are, Fire. Earth. Water. Wood. Gold. They say that in order for man to be healthy there has to be the right equilibrium, which is basically achieved if there is a balance between the yin and the yang, the masculine and the feminine, the creative and the receptive. (See: Talmud. *Baba Batra*, 74b. "Everything that the Holy One blessed be He created in His world is Male and Female." See also: *Zohar*, Part 1, p. 157b.)

22. *Sharei Kedusha.* Part 1. Shar 2. Here Rabbi Chayim Vital explains how these four elements represent the four basic negative traits in man: Fire—haughtiness and anger, Wind—idle talk, lies and deceit, Water—lust and jealousy, and Earth—depression and laziness. (See also: Rabbi Schneur Zalman of Liadi *Tanya*, Chapter 1.) Their positive counterparts are Fire—humility, Wind—silence, Water—disgust of excessive earthly pleasures, and Earth—happiness.

23. "My heart spills forth like water." *Lamentations* Chapter 2. Verse 19.

24. In the animalistic soul of man, it is the will to be consumed in greater physical pleasures; in the Godly soul, it is the will to be consumed in its source above, to become one with God alone. See: Rabbi Schneur Zalman of Liadi. *Tanya.* Chapter 19.

25. The Midrash (*Midrash. Rabbah Genesis.* Parsha 14, verse 9.) enumerates five parts, Nefesh, Ruach, Neshama, Chaiyah, and Yichidah. The reason I discuss only four is that what is relevant here is the animal soul, and the need to elevate it during prayer, and the animal soul does not have a counterpart for the level of Yichidah. The fifth part of the Godly soul has no counterpart in this physical and mundane world, for it is a higher level of spirituality, which has no manifestation in the physical. *Likutei Sichot.* The Lubavitcher Rebbe. (New York: Kehot Publication Society, 1972) Vol. 6, p. 107.

26. The reason the term sacrifice is used, although, perhaps it has negative connotations, is that in the Talmud, prayer is likened to a *karban*—sacrifice, offering. (see: Talmud *Berachot* p. 26a.) Note, that the root of the word Karban is 'Karov' which means to draw closer. *Sefer HaBahir.* Chapter 109.

27. The reason is that the source of the divisions of four, the four elements, originates from the name of God,—the tetragrammaton, which has four letters. Yud—Hei—Vav—Hei. Rabbi Chayim Vital. *Sharei Kedusha.* Part 1. Shar 1. By the same author. *Sharr Hagilgulim.* Hakdamah 18. Rabbi Avraham Azulay. *Chesed Le'Avraham.* Part 4. Chapter 5. Rabbi Schneur Zalman of Liadi. *Torah Or.* (New York: Kehot Publication Society. 1996.) Bereshit, p. 3:d. By the same author. *Tanya.* Chapter 38. Rabbi Dovber. The second Chabad Rebbe. *Imrei Binah.(1)* (New York: Kehot Publication Society. 1975.) p. 78b. Rabbi Yakov Yoseph of Polonnoye. *Taldot Yakov Yoseph.* Hakdama.

28. These four worlds are alluded to in *Isaiah.* 43:7, and the four letters of the name of God, the Tetragrammaton, allude to these four worlds. Yod—Atziluth, the first Hei—Beriah, Vov—Yitzirah, and the final Hie—Asiyah. See: Rabbi Chayim Vital. *Sharei Kedusha.* Part 3. Shar 1.

29. The root of the word Atziluth is Etzel, which means near. This world is a reality, a separate existence which really does not exist the way man perceives existence. However, the world of *Beriah* is the first world to exist as a separate reality. Thus the word *Beriah* means cut off. Rabbi Moshe Cordovero. (1522–1570) *Pardas Rimonim.* Shar 16. Chapter 1.

30. The four parts are as follows: 1) Birchot Hasachar (the morning blessings, and the recitation of the sacrifices) Asiyah, 2) Pisukei D'zimrah (the verses of praise) Yitzirah, 3) Keriat Shema (the blessings and reading of the Shema) Beriah, and 4) Shmone Esrei (the eighteen benedictions) Atziluth. See: Rabbi Chayim Vital *Pri Eitz Chayim. Sharr Hatafila.* In the beginning. *Olat Tamid* Shar Hatefilan p. 7A. Rabbi Moshe Chayim Luzzatto. *Derech Hashem.* Part 4. Parek 6: 14. See also: The fifth Chabad Rebbe. Rabbi Shalom Dovber. *Kuntres Ha'avadah.* (New York: Kehot Publication Society. 19–) In the beginning. [For another way of dividing the prayer in four, see: *Sefer Hama-*

amorim—Kuntreisim. By the Sixth Chabad Rebbe, Rabbi Yoseph Yitzchak. (New York: Kehot Publication Society. 1986), Vol. 2, p. 638.

31. Rabbi Schneur Zalman of Liadi, writes, that the Pisukei D'Zimrah are called *songs* of praise, because through reading these words of praise one becomes spiritually aroused. It is a song which arouses emotions. See: *Torah Or.* (New York: Kehot Publication Society. 1996) Parshat Beshalach, p. 62c.

32. See: *Tur* Rabbi Yaakov ben Asher (c1275–c1340) *Shulchan Aruch.* Orach Chayim. Chapter 63. See also: *Midrash Rabbah Genesis.* Parsha 48. Chapter 7.

33. An integral part of reading of the Shema, is the recitation of blessings which precedes the Shema. The blessings which speaks of the angels singing God's praise. In Halacha these two, the introductory blessing, and the actual reading of the Shema, are considered as one. See: *Rambam.* Hilchot Keriat Shema. Chapter 2. Halacha 13. The commentary *Kessef Mishna.* Ad loc. Rashba. Rabbi Shlomo Ben Aderet. *T'shuvat Harashba.* (Responsa) Part 1. T'shuvah 320. Rabbi Schneur Zalman of Liadi. *Tanya.* (New York: Kehot Publication Society. 1965) Chapter 49.

34. Shemone Esrei, means eighteen, for when this prayer was instituted by the "men of the great Assembly," it had eighteen blessings. (See: Talmud. *Megillah.* 17b.) Later on, some time after the destruction of the second temple, during the period when Rabbi Gamliel was the *Nassi*—prince, leader of Israel, a nineteenth blessing was added. In the Talmud, this prayer is referred to as simply "the prayer."

35. See: *Shulchan Aruch.* Orach Chayim. Chapter 98.

36. The Talmud *Berachot* (p. 10b) says that one should pray this prayer with feet together, but does not give the reason. The Jerusalem Talmud *Berachot*, Chapter 1. Halacha 1 says that this allows us to resemble angels and priests in the Temple. See: Rabbi Mordecai Jaffe. (1530–1612) *Levush.* Orach Chayim. Chapter 90:1. There is also the reason why the feet are together, and that to show that you are completely bound and helpless without God. Rabbi Shlomo Ben Aderet. *Rashba.* Berachot. Page 10b. *Rabbeinu Bachya Numbers* 16:22. It is also to show that the right powers, the Godly inclination, and the left powers, the evil inclination, are both unified in serving God. Rabbi Moshe Metrani. *Beit Elokim.* Shar Hatefila. (Jerusalem: Otzer Hasefarim. 1985), Chapter 7, pp. 27–28. Rabbi Chaim Ben Betzalel. (1515–1588) *Safer HaChaim. Safer Selicha U'Mechila.* (Jerusalem: Machon Sharei Yoshar. 1996) Chapter 8, p. 185.

37. See: *Zohar.* Part 3, p. 218b. Rabbi David *Avudrham. Shulchan Aruch* Orach Chayim. Chapter 48. The *Rama*: 2. See also: Rabbi Yehudah Halevi *The Kuzari* Maamor 2. Chapter 79–80. Rabbi Yehudah Ha-Chassid. *Sefer Chassidim.* Chapter 57. *Shibolei Haleket.* Chapters 17 and 20.

38. *Shulchan Aruch* Orach Chayim. Chapter 48. *Magen Avraham.*4. See also: Rabbi Menachem Azaryah De Fano. (1548–1620) *Asarah Maamorot. Maamor Aim Kal Chai.* Part 1. Chapter 33. Rabbi Chayim Yoseph David Azulay. *Avodat Hakodesh. Kesher Gudal.* Chapter 12: 1. In the name of the Kabbalists. See also: Rabbi Yeshayah Halevi Horowitz. Shalah HaKodosh. *Shenei Luchot Habrit.* (Jerusalem: 1963) Part 2. Inyana Tefila, p. 79.

39. See: Rabbi Yehudah Lowe. (1512–1609) *Nesivoth Olam. Nesiv Ha'Avadah.* Chapter 6.

40. Rabbi Yakov Emdin. *Sidur Beit Yakov.* Before "Shemone Esrei," in which he refers to this part of prayer as the holy of holies, as if entering the Kodesh HaKodashim in the holy temple.

41. Thus, it is understood in the saying by the Baal Shem Tov, that it is an act of kindness from God that after prayer, one remains alive, because how indeed can one survive in the physical body, after praying with such intensity. *Tzavoas Horivash.* (New York: Kehot Publication Society. 1982) Chapter 42.

42. Rabbi Pinchas of Koritz. *Midrash Pinchas,* (Jerusalem: 1971.) p. 18. Chapter 52.

43. The Lubavitcher Rebbe. *Likutei Sichot.* (New York: Kehot Publication Society. 1982.) Vol. 19, pp. 291–297.

44. Rambam. *The Guide To The Perplexed.* Part 3. Chapter 45.

45. Rabbi Shem Tov Ben Yoseph Ibn Falaquera. *Safer Hamevakesh,* (Jerusalem: Mekorot. 1970) p. 86. Rabbi Moshe Yichiel Elimelech of Levertov. *Safer Shemirat Hada'at.* Aimrei Tal. Ma'amar Nigun. (Bnei Brak Israel: Ginzei MaHaritz. 1986), pp. 8–9.

46. Rabbi Dovber. The second Chabad Rebbe. *Maanorei Admur Hoemtzoee. Kuntresim.* (New York: Kehot Publication Society. 1991) Kuntras Hispalous, p. 66. The Chinuch writes, that music was played to assist the Cohen in his intention. *Sefer Hachinuch* mitzvah 384.

47. A place of worship is considered a small temple. Talmud *Megillah* 29a.

48. See: Talmud, *Berachot* 26a.

49. Rabbi Schneur Zalman of Liadi, *Sirrur Im Dach.* (New York: Kehot Publication Society. 1965) At the end of 'Intentions for the Mikvah,' p. 159.

50. There are various ways the concept of Mikvah can be accomplished when there is not a Mikvah, washing one's hands, learning the laws of the Mikvah. See: *Sharrei Halacah U'Minhag,* (Jerusalem. Hechall Menachem. 1993. p. 95.

51. See: *Sifron Shel Tzadikim,* (Jerusalem: Israel. 1959) p. 51. 5. See also: Rabbi Moshe Yichiel Elimelech of Levertov. *Safer Shemirat Hada'at.* Aimrei Tal. Ma'amar Nigun, (Bnei Brak Israel: Ginzei MaHaritz. 1986) p. 23.

52. See: I. Klapholtz. *Beit Rushin,* (Bnei Brak Israel: Mishor. 1987) p. 120.

53. The Talmud says that one shall begin prayers in a happy mood. *Berachot.* 31a. Jerusalem Talmud *Berachot.* Chapter 5. Halacha 1. Furthermore, Simcha—happiness, is an integral part of prayer itself. Rabbi Eliyohu Ben Moshe Di Vidas. *Reshit Chochmah.* Shar HaAhavah. Chapter 10, thus, singing before prayers is indeed an appropriate behaviour. See: Talmud *Berachot* 31a. *Tosefot* titled *Rababan.*

54. The sixth Chabad Rebbe. Rabbi Yoseph Yitzchak. The nineteenth of Kislev 5708 (1948).

55. See: *Isaiah.* Chapter 25. Verse 5. *Exodus.* Chapter 15. Verse 2. *Rashi.* Ad loc. Rabbi Yoseph Gikatalia. (1248–1323) *Shaarey Orah.* (New York: Mariah. 1985.) Shar 1: p. 7. Rabbi Schneur Zalman of Liadi. *Likutei Torah.* (New York: Kehot Publication Society. 1996) Parshat Nitzavim, p. 51d. The sixth Chabad Rebbe. Rabbi Yoseph Yitzchak. *Sefer Hamaamorim 5687* (New York: Kehot Publication Society. 1986.) p. 205. See also: Rabbi Meir Ben Gabbai. *Tola'at Yakov.* (Jerusalem: Mokor Chaim. 1967) Sod Pisukei D'zimrah. p. 21. Rabbi Chaim Ben Betzalel. *Safer HaChaim. Safer Selicha U'Mechila.* (Jerusalem: Machon Sharei Yoshar. 1996) Chapter 8, p. 185. Rabbi Yitzchak Lamfronati. (1697–1757) *Pachad Yitzchak.* (Jerusalem: Mokor. 1971) Erech Zimiras.

56. Rabbi Nachman of Breslov *Likutei Aytzot* Tefilah. P 157. See also by the same author: *Likutei Moharan*. Part 1. Chapter 46.

57. See: Talmud. *Keritot*, 6a, in which the Talmud says that if one studies next to the rush of water, one will understand the studies better.

58. As the Sufis, who are known to use their own body movements, in dancing, as a form of meditation. Rabbi Avraham Ben HaRambam, cites various meditative techniques of the Sufis. (Dervishes) See: *Safer HaMaspik Leovedei Hashem*. Hisbodedut, p. 185.

59. Many Chassidic Rebbes use dance to reach *Hitpashtut Ha'Gashmiyut*—the taking off of materiality.

60. See: Rabbi Moshe Yichiel Elimelech of Levertov. *Safer Shemirat Hada'at*. Aimrei Tal. Ma'amar Nigun, (Bnei Brak Israel: Ginzei MaHaritz. 1986.) p. 16. He writes that it is only natural that when one is inspired or overwhelmed, he will sing. He says that younger people are more ready to sing and dance on any given occasion. Because they are less rigid and set in their ways, they are more easily inspired and moved.

61. Retold by the sixth Chabad Rebbe, Rabbi Yoseph Yitzchak, on the nineteenth of Kislev 5706. (1946)

62. See: Rabbi Yisrael Baal Shem Tov. *Tzavoas Horivash*. (New York: Kehot Publication Society. 1982.) Chapter 66. Rabbi Schneur Zalman of Liadi. *Likutei Torah*. (New York: Kehot Publication Society. 1996) Parshat Naso, p. 20d.

63. The Baal Shem Tov said that just as begetting children can only be done through happiness and gladness of the heart, so it is with prayer; in order for prayer to beget fruits, and have an effect on your actions, it must be done with happiness. *Kesser Shem Tov*. (New York: Kehot Publication Society. 1974) Chapter 16. The Ari Zal. Rabbi Yitzchak Luria warns against praying in a depressed state of mind. See: *Shar HaKavanot*. In the beginning. During the prayers, one expresses fear and love concurrently. Rabbi Yoseph Yitzchak. The sixth Chabad Rebbe. *Safer Hamaamorim*. *5705*, (New York: Kehot Publication Society. 1986) p. 143.

64. Prayer is a synthesis between feeling God's immanence, and His transcendence. A traditional blessings starts with "Bless You God . . . who has sanctified us with His commandments." At first you start by speaking to God as You, then you shift to the third person, 'Who has sanctified us with His. . . . The Chassidic master, Rabbi Elimelech of Lizhensk (1717–1787), explains, that in the beginning, before you start to pray, you feel close, you feel God's immanence. You are happy. However, once you start praying, you realize how far away you really are, and you are sad. See *No'am Elimelech*. Parshat Bechukotai. See also: Jerusalem Talmud. *Berachot*. Chapter 10. Halacha 1. Rabbi Shlomo Ben Aderet. *T'shuvat HaRashba*. Part 5. T'Shuva 52. Rabbi David Ben Yoseph *Avudraham*. (Jerusalem: 1963) Birchat Hashachar, pp. 33–34.

65. The sixth Chabad Rebbe. Rabbi Yoseph Yitzchak. *Likutei Diburim* (New York: Kehot Publication Society. 1980) Vol. 1. p. 109.

66. *Tikunei Zohar*. Tikkun 21. *Zohar*. Part 3, p. 227b. Rabbi Mordechai Ashkenzr. Teachings by Rabbi Avraham Ben Rephael (?–1714) *Eishel Avraham*. In the beginning. Rabbi Yehudah Muscato. (1520–1590) *Nefutzhot Yehudah*. Derush 1. *Higoan Bechinor*. (This is a discourse dedicated to the mystical evaluation of music. And how the four letters in the name of God, *Yud. Hei. Vav. Hei*, relate to the musical scale.)

Rabbi Schneur Zalman of Liadi. *Maamorei Admur Hazoken. Maarezal,* (New York: Kehot Publication Society. 1984.) pp. 25–28. By the same author. *Torah Or.* (New York: Kehot Publication Society 1996.) Parshat Bereshit, p. 7c. The second Chabad Rebbe Rabbi Dovber. *Shaarei T'shuva. 1,* (New York: Kehot Publication Society. 1983.) p. 35.

67. The second Chabad Rebbe Rabbi Dovber. *Shaarei T'shuva. 1,* (New York: Kehot Publication Society. 1983.) p. 35. He writes that the reason it is called by this name, is, that the source of these tunes come from *da'at* which is the fourth (in the order of Sefirot) level of intelligence, the capacity to divide and separate.

68. This is the beauty of song. Just as an exquisite painting incorporates a myriad of hues, music composed of an abundant emotional spectrum is infinitely more beautiful. Rabbi Shlomo Zalman of Kapust. *Magen Avot* Parshat Yitro.

69. See: Talmud. *Baba Kamma.* 82a. *Rashi* Machnis.

70. Rabbi Dovber. The second Chabad Rebbe. *Maanorei Admur Hoemtzoee. Kuntresim.* (New York: Kehot Publication Society. 1991) Kuntras Hispalous, p. 159.

71. Rabbi Abraham Kalisk (1741–1810) The idea of a somersault (turning oneself over) expresses the concept of *bittul*—self nullification.

72. Rabbi Nachman of Breslov. *Likutei Moharan.* Part 1:156. See also: *Tzavoas Harivash.* (New York: Kehot Publication Society. 1982.) Chapter 68.

73. Rabbi Pinchas of Karitz. *Aimrei Pinchos,* (Benei Brak: Mishor. 1988.) p. 205.

74. The sixth Chabad Rebbe. Rabbi Yoseph Yitzchak. *Likutei Diburim* (New York: Kehot Publication Society. 1980) Vol. 3, p. 445. See also: Rabbi Schneur Zalman of Liadi. *Torah Or.* (New York: Kehot Publication Society. 1996) Parshat Beshalach, p. 62c.

75. Parenthetically, Rabbi Dovber was known to love music. (See: The Lubavitcher Rebbe. *Hayom Yom.* (New York: Kehot Publication Society. 1965, the twenty-fifth of Tishrei.) Rabbi Dovber had a group of musicians and a choir, who were specially designated to compose Chassidic melodies for his court.

76. See: *Maanorei Admur Hoemtzoee. Kuntresim.* (New York: Kehot Publication Society. 1991), pp. 39–185. Kuntras Hispalous. In the beginning.

77. Interestingly enough, the founder of Chabad *Chassidim,* Rabbi Schneur Zalman of Liadi (the father of Reb Dovber), was known to pray with externally displayed emotions. Once his Rebbe, Rabbi Dovber, wanted to deliver a Chassidic discourse; however, he asked first that his student, Reb Schneur Zalman be present. So his disciples went to the synagogue to call him. When they entered the synagogue, they found Reb Schneur Zalman in the middle of prayer, saying "All your creations shall realize that you are their creator." While he was pronouncing these words with tremendous rapture, he held the table in front of him, and kept banging it up and down, as if saying to the table, "Recognize your creator." It is also known in Chassidic circles that in his personal study, where he would pray, the walls were covered with a soft covering, because many times, while praying in tremendous ecstasy, he would fall to the ground and start rolling on the floor, and would bang his head on the walls. Therefore they covered the walls with a covering. This may be best explained by examining the development of any group, and especially a mystical group. In short, the first generation operates always with more excitement and vigor, for the doctrines are still new and fresh. The second generation, if they are led by a capable leader will take these immense feelings and inspirations felt in earlier stages in the development

of the movement, and internalize them. They bring the fervor to their own level, and give the movement more focus and direction. In Chabad circles it is known that Rabbi Schneur Zalman, the originator of the movement was the level of *chachma*—intuition, the flash of insight, while his son, Rabbi Dovber, was *binah*—understanding, consciousness, internalizing and giving focus. *Sefer Hasichot 5705.* The disciples of Rabbi DovBer would pray with song, albeit, their tunes were more composed and meditative. See: Rabbi Yoseph Yitzchak. The sixth Chabad Rebbe. *Sefer Hasichot. 5703,* p. 60. (New York: Kehot Publication Society. 1986) p. 125.

78. Rabbi Moshe Cordovero. (1522–1570) *Pardas Rimonim.* Shar 10. Shar Hagvanim.

79. Rabbi Shlomo Zalman of Kapust. (1830–1900) *Magen Avot.* Parshat Yitro.

80. Rabbi Dovber. *Shar Ha'Emunah,* (New York: Kehot Publication Society. 1979) pp. 105–107.

81. When we speak of intellect, we refer to going through one level at a time; for example, one can not teach a child who has never even learned basic math, an equation of Einstein, because intellect works a step at a time. In order to know $2+2 = 4$, one must first know $1+1 = 2$.

82. For instance, a small child can have the same exact feelings as the greatest of scientists, since feelings are and can be "above" intellect (which differentiates between a child and an adult.) Thus, a feeling does not need to be experienced "one level at a time." A child can experience the same pain or the same happiness as an adult.

83. See: *Safer Chassidim.* Chapter 158.

84. Talmud, *Berachot,* 21a.

85. It is well documented in Chabad circles how each of the Chabad Rebbes had his particular melodies, which he would sing during prayers. Indeed, many of their *Chassidim* as well had their distinct tunes, or tune, which they would sing during their prayers.

86. The sixth Chabad Rebbe. Rabbi Yoseph Yitzchak. *Sefer Hasichot 5702,* (1942) (New York: Kehot Publication Society. 1986) p. 109.

87. Rabbi Yisrael Baal Shem Tov. *Kesser Shem Tov.* (New York: Kehot Publications Society. 1987) Part 2, p. 60.

88. See: Talmud. *Niddah.* 30b. See also: Rabbi Schneur Zalman of Liadi *Tanya.* Chapter 1.

89. Eliezer Shtainman. *Yalkut Meshalim U'sipurim,* (Israel: Keneset. 1958.) p. 63–64. In the name of the Baal Shem Tov.

90. A ram's horn, blown on this holiday.

91. There is a sound, a pure cry which emanates from the inner essence of one's being. See: Rabbi Dovber. The second Chabad Rebbe. *Torat Chaim Shemot,* (New York: Kehot Publication Society. 1974.) p. 200a.

92. *Zohar.* Part 1. Parshat. Chayei Sarah. *Tikunei Zohar.* Tikkun 12.

93. Talmud. *Berachot.* 32a.

94. See: Talmud. *Avodah Zarah.* 7b–8a.

95. Man is refining himself by saying God's praise. Rabbi Meir Aldavie *Shevilei Emunah* (Jerusalem. 1990.) Nosive 1, p. 28. Furthermore, he writes, the purpose of prayer is not that God should change His will, rather that man changes through prayer. The third Chabad Rebbe. Rabbi Menachem Mendel. *Derech Mitzvosecho.* (Israel: Kehot

Publication Society. 1986), *mitzvahs Tefilah*. Chapter 9. Rabbi Moshe Metrani. (1500–1580.) *Beit Elokim*. Shar Hatefila. (Jerusalem: Otzer Hasefarim. 1985). Chapter 2, p. 7. Rabbi Yehudah Loew, writes that the entire prayer in fact is to complete and elevate the human being. *Nesivot Olam. Nosiv ha'avodah*. Chapter 2. See also: *Ma'arechet Elokut*. (Jerusalem: 1963) Chapter 10. (Rabbi Eliyohu Ben Moshe Di Vidas. *Reshit Chochmah*. Shar HaAhavah. Chapter 10. He writes that praising God during prayer brings about a closeness between man and God.)

96. The Lubavitcher Rebbe. *Sefer Ha'maamorim. Meluket*. (New York: Kehot Publication Society. 1988), Vol. 2, p. 301. See also: The third Chabad Rebbe, Rabbi Menachem Mendel. *Derech Mitzvosecho*. (Kfar Chabad Israel: Kehot Publication Society. 1986) *mitzvot* Hallel. By the same author. *Sefer Thilim. Yahel Or*. (New York: Kehot Publication Society. 1984) *Psalms*. Chapter 146. Verse 1, pp. 558–559.

97. See: *Zohar*. Part 3, p. 144b.

98. *Proverbs* 22:6. says, "Educate the youth according to his way, (so that) when he grows older, he won't stray from it." What is "his way?" Perhaps this means that when one educates, one must discern the way of the child, what the child's inherent talents and abilities are and help him to articulate them. One must educate the child to follow his own unique way, so that he shall be happy his entire life. Thus, "When he grows older . . ."

99. Any connection with others, he felt may have caused a spiritual descent. Rabbi Yisrael the Magid of Koznitz. (1733–1814) *Avodat Yisroel*, (Jerusalem. Mochon Sifrei Tzadikim. 1998), p. 276.

100. By analyzing one's own attributes, man is able to comprehend "God's personality" because, In the image of God He created . . . man (*Genesis*. Chapter 1. Verse 27), and since God created man in his image, man can understand God by drawing parallels from his own life. As it says, "In my flesh I see God. (*Job*. Chapter 19. Verse 26.) The reason for this is that God, so to speak, chose to reveal himself in this fashion. So man can indeed draw parallels, and make it more real.

101. Rabbi Schneur Zalman of Liadi. *Likutei Torah*. (New York: Kehot Publication Society. 1996.) Parshat Kedoshim, p. 29b–29c.

102. The sixth Chabad, Rabbi Yoseph Yitzchak. *Sefer Hamaamorim—Yiddish*, (New York: Kehot Publication Society. 1986.) p. 138.

103. *Psalms*, 22:3.

104. Kodesh, holy, is a level of complete transcendence. See: Rabbi Schneur Zalman of Liadi. *Tanya*. Chapter 49. Rabbi Yehudah Loew. *Gevurath Hashem*. Hakdamah 2.

105. God lowers himself so to speak, and connects with this lowly world. Thus when the Torah uses the word sitting for God, it means connection. See: Rabbi Meir Ben Gabbai (1480–1547) *Avodot Hakodesh, Cheilek HaTakhlit* Chapter 42. Rabbi Moshe Coredovero. *Shiur Komah*. (Jerusalem: 1966) Chapter 21. In addition sitting means permanence, being everlasting. See: Rambam. *The Guide To The Perplexed*. Part 1, Chapter 11.

106. It is worth noting that in the Kabbalah it says that through the act of singing in the worlds above, a revelation of Godliness, of the "ein soft," God's infinite light, is revealed to this world. Rabbi Avraham Azulay. (1570–1643) *Chesed Le'Avraham*. Part 1. Chapter 7. Furthermore, he writes, it is known that every physi-

cal existence has a unique song that it sings; thus if a human being knows his tune, and knows the intention of the tune, through singing this song one brings down a great revelation upon this earth. See: *Chesed La'Avraham*. Part 4. Chapter 3. See also: Rabbi Chayim Yoseph David Azulay. *Shem Hagdalim Marrechess Siforim Pei*. 147. In the name of the AriZal.

107. The Lubavitcher Rebbe. *Likutei Sichot*. (New York: Kehot Publication Society. 1972.) Vol. 7, p. 135.

108. *Aimrei Pinchos*, (Benei Brak: Mishor. 1988.) p. 196. See also: Eliezer Shtainman. *Be'er HaChassidut*. Me'orei HaChassidut, (Mochon Kemach. Israel.) p. 47. Note: *Midrash Rabbah Exodus* Chapter 23. Parsha 1.

109. The question is not if you can say the praises of prayer in the language you understand best, for that is permitted. If one understands English better than Hebrew he can surely pray in English. (See: Talmud. *Sotah*. 33a. Rabbi Yehudah Ha-Chassid. *Sefer Chassidim*. Chapters 588 and 785. *Tur. Orach Chayim*. Chapter 101. *Shulchan Aruch Orach Chayim*. Chapter 101: 4. *Chatam Sofer* Orach Chaim. Chapter 84. 86.) The question is, why translate? Why not use your own personal expressions of praise? The truth is, when you think about the idea of praise, it seems trivial, especially when it comes to praising God, albeit as explained, praise "reveals character." For how can man be certain that these praises are not trivial and completely off the mark. They may be even embarrassing, like praising a wealthy man for having five dollars (See: Talmud. *Berachot*. 33b.) How can a human, finite being, dare utter praise to God? The Talmud resolves this issue by asserting that the praises we use in prayer were first said by the master prophets, who did to an extent have understanding of God, as much as is allowed for humans to comprehend. For this reason, and so that we should not be completely off the mark, we use their praises. (Talmud *Yuma* 69b. See also: Talmud. *Megillah*. 18a. *Berachot*. 33b.) [Rabbi Klunmus Kalmish elucidates this theme.]

110. Rabbi Tzadok HaKohen of Lublin. (1823–1900) *R'sisei Layla*. Chapter 8. He writes that true "Shirah," song, can only be composed when there is immediate revelation, when Godliness is openly revealed. Rabbi Yakov Emdin. *Sidur Beit Yakov*. Hakdamah LeShir Hayichud. He writes in approval of even singing new praise during prayer, although he writes that the praise must be composed by men of great spiritual stature. The praise then will assuredly befit the prayer.

111. *Chavat Hatalmidim*. (New York: Taryag Publishers.) Ma'amor Beit.

112. Regarding praise within prayers, the question of set prayers as opposed to spontaneous praise was raised. This question can be expanded to include all the traditional prayers. Why, one may ask, do we all pray for the same things? One person may need health, while the other is in need of sustenance. So why is it that when we pray to God, we all pray from the same text? The answer to this question lies in the fact that we pray in first person plural (May God grant "us" . . .) and not first person singular. It is written that the reason that *Tzadikim*, the righteous men, must also say the confessions of sins committed during the prayer is that a person prays not only for themselves but on behalf of the whole of Israel. (Rabbi Chayim Vital. *Likutei Torah. Taamei HaMitzvot*. Kedoshim. The third Chabad Rebbe. The Tzemach Tzedek. *Derech Mitvosecho*. (New York: Kehot Publication Society. 1986.) Mitzvhat. Ahavat Yisroel.) It is not only an individual prayer, but a collective prayer. One joins together with all one's brethren, to pray as a whole. It is for this reason

that we all pray from the same text. Furthermore, through praying in a liturgy which was prayed for hundreds of years by millions of people, we are, in a sense, connecting ourselves with the whole history of the Jewish people. These set prayers, however, do not negate the spontaneous prayers, which, at times, are permitted even during the formal parts of prayer. And it surely does not negate the spontaneous prayers that we utter throughout the day, in an informal setting. See: Rabbi Eliezer Ezcary. (1522–1600) *Safer Cheraidim*. (Jerusalem: 1990) Chapter 65. Where he writes of spontaneous prayer.

7
Torah/The Wisdom of the Infinite
Expanding Consciousness

Once a Chassid complained to the Rebbe that his mind was not capable of understanding *Chassidut*. The Rebbe replied that the expansion of his mind will occur with song.[1]

In the previous chapter, we discussed how prayer impacts a human being, and how the experience recreates the person. In this chapter, we will discuss the transformative quality of Torah study.

Prayer is connection, communication. Prayer is a dialogue between the finite human, and the infinite God. Prayer is the way through which a finite can merge with the infinite. Furthermore, during the prayers, one loses his entire existence in the oneness of God, and, as explained, it is the foundation of the relationship between man and God, which is reinforced with every good deed, every mitzvah that we perform.

There are, however, always difficulties with any relationship when it is only one way, when you are always the one giving, and the other partner in the relationship always receives. A healthy relationship is one in which there is a two way street; there are times when you are the one who gives, and there are times when you are the one who receives. A sound relationship is one of give and take. The same is true with a human being's relationship with God.[2] In order for the relationship to be healthy, secure, and everlasting, it must be mutual. It must have the elements of both giving, which is prayer, where one offers himself to God, and receiving, which is Torah study, where one studies God's thoughts, and receives inspiration from above.

In Chabad terminology, prayer is termed *MilMatah LeMalah*, from below upwards. Here the human being is the initiator of the relationship, and it is the human who aspires to be close and one with God. And thus one prays and connects. Torah is termed *MilMalah LeMatah*, from above downwards.[3] One takes inspiration from above; one opens himself to a greater heavenly wisdom, and becomes a vessel through which the holy Torah can be manifested and revealed.

There are areas that seem counterintuitive to experiencing God through prayer on a continuous basis. One is that, being that the connection comes from man's own initiative,[4] and it is a finite being who creates the process, thus, the connection by definition is finite. This means that the connection is limited, and not everlasting.[5] What occurs during the prayers is no indication of what will occur after the "high" of prayer ceases to be felt. The experience of prayer has its limitations.

Additionally, an aspect of being human is to be invested in the physicality. We are trained to negotiate a three-dimensional universe, and we use the tools that promote survival, if not success, in that universe. The brain is not designed to hold the paradox; it is antithetical and unnatural for the human mind (in its human form) to maintain the great spiritual and transcendental experience of prayer for too long a time.

Being that the experience may have been enormous and momentous for most people, thus, what may occur to those who are untrained in such spiritual matters is that they will reduce the overwhelming experience to memory. They will immediately following their prayers, forget the entire experience. Since the experience of prayer was never really part of them, and never truly permeated their consciousness, their minds never fully understood the experience. Neither did their hearts ever really feel at ease with what they were feeling; thus, once the prayers are over, so are the feelings. Some people may find it difficult to forget the experiences they had during prayers. They may not have the necessary tools to handle the immense spiritual feelings that they carry with them from the sanctuary back to the workplace. Hence, not being properly equipped, they force these feelings into memory. It is as if one goes through a traumatic and overwhelming experience that he cannot mentally endure; the person experiencing this often subconsciously forces these feelings and memories to be suppressed. A person who was traumatized chooses (subconsciously) to forget the experience; the subconscious mind erects a barrier to protect him from the overwhelming experiences.

The opposite response may occur as well, although perhaps only to a select few. For them, the ecstasy they felt during prayer was so overwhelming, and meant so much to them, that they lose focus of physical reality. The ecstasy they feel during their prayers leads them to a total withdrawal from all physicality. Since the experience came too quickly, they easily lose their focus on life. They never really had the proper time to absorb and process the experience with introspection, to internalize and make the experience real. They become so caught up with their own feelings that they may lose the proper balance of life. This is contrary to the ultimate purpose of the creation of man, which is to be holy and spiritual within this physical world, and to "draw down" Godliness into this earthbound reality. "To be" and "not to be," which is to say to be within this world, and yet stand above it; to be unaffected negatively by the world, but to have a positive effect upon it. Thus, the proper experience of prayer is to take the inspiration, the ecstasy experienced, and draw it down and internalize it into one's personal reality. However, if the experience occurred too quickly, and there was an instant high, one may become "stuck above" with the experience, and never "return." (Such ecstasy may lead even to death, a complete withdrawal from all that is physical forever.[6])

Torah is the befitting complement. Torah creates the proper balance of achieving great spiritual heights, while remaining connected with the earthbound reality. With Torah, the experience comes more slowly, and additionally, its source is from above. Torah is a Godly gift given to man. It is a "part of God,"[7] which was given into the possession of man. In addition, as much as studying Torah is a religious and spiritual experience, it is also a rational and logical endeavor. Torah is God's wisdom revealed to man. It is an "infinite wisdom," which manifests itself within the confines of this physical, finite world.

Because it is wisdom, it contains within it two realms. On one hand, it is a thought that has rational dimensions. The Torah follows a logic; its study has a systematic thought process. And yet on the other hand, it is a "Godly logic,"[8] a divine thought, a logic that by its very definition defies all logic.

To the untutored, untrained in Talmudic thought, the reasoning used in Talmudic study may appear illogical. The methodology the Talmud uses, may feel absurd and unsound; however, once mastered, one finds that there exists a consistent pattern of "Talmudic logic." There exists a logic, albeit a "Godly logic," which weaves through the entire Talmud.[9]

Consequently, what the experience of prayer lacks, the Torah experience supplements. The connection with God through the Torah is not from the bottom upwards, that is, a human's initiative to connect with God; rather, Torah is "God's wisdom" which was, and is, continuously being revealed to man here on earth. Therefore, when one studies Torah, one becomes connected and unified with God on His infinite terms. And since the Torah is also a comprehensive and rational intellectual pursuit, the experience is not overwhelming. It is with one's own intellect that one becomes connected. As explained earlier, when one works to reach spiritual heights, through one's intellectual capacities, one is elevated only one step at a time. In a sense, the inspiration, and great spiritual high one experiences during prayer, is "drawn down" and internalized through studying Torah. Thus, the Talmud says, one should immediately proceed to a house of study following prayer.[10]

However, there are also difficulties with experiencing a connection only through Torah.[11] The trouble is that since Torah is knowledge (albeit a Godly knowledge) it is possible for someone to sit and study Torah the entire day, and entirely forget that it is God's Torah they are contemplating.[12] One can study the wisdom of Torah as he would ponder any other thought. This is especially true if one is studying the revealed parts of the Torah, that is, the law, which concerns itself mostly with materialistic subjects. For example, if someone loses an object and another finds it, to whom does the object belong, and the like. For this reason the Talmud says[13] that for some, the study of Torah is in fact poisonous. Therefore, an appropriate introduction to studying Torah, and hence the very first thing one should aspire to accomplish each morning, is prayer,[14] since prayer is designed to nullify the ego, and through prayer one sacrifices one's entire being to God; thus, afterwards, when one sits down to study Torah, he will remember the "Giver of the Torah."[15] When one gets oneself out of the way, then the giver and the author of the wisdom is remembered, even while learning about the mundane and the quotidian.[16] Consequently, both these connections with God, from below to the above (prayer) and from above to the below (Torah), are extremely important in the spiritual experience.[17]

Just as there are tunes that accompany prayer, assisting the concentration and the elevation, there are also tunes geared especially for the study of Torah.

The Talmud speaks harsh words against one who studies Torah without song.[18] Singing while studying shows that one truly appreciates, and is inspired by, the sweetness and beauty of the Torah, so much so in fact, that they are moved to sing from this overwhelming joy.[19]

Additionally, when feeling depressed, albeit a constructive type such as *Marirrut*, a person needs the hope that he can overcome and shift to happiness. The anodyne and the cure, says the *Zohar*, is to study Torah with joy.[20]

Generally, the melodies that one sings as an introduction to the study of Torah or during one's study, are not emotional melodies, fast-paced or light-hearted tunes, but rather are of a meditative character. They are slower, more subtle tunes, tunes that appeal to the mind, for an appropriate meditative song can awaken within man the power of his intellect.[21] As we explained in the introduction, Western music is generally goal-oriented, with a well-defined structure and pattern. Recent studies have shown that classical music, which fits into the category of Western music, can have a tremendous impact on the development of one's intellectual capacities. Even at a very young age, music can assist in a child's intellectual development.

Music can be relaxing and can get one into the right mood for contemplative, arduous study.

Why is it that when a child is crying hysterically, a soothing tune will calm him? Why will singing a lullaby to a frantic child cause the child to fall into a slumber? The Kabbalah teaches that the inner reason that a person is moved by a rhythm, a tune, or a symmetrical sound wave is that the soul of man is accustomed to hearing the sounds of music from the heavenly angels above.[22] Even a child, and in a sense, especially a child (for children are closer to the original source above), will be soothed when he hears music. Music below is a reminder of the music above, and thus soothes the soul. Hence music can serve as a relaxing agent; it can place a person in the right state of mind for study.

At times, music and song can be used to clear the mind of any extraneous thoughts, and make it a fitting receptacle in which "Godly thoughts" can flow. These meditative melodies are found more frequently within the Chabad, the intellectual branch of *Chassidim*, while *Chagas*,—emotional *Chassidim* melodies, are for the most part lighter and more joyful.

The founder of the Chabad *Chassidut*, Rabbi Schneur Zalman of Liadi, was known to be very fond of Chassidic song. In fact, everything he said would be with a tune.[23] The Rebbe strongly urged his disciples to learn an appreciation of a fine melody. When he first founded his school, where he taught students the Chabad doctrines, he attracted an elite group of young scholars. (To become a student at the Rebbe's school, one had to qualify by satisfying the Rebbe's high standards of required Torah knowledge.) Two of the Rebbe's early disciples related how they were accepted.

They said that after the Rebbe tested their knowledge, their intellectual capacities, he sent them off to a celebrated Chassid, who was well-known for his appreciation of Chassidic melody, and who himself was a composer of Chassidic song. The Rebbe sent them to that Chassid to learn song, and to learn how to appreciate a melody. The Rebbe felt that in order for one to really understand Chassidic mysticism, one needs to know and appreciate Chassidic melody.[24]

To become one with God, to lose one's self in the greater existence of the Creator, this is the purpose of Chassidic thought and study. The goal of Chassidic song mirrors the goal of Chassidut itself, which is to lose one's self within the tune where one's entire being is absorbed and consumed within the song, until, one becomes song.

Rabbi Schneur Zalman was first introduced to Chassidic doctrines when he went to the Magid of Mezeritch, Rabbi Dovber. The Magid told him three things:[25] who he was, what the unique purpose was of his soul's descent into this world, and the fact that in order for one to properly understand Chassidic mysticism, one needs song. He explained that song elevates and opens one to Godly thoughts, while also enabling one to encounter these lofty thoughts at one's own level of understanding.

There are basically two types of questions that people ask. One is intellectual questions, questions of the mind, and they require intellectual answers. This type of answer, by satisfying the intellectual requirements, eradicates the question. The other is a question rising from the emotions. This is a more difficult one to satisfy, because it is not rooted in logic. Thus, while an answer may be factual and reasonable, the questioner is only temporarily satisfied. Interaction with children is a prime example of the latter type. Because the organizing principles differ between the question and the answer, a gap always exists, and is never satisfied. The questions asked about God are articulated linguistically and logically, but are inquiries about the insubstantial (spiritual/emotional) and defy a comprehensive linguistic description. The existence of evil, or the prospering of the wicked, defies the consistent logical construct that we believe should exist in the world. So the answers sought for these profound questions come from another plane than the linear reasoning we are accustomed to, (eg: $1+1 = 2$ and so on). Chassidic mysticism undertakes these questions based on Torah study and Torah logic. However, to access and be in tune with that plane, which subsumes and supersedes ordinary logic, an appropriate tune eases and accelerates the process. A proper tune can transplant and elevate a person entirely, one's intellect as well as one's emotions, to the higher plane.

At times, when there are strong emotional questions, the melodies one sings as a preparation for intellectual study can be so powerful that one no longer needs the actual study to appease the mind, for the songs themselves are sufficient.

There is a story told of the first Chabad Rebbe, Rabbi Schneur Zalman of Liadi.[26] At the beginning of the Chassidic movement, there were many adversaries who questioned this new approach to life. The Rebbe came to the famed scholarly city of Shklove, where the great scholars called for an assembly, to use this opportunity to interrogate the Rebbe. After they had all posed their questions before the Rebbe, the Rebbe closed his eyes, and began singing a song. He sang with his beautiful, powerful, and awe-inspiring voice, a deep and penetrating melody, a melody of great *Deveikut*. When the Rebbe sang, the entire assembly became quiet, motionless, until they were all transported by the tune into a higher level of *Deveikut*. When the Rebbe completed singing, there were no more questions to be asked. The Rebbe, with the power of song, elevated the entire assembly to a lofty level of spirituality where there are no questions. This is the highest level of elevation through song, where through song one transcends all questions; one lifts himself to a spiritual state of being where there are no questions, where there are no artificial distinctions created by the mind, but only the satisfaction of wholeness.

On a more simple level, a Chassidic tune can elevate man as an introduction to the actual studying of the *Chassidut*. It puts the mind, as well as the heart, in the right state of consciousness, and enables the person to understand these lofty thoughts.

Song elevates the person, and opens one to Godly thoughts, yet, song also enables one to encounter lofty thoughts at one's own level, meaning, to take lofty concepts and allow them to penetrate the mind, so that they are retained. The Talmud says that one should learn Torah with a melody.[27] The commentaries[28] explain that the tunes, when associated with the wisdom, make it more memorable and more attainable. (This was especially true in those times before the Torah was written down, and the scholars had to learn the Torah through oral instruction, and commit it to memory.)

Many Chassidic masters while writing deep Chassidic thoughts, would pause for a few moments, and sing Chassidic melodies. They would do this so that they could reevaluate and process what they had just written.[29] This is a practice that still prevails amongst *Chassidim*; they pause during their study to sing. This helps them to assimilate the knowledge.

A higher purpose in singing while studying is to 'humble' the thoughts, so that they may become "engraved" into the consciousness. One can then become one with the Torah he is studying. When an artist engraves words on a stone, the words are not extraneous to the material upon which they are written. When one writes on a sheet of paper, the ink is added to the paper, but with engraving, the words are made from the stone itself.[30] So it is with studying Torah; a person should aspire to study the Torah until he becomes one with the Torah; they become inseparable, and part of the same entity. This level of study can be attained through song, because through song, one can grasp a concept, and allow it to slowly penetrate and invade one's entire being. A Chassidic master said, "If you accept the yoke of Torah completely, to the degree that you are one with it, then you will demonstrate it in your appreciation for song."[31]

The preceding reasons for singing during the studying of Torah applies to the revealed components of Torah, the Talmud, Midrash, Halacha, and so on, as well as to the inner components, the mystical dimensions of the Torah. Nevertheless, there are pertinent reasons for song that apply and have a greater relevance when one is engrossed in the study of Kabbalah, mysticism.

As a child, the *Tzemach Tzedek* displayed a natural gift for music.[32] He possessed a genuine comprehension of music, and showed tremendous talent for composing. However, as a child, he felt that having these talents squandered precious time from his studies. He therefore disciplined himself to annihilate his talent for music. Many years later, he said that he regretted losing that gift. Once, he related, he saw a group of *Chassidim* complaining to his grandfather, Rabbi Schneur Zalman of Liadi, that they did not understand the Tanya, the magnum opus of that Rebbe, the monumental and foundational book of Chabad Chassidism. The Rebbe answered that in order for them to fully understand Chassidic mysticism, they needed song. When the *Tzemach Tzedek* heard this, he regretted bitterly suppressing his own talent for music.[33]

What exactly does this anecdote suggest? Why is it that only through song can one truly understand Chassidic thought?

Being that the source of Torah is God, who defies definition and description, thus the Torah which is "God's wisdom," is super-rational thought. It is thoughts that are above and beyond any rational conventionality. This truism applies to both parts of the Torah, the revealed, the body, as well as the hidden, the soul. Nonetheless, there is a distinction between the two. The revealed parts of Torah is 'God's wisdom,' manifested within the physical reality. It is the Divine wisdom of all creation. Torah is the inner will, plan, and structure of how creation should appear.[34] For this reason most of the Talmud concerns itself with materialistic realities, with physical subjects, notwithstanding the fact that, as the Kabbalah explains,[35] even the revealed parts of the Torah, which seem to be speaking of the physical, are in actuality speaking of the spiritual, and are merely alluding to the physical.[36] However, the mystical components of Torah, the hidden secrets, are pure transcendent thoughts. They are the segments of Torah that never truly manifest themselves within the confines of the physical; they remain throughout their descent from above, transcendent and infinite.[37] Kabbalah/Chassidic thought trains the mind to rise above its normal modality of thinking, and think infinitely, the idea being to go beyond the physical, finite appearance, and come to the source. This "place" has no physicality, rather this is where the physical emanates from. Music has the facility to transport one to that "place." It has the power to touch, and make real that which is beyond.

Chassidic thought asserts that there are two domains of consciousness. One is called *mochin d'gadlut*—consciousness of maturity, and the other is *mochin d'katnut*—consciousness of immaturity. This means that humans can experience two states of being; either one can have expanded consciousness, or one can experience constricted consciousness.[38] On a simple level, this translates coming from love, happiness, and inclusion, or coming from fear, depression, and exclusion.

Coming from a fearful ground of being is to view life and its contents as potentially threatening: occurrences do not present themselves as opportunities, and existence feels fragile. This perspective, and state of being, comes from being depressed. Life in this state is continuously trying and tiring. The possibilities in this consciousness are none.[39] The spirit is constricted, and one may feel as if operating with the mind of a child.[40]

In *Mochin d'gadlut*, expanded consciousness, one is more integrated and happy,[41] and consequently one views life from that perspective. Events are opportunities, and the possibilities are aligned with a higher purpose. Living is much more joyous, and less effortful, and thus more energy is available to the person.

Sometimes, experiencing "constricted consciousness" can be a sign of depression, or can cause depression, because when one is depressed, he is constricted. When a human being, at any stage in life, cannot make appropriate distinctions, cannot distinguish right from wrong, and fails to discern the Godliness within creation, then a frustration and a vexation comes in. This is accompanied by irritation and anger in one's relationship with life, and unless intervention occurs, there is a downward spiral to *Atzvut*—depression. The Torah is man's guidebook in life, and through it man learns to acquire the ability to cope, and to be appropriate and competent in the journey of life. Chassidic melodies, and especially Chabad melodies, are geared to the expansion of the spirit and the pursuit of wisdom.

There is a type of meditation, which is called "inner directed, constructed meditation." This means that a Torah thought is taken and thought about repeatedly with intense concentration until one reaches a higher state of consciousness. And melody can perform an important role in such meditations. Repetitive thoughts remain focused when put to repetitive tunes.

The venerable Chassid Rabbi Hillel of Poritch (1795–1864) once said, "He who does not appreciate and understand song, can never really understand *Chassidut*."[42] In order for one to truly comprehend *Chassidut*, one needs expanded consciousness, of which the expansion can be achieved through song.[43]

There is another element with regard to study and music. The Talmud reports on a debate between two Talmudic sages, Rav and Shmuel.[44] It begins with both sages stating their opinions. Then Shmuel asks Rav a question of such power that it seems to eradicate Rav's opinion. Nonetheless, though Rav demurs, it is widely held that he maintained his opinion,[45] which leaves many to wonder why he had not changed his line of thinking.[46]

This Talmudic tale is illustrative of a process in which there is a beginning and an end, but as yet no middle to connect the two. The premise is there, and so is the conclusion, but there is no logical construct on which to base the latter. In such an instance intuition, more than rationality, is in charge, and the linguistic distinctions have not yet been formulated. On this level of thought, a flash of insight comes to mind, and one may feel as if "seeing" the issue in all its clarity without comprehending the issue in linguistic intellectual terms. This phenomenon is called *chochmah*; it is the level of soul or psyche, where ideas are understood above and beyond the conventional language of words.

It was for this reason that the Talmud sage, Rav, remained quiet, and yet did not relinquish his opinion, for he understood his opinion on a level of thought that exists before it descends into conventional, rational words. He saw the thoughts in his mind, but was not yet able to articulate them in rational, defined words.[47]

Here again music can be a facilitator. According to the Kabbalah[48], when one is confronted by a problem that is frustrating in being languaged, at any stage of its development, then the usage of song will relieve the frustration and accelerate a solution. By joining song with thoughts, one "lifts" the thoughts to the level of song, which is the level of soul where one can "see" the thoughts. At this plane thought exists prior to "descending" into intellect, before it has been "dressed" in rational words.

NOTES

1. Told over by the sixth Chabad Rebbe. Rabbi Yoseph Yitzchak. *Sefer Hasichot 5703* (1943) (New York: Kehot Publication Society. 1986), p. 108.

2. Man's relationship to God is likened in the Midrash to marriage. See: Talmud *Taanit*. 26b. *Midrash Rabbah Exudos* Parsha 15: 31. And with every mitzvah one reinforces the relationship. The Lubavitcher Rebbe. *Sefer Ha'maamorim Meluket.* (New York: Kehot Publication Society. 1988.) Vol. 2, p. 82.

3. The general idea of MilMatah LeMalah and MilMalah LeMatah, with regards to a revelation of Godliness, is found mentioned in *The Bahir.* Chapter 171. [The Bahir, one of the earliest circulated Kabbalistic texts. First published in 1176.] See also: Rabbi Moshe Cordovero. *Pardas Rimonim.* Shar 15. Chapter 4. This idea of a two way path of prayer, and study, is developed at length in Chabad thought. See for example: Rabbi Schneur Zalman of Liadi. *Tanya. Igeret Hateshuvah.* Chapter 10. By the same author. *Torah Or.* (New York: Kehot Publication Society. 1996.) Parshat Berieshit, p. 1: c. The Lubavitcher Rebbe. *Sefer Ha'maamorim Meluket.* (New York: Kehot Publication Society. 1993), Vol. 4, p. 384–385. See also: Rabbi Chayim Volozhine (1749–1821) *Ruach Chayim. Avot.* Chapter 1. Mishnah 2.

4. This is especially so if we go according to the opinion of the Halachic authorities who say that 'Tefilah' is only a commandment by the sages. See: Chapter 6, footnote 6.

5. The Lubavitcher Rebbe. *Likutei Sichot.* (New York: Kehot Publication Society. 1964) Vol. 3, pp. 757–758. With regards to *mitzvot* that the forefathers performed before there was a direct commandment from God at Mount Sinai.

6. As mentioned before (chapter 6, footnote 41.) in the name of the Baal Shem Tov, "that man continues to live after prayer, is a pure act of kindness from God."

7. See: *Zohar.* Part 3, p. 73a. *Zohar.* Part 1. p. 24a. 'I have given Myself in My writings. (ie; Torah)' Talmud. *Shabbat.* 105a. *Ayin Yakkov.* See also: *Midrash Rabba. Exodus.* Parsha 33. Chapter 1.

8. Rabbi Yehudah Loew. *Nesivot Olam. Nosiv Hatzniut.* Chapter 3. See also by the same author: *Nesivot Olam. Nesiv HaTorah.* Chapter 2.

9. Rabbi Asher Ben Yechiel (1250–1327) (known as the Rosh.) writes, that there exist two distinct forms of knowledge. One is the natural sciences, while the other is

a Divine wisdom. (ie; Torah) If a person has mastered one distinct pattern of thought, it will then be very difficult for that same person to become proficient in the other thought. Each knowledge operates within its own rules and principles. See: *Responsa of the Rosh.* (New York: Grossmans Publishing House. 1954) Klal 55. Chapter 9.

10. Talmud. *Berachot.* 64a. See: *Tur Shulchan Aruch. Orach Chayim.* Chapter 155:1. *Rabbienu Yona of Gerondi* (1194–1263) *Safer HaYirah,* (Israel: Eshkol. 1978.) p. 167. Rabbi Chayim Vital (1543–1620) *Sharei Kedusha.* Part 1. Shar 6. The Baal Shem Tov once said that one must be exceedingly cautious with one's actions proceeding one's daily prayers. For the emotions that are called up during one's prayers, linger on afterwards and must be channelled properly lest they be used for unholy purposes. For example; one's passion and love towards God during prayer, can extend into the day and be used in an unholy manner. Therefore, the Baal Shem Tov said that it is most crucial, that one learn Torah immediately after the prayers, so as to channel these potent emotions into Divine service. See: Rabbi Moshe Chayim Ephraim of Sudylkov. *Degel Machanah Ephraim,* p. 131.

11. See: Talmud *Yevamot.* 109b.

12. They may forget the 'Giver of the Torah.' See: Talmud *Nedarim.* p. 81a. The commentary by the *Ran,* Devar Zeh. *Shulchan Aruch Orach Chayim.* Chapter 47. In the commentary by Rabbi Yoel Sirkes. *Beit Chadash.* See also Rabbi Yehudah Loew. *Tifferet Yisrael.* The author's introduction.

13. See: Talmud. *Yuma,* 72b.

14. See: Talmud, *Berachot* 5b. *Rashi.* Samuch Lemitasi.

15. Rabbi Schneur Zalman of Liadi. *Likutei Torah.* Parshat Behar, p. 40 . . . , Parshat Beracha, p. 96b. The Lubavitcher Rebbe. *Sefer Ha'aamorim Meluket,* (New York: Kehot Publication Society. 1987) pp. 230–231.

16. The Chassidic custom is to study the mystical dimensions of Torah before prayer. This study is an appropriate introduction to prayer, because before prayer one should contemplate the greatness of God, and his own lowly level. See: *Shulchan Aruch. Orach Chayim* Chapter 98. *Rama.* Ad loc.

17. For this reason, the Talmud says, one should study in a place of prayer (Talmud. *Megillah.* 29a) and pray in the location they study. (Talmud. *Berachot.* 8A.)

18. Talmud, *Megillah.* 32a.

19. See: Rabbi Moshe Yichiel Elimelech of Levertov. *Safer Shemirat Hada'at.* Aimrei Tal. Ma'amar Nigun, (Bnei Brak Israel: Ginzei MaHaritz. 1986) p. 19.

20. See: *Zohar.* Parshat Vayikrah. p. 8. See also: Rabbi Eliyohu Ben Moshe Di Vidas. *Reshit Chochmah.* Shar HaAhavah. Chapter 10.

21. See: *Radak.* Rabbi David Kimchi. (1160–1235.) *Psalms.* Chapter 33: 2.

22. Rabbi Meir Ben Gabbai (1480–1547), *Avodot Hakodesh, Cheilek HaTakhlit* Chapter 10. In the name of *Levinat Hasapir.* Parshat Noach. Rabbi Shlomo Alkabatz. (1505–1584.) *Manot HaLevi* The Hakdamah. p. 36. (Reprinted in *Kal Sifrei Reb Yoseph Yavetz.* Book 2. (Israel: 1990.) Likutim. p. 33.) Rabbi Yisrael of Modzitz. (1848–1920.) *Divrie Yisrael.* Parshat Mikketz. Maamor Echad M'Remazei Chanukah. Rabbi Moshe Yichiel Elimelech of Levertov. *Safer Shemirat Hada'at.* Aimrei Tal. Ma'amar Nigun, (Bnei Brak Israel: Ginzei MaHaritz. 1986.) p. 5. See also: *Zohar.* Parshat Vayakel, p. 195b.

23. A talk by the sixth Chabad Rebbe. Rabbi Yoseph Yitzchak. On the twelfth of Tammuz 5692 (1932).

24. The sixth Chabad Rebbe. Rabbi Yoseph Yitzchak. *Sefer Hasichot 5702*, (1942) (New York: Kehot Publication Society. 1986) p. 134.

25. The sixth Chabad Rebbe. Rabbi Yoseph Yitzchak. *Sefer Hasichot 5700*, (1940) (New York: Kehot Publication Society. 1986) p. 160.

26. The sixth Chabad Rebbe. Rabbi Yoseph Yitzchak. *Sefer Hasichot 5703*, (1943) (New York: Kehot Publication Society. 1986) p. 111.

27. Talmud, *Megillah*, 32a.

28. See: Ibid. *Tosefot*. Ad loc. Rabbi Chayim Yoseph David. *D'vash L'phi Zayn*.

29. A talk by the sixth Chabad Rebbe. Rabbi Yoseph Yitzchak. Shabbat Parshat Noach. 5706 (1945).

30. The first Chabad Rebbe. Rabbi Schneur Zalman of Liadi. *Likutei Torah*. Parshat Bechukotai, (New York: Kehot Publication Society. 1996) p. 45.

31. Rabbi Nachman of Breslov. *Likutei Moharan*. Part 2: 31. By the same author. *Sefer HaMidot*. (Brooklyn: Moriah. 1976.) Neginah, p. 218.

32. Told over by the sixth Chabad Rebbe. Rabbi Yoseph Yitzchak. *Sefer Hasichot 5704* (1944) (New York: Kehot Publication Society. 1986) p. 92.

33. Although he may have lost his talents, nonetheless, the Tzemach Tzedek was still always very fond of singing, especially singing while studying. His son, the fourth Chabad Rebbe, Reb Shmuel, said, from the tune his father was humming during study, one could discern which subject he was studying. For every subject he studied, he had a unique tune which he associated and connected with the study. See: The Lubavitcher Rebbe. *Hayom Yom*. (New York: Kehot Publication Society. 1961) The thirteenth of Sivan.

34. Thus it says, "God looked into the Torah and created the world accordingly." Torah is the blue print of creation. *Zohar*. Part 2:161a. See also: *Midrash Rabbah Genesis*. Parsah 1. Chapter 1. *Midrash Tanchuma* Bereshit. Chapter 1.

35. Rabbi Menachem Azaryah De Fano. (1548–1620) *Asarah Maamorot*. *Maamor Chakur Din*. Part 3 Chapter 22. See: The Lubavitcher Rebbe. *Likutei Sichot*. (New York: Kehot Publication Society. 1984) Vol. 23, pp. 37–41.

36. However, in this physical world the spiritual dimensions of man are concealed within the body; Godliness is concealed in physicality. In this world, when one studies the revealed parts of the Torah, one comprehends the Torah only in the way it manifested itself in the physical. However, when one reaches the spiritual worlds above (after 120 years, or, if one can reach this intense level of spirituality in his own lifetime), he will be able to comprehend the Torah in its spiritual dimensions as well. The Talmud relays a story (*Baba Batra*, p. 10b.) how once a great sage was very sick, so sick that his soul actually departed his body. He did not, however, pass away. It was sort of what is called today an out of body experience. When he returned, his father asked him what he had observed. He answered him, "I saw an opposite world. Everyone who in this world is from "high society" is in those worlds, below, and anyone who is below here is on the top there. Moreover, I heard them saying. Honorable is one who enters this world with the Talmud, the revealed Torah, in his possession.' This means that if one has already learned

the Torah in this world, in its physical dimensions, then when he learns the Torah above, he would have a head start, because in this world, one learns the concepts, and in the next world, one comprehend inner meanings. It is as if a blind person has learned about colors all his life, and one day, can open his eyes and actually see colors. It is then that he can comprehend what he was learning about all those years.

37. See: The Sixth Chabad Rebbe. Rabbi Yoseph Yitzchak. *Sefer Hamssmorim. 5705*, (New York: Kehot Publication Society. 1986) p. 193.

38. See also chapter 4, footnote 6 (the story with Reb Dovber and Reb Schneur Zalman of Liadi) for another perspective on the difference between these two states of being.

39. In constricted state of being, as hard as one attempts to concentrate on an idea, the thoughts do not become comprehended. Rabbi Yisrael Baal Shem Tov: *Tzavoas Horivash*. (New York: Kehot Publication Society. 1982) Chapter 129. *Kesser ShemTov*. (New York: Kehot Publication Society. 1987) Part 1. Chapter 102.

40. *Tzavoas Horivash*. (New York: Kehot Publication Society. 1982) Chapter 67. Rabbi Schneur Zalman of Liadi. *Maamorei Admur Hazoken. Inyonim.* (New York: Kehot Publication Society. 1983.) p. 201. Rabbi Nachman of Breslov. *Likutei Moharan*. Part 1. Chapter 106.

41. Happiness is the appropriate solution to bring about Mochin d'gadlut. See: Rabbi Yisrael Baal Shem Tov. *Kesser ShemTov*. (New York: Kehot Publication Society. 1987) Part 1. Chapter 37. Rabbi Schneur Zalman of Liadi. *Maamorei Admur Hazoken. Inyonim*, (New York: Kehot Publication Society. 1983) p. 202.

42. In a talk by the sixth Chabad Rebbe, Rabbi Yoseph Yitzchak. On the first night of Passover 5697 (1937). See also: The Baal Shem Tov. *Kesser ShemTov*, (New York: Kehot Publication Society 1987) p. 82.

43. See: Rabbi Avraham Ben HaRambam. *Hamaspik Leovedei Hashem* Erech. Kevishas Hakochot VeHamasim. About the importance of sound-music for religious and secular study.

44. Talmud. *Beitza.* 6a.

45. Although there are those who argue, that he did indeed change his opinion, and the reason he remained quiet was out of concession. See: Talmud. *Baba Batra.* 62a. *Tosefot*. Titled Umode Rav. However, since the final law is like the opinion of Rav, this would seem to indicate that he did not concede, for whatever reason, but just remained quiet. See: *Rambam. Hilchot Yom Tov.* Chapter 2. Halacha 1. *Shulchan Aruch Orach Chayim*. Chapter 513: 8. (The *Rosh Talmud. Beitza.* 6a. says that the reason that the law remains like Rav is that Rav's opinion is the more stringent; thus we uphold his opinion with regard to the law.)

46. There are those who assert that Rav had a mystical reason for his opinion; however, he felt that it was not fitting to state his reason openly, to reveal the mystical concept to all. Thus he remained quiet. However, quietly, he told his mystical reason, which made sense, and therefore, the Halacha (law) agrees with his opinion. Rabbi Menachem Azaryah De Fano. *Asarah Maamorot. Maamor Shivrie Luchot*, p. 10b. (Printed in *Kal Sifrei Reb Yoseph Yavotz*. (Israel. 1990.) Book 2, in the back of the book.)

47. Rabbi Yoseph Yitzchak, the sixth Chabad Rebbe. *Sefer Hamaamorim 5708–5709*, (New York: Kehot Publication Society. 1986.) p. 102.

48. The second Chabad Rebbe Rabbi Dovber. *Shaarei T'shuva. 2*, (New York: Kehot Publication Society. 1983.) p. 15. See also: Rabbi Moshe Cordovero. *Pardas Rimonim*. Shar 23. Chapter 21. He writes that Shir (song), is the level of Chachmah, which are thoughts the way they exist before entering words, when one "sees" the thought as an intuition, as a flash of insight.

8
Yichudim/Unification
Merging Heaven and Earth

Rabbi Yehudah Ha'Chassid writes, "For the one who has a delightful voice, and is able to sing songs of praise, and does not, it would have been more desirable if his soul would not have descended upon this world."[1]

According to the Talmud,[2] there is a small verse in the Torah that the entire Torah is connected with, and that is, "In all your actions you shall know Him."[3] This means that whatever one does, God should be present in the doer's consciousness.[4] An ordinary person's day has two aspects. One is the quotidian actions, such as eating, sleeping, and the other is the performing of *mitzvot*.[5] It is man's secret and inner desire (though we do not always express it) to have an extraordinary life, where every moment of life is special and holy. This is attainable by melding the two and imbuing each mundane act with a God consciousness. For example, the blessings we recite before eating, brings an elevated *Kavanah* to living.

Kavanah, intention, has two levels.[6] On the first level, one accepts that the daily routine is necessary. Working, sleeping, and the like, are needed but there is the realization that they are only a means to an end, which is to serve the Master of the universe.

One knows that all his actions are geared toward a higher purpose such as study or prayer. As it says, "All your deeds shall be for the sake of heaven."[7] This means that one's mind should always be focused on the end, on the ultimate purpose. All that is accomplished throughout the day is only a means to a loftier end. On the second, loftier level, one's intention or *Kavanah* is expressed in the verse, "In all your actions you shall know him." As the Baal Shem Tov once explained,[8] the Hebrew word that the verse uses for "know" is *Da-AieHu*, which can be divided into two separate words, *Da* to know, to connect,[9] and *Hu*, which is one of the names of God. Thus, says the Baal Shem Tov, the verse is saying that every action that a person takes in this world, from the most holy to the most seemingly mundane, should be recognized as being performed as a service to the Creator, *Hu*, and consequently, as an action that connects and unifies God with the world. In other words, not only are your mundane and earthly matters a means to an end, a means to reach a higher purpose, but they are in fact an end to themselves. There is a holy and Godly purpose in every action that occurs on this earth.

This idea was innovative, if not revolutionary. The Baal Shem Tov came to teach the world the notion that man can, and should, overcome the separation between the sacred and the secular. It expresses the idea that every action taken, however mundane it may appear, becomes a sacred act when done with the proper *Kavanah*, intention.

To understand this idea better, one must go back to a primary teaching of the holy *AriZal*, Rabbi Yitzchak Luria (1594–1572). He taught that all that exists in this physical world contains within it a spark of God, which after layers of concealment from its original source, has become invisible to the naked eye. He taught that the purpose of man's creation is for *Tikkun*, rectification, elevation, so that man can manifest and reveal the Godly spark contained in all creation. It is man's actions, that cause this to occur, so every act is sublimated to the purpose of *Tikkun*. It is incredibly empowering to realize that God entrusted humans by giving them the freedom to choose to fulfill the task of revealing and manifesting Godliness. In a sense, we are liberating Godliness from its prison of concealment and physicality, which can only occur if we are willing to free ourselves by revealing the Godliness within us, that is, our Godly soul, a true symbiotic relationship.

Tikkun, the notion that man can perfect and restore the materialistic world to holiness, found a new home within the teachings of the Baal Shem Tov. In the verse, "Hungry as well as thirsty, my soul withers from within,"[10] the Baal Shem Tov questioned,[11] "Why does the Psalmist say, the soul withers? Why does the soul suffer if the body is hungry?"[12] The Baal Shem Tov then responded that when a person's physical body hungers for food, in truth it is his soul which is hungry. The soul hungers to elevate the sparks within the physical food, so the physical hunger only reflects the spiritual one. Furthermore, the reason that different people have distinct tastes in food, with one liking sweets, and another preferring spicy foods, is that, in the same way that every individual soul is different from the other, each soul is distinct in its character from others. Consequently, every soul has its distinct spark which it is connected to, and desires to elevate. Thus, the reason different people enjoy different foods is that the soul which is within them is hungry for those particular sparks within those foods, to which they are connected.[13]

Even a routine such as eating can be a sacred and holy expression, an act of *Tikkun*, rectification, and unification, where one reunites the holy spark with its source. Eating has the potential to be like a *Karban*, a sacrifice in the holy Temple, in which one would take an animal, and bring it as an offering to God. Therefore, the Talmud equates the table where one eats with the altar in the Holy Temple.[14]

It is axiomatic that before one eats, or does any type of action, one should be certain that his mind is entirely focused, so that he will eat with the proper intentions. Accordingly, it is the custom of many who are mystically inclined, to sing a song of *Deveikut* before they begin eating, in order to arouse a yearning to be close to God, so that they will eat with the right intentions.

There are times when the songs themselves can do the *Tikkun*, the elevation, and the food does not need to be physically consumed. A story is told of the Baal Shem Tov's visit for Shabbat to the city in which Rabbi Yakov Kopel lived.[15] (Reb Yakov was a discreet and unassuming person; no one knew of his greatness. He supported himself with a small shop which he owned.) While the Baal Shem Tov was reciting his evening prayers, he felt a tremendous holiness present in the city. Immediately following the prayers, he proceeded to walk about the town investigating the source of the holiness. When he walked past the residence of Reb Yakov, he felt extreme holiness emanating from within. He entered the house at once, imagining that he would find Reb Yakov in the midst of intense prayer. However, the reality he found was Reb Yakov standing in front of his Shabbat table, singing and dancing with tremendous exhilaration. The Baal Shem Tov waited until he concluded singing, and then asked him, "Why don't you eat your Shabbat meal first and then sing songs?" (The prevailing custom is to sing songs during the Shabbat meal.) He answered, "First I delight in the spiritual aspects of the food, and only then do I consume the physical food itself."

By singing a tune, which expressed the deepest parts of his soul's yearning, he connected with the soul of the food, the Godly spark contained within the food. That spark was connected with his soul, and through his singing he elevated the soul of the food to its source. Only then did he partake of the physical, the body of the food, which was the nourishment for his physical form.[16]

Here two types of elevation are available. One is the elevation of the Godly spark within the food, the soul of the physical object to its source above. That is achieved through song. The second, is a higher and deeper level in *Tikkun* where one not only elevates the soul within, and through elevating the soul, elevates the body, rather where one actually elevates the physical itself. For example, while eating, one has the intention that "everything God created, He created for His glory."[17] To accomplish this, one needs to actually consume the food. Thus, although Reb Yakov achieved elevation through song, he also digested the food itself, to cause a transformation of the physical aspect of the food, to the spiritual.

This concept of *Tikkun* is not only with regard to food, rather with reference to everything one does. A person can utilize every single opportunity in life, even the most mundane of actions, in the service of the Creator.

Dancing can be the ultimate expression of *Tikkun*. When one dances a holy dance, one elevates his entire physical form to God.

A Chassidic master would say that on the morning following Simchat Torah, following a full night of the *Chassidim* remaining awake and dancing joyously with the Torah, *Gan Eden*, Paradise, is cluttered with torn shoelaces, broken heels, and muddy footprints that were created the night before while dancing with the Torah.[18] This was not necessarily said in jest. The deeper meaning, is that when a person dances a holy dance, then everything, objects as well as people, are elevated through that act. The same is true with every single physical action that a person takes. Hence, the idea of dance is taken very seriously by *Chassidim*. There is an actual prayer taught by Rabbi Nachman of Breslov, which he would recite before dancing. The following is an excerpt of the prayer; please God, I implore you that all the functions of my body, my hands, my feet, and so on, should be exercised only for Godliness . . . and the happiness that I experience in serving You, shall overtake my entire existence, until it permeates even my lowly feet."

The concept of someone's dancing, and through that dance, unifying the physical with the spiritual, specially occurs when it comes to the dancing of a *Tzadik*.

A *Tzadik* has the ability to combine the physical with the spiritual, when it comes to dancing or any other act. He is at a level of egolessness where he becomes a *merkavah*, a wagon or vehicle through whom God is manifested. He is a conductor, much like an electric main line, that brings God's energy into the world. His aspirations having been realized, he is in a state of being, where he is simply an instrument. The Mishnah says, "Make your will as His will. Nullify your will for His will."[19] There are two levels of *Bittul*, self-nullification. The lower level is where one has a personal will, but it is surrendered to the will of the Creator. One makes his will to be like God's. There is, however, a higher level of *Bittul*, and this is where one has given up all personal desires, and all that is left is the oneness with God.

Those who attain the lofty level of *Tzadik* live their lives in complete spontaneity, responding instinctively to all of life's situations.

In this lofty condition when a *Tzadik* of such distinction dances (either to music, or his inner tune which is in sympathetic vibration with the heavenly music), his dance is a spontaneous response of purity and holiness.

Once,[20] Rabbi Leib, known as the Grandfather of Shepole, went for the Shabbat to visit the grandson of his Rebbe, Rabbi Dovber, who was himself a Rebbe, Reb Shalom. They did not converse during the entire Shabbat meal. After the meal Reb Leib asked his host, Reb Shalom, if he knew how to dance. The Rebbe answered, "No." Reb Leib then said, "I will show you how a person is supposed to dance." He then stood up, and began dancing with such intensity and fervor that when he concluded dancing, Reb Shalom remarked to his disciples, "You should know that with every step and body movement Reb Leib took, he was creating unifications in the worlds above." In Hebrew, the concept of unification is called *yichudim*. To fully comprehend the idea of *yichudim*, one may need a short "tour" of the basic teachings of the Kabbalah with regard to creation.

The Kabbalah explains that the essence of God is *Ein Sof*, the infinite. Unlike the mathematical or philosophical definition of infinite, meaning unmeasurable or nondimensional, the infinity of God is beyond even those definitions. In mathematics, the word infinite means beyond grasp or measurement, but the infinite of something finite is by its very definition a finite entity. For instance, infinity refers to an infinite quantity of finite numbers, that is, one, two, etc., unto infinity. However, God's infinite is beyond all possible limitations. The only description humans can use to describe His infinite is the negative; we could say, what He is not.

He is beyond any definition we could ascribe to him, beyond any negative or positive definition and description. This is because just as God is not matter, neither is He spirit. Moreover, even this definition of His being beyond all definitions, of being beyond our grasp, is in itself a definition, a definition of being beyond a definition. Furthermore, God is even higher than this definition itself; He is beyond our saying that He is beyond. God is beyond the definition of being infinite.[21]

Since God is infinite and all that He created is finite, it would seem that there is an abyss stretching between God, who is beyond all limitations and definition, and the finite world He created, which is a universe defined and confined within the parameters of a time-space capsule. This would be true of the physical world as well as the spiritual worlds, for however sublime and lofty those worlds may be, they are still a finite creation. Thus, given the limitations of the human equipment of comprehension, the mind, a gap seems to exist between the infinite and the finite. It would seem that there is no connection between God, the *Ein Sof*, and his creations, the finite!

Furthermore, there seems to be another difficulty with creation as such. Since God is *Ein Sof*, infinite, how is it that finite creatures came into existence? How can there be a transformation from infinite to finite? From absolute unity, One, to diversity? A process of spiritual evolution cannot be possible as the solution, because infinite and finite are not only different in quantity, but in their essential quality. Infinite, no matter how gradual the descent, will always remain infinite. Therefore, the question is, how does this world, one of time and space, come into existence?

The question is not one of God's capabilities, for God is all-powerful and above limitations. Rather, the question is, how does a finite being maintain its existence in the presence of the infinite? If in truth, all is infinite, how do we perceive the existence of this world to be finite, in the presence of God, the infinite? In other words, the infinite should overwhelm the finite; it should not allow the finite to come into its own defined, limited existence. Conversely, the finite should find the infinite intolerable.

In addition, how does one reconcile the concept that there exists a finite, divided universe, with the notion that it was created by God, the true oneness. How can diversity emerge from an absolute, undividable unity, God?

To overcome these difficulties, and to make it more comprehensible, the Kabbalah says that God created the finite world through a construct called, *Tzimtzumim,*: contractions or concealments.[22] Creation was not a slow process of evolution from infinite to finite, from spiritual to physical, from ether to nether, but rather was accomplished by a leap and bound. God, figuratively speaking, hides His essential being, his endless light,[23] and through the process of withdrawal, leaves space for the concept of a finite being to be revealed and to emerge into existence. Hence, once there was the idea of the finite, there began a process of evolution and emanation from that light; a transformation took place of the divine, finite light, at first into higher spiritual realms, and then, into something defined and limited, this physical world.[24]

This process is what the Kabbalah calls *Seder Hishtalshelut*—a spiritual evolution. This means that there exists a link, a thread, of finite light that weaves, from the first manifestations, throughout all the spiritual worlds above and down to this universe. All of creation is really one continuous loop.[25] Therefore, although it may feel that this world exists on its own, the truth is that this world is only one of many worlds. This world is actually the last of the link, and therefore the lowest, because spiritually it is the furthest removed from its source above.

The manner in which God operates and sustains all worlds is through a system of ten *Sefirot*.[26] These ten *Sefirot* are the inner pattern and paradigm of the world.[27] In order for these worlds to be sustained, the Divine energy manifests itself through these ten *Sefirot*. These are the essential channels and forces through which the Divine energy flows into the worlds. The *Sefirot* are 1) *Chochmah*—wisdom, intuition, 2) *Binah*—understanding, comprehending, and 3) *Da'at*—knowledge, internalizing the thought. These are the first three *Sefirot*, the cognitive. Then there are the three emotional *Sefirot*: 4) *Chesed*—kindness, benevolence, 5) *Gevurah*—severity, strength and 6) *Tiferet*—beauty, a synthesis between the two; compassion. The next three are the functional, the implementation of actual thought or emotion: 7) *Netzach*—eternity, conquest; the capacity to overcome and persevere, 8) *Hod*—splendor, persistence; also the power to overcome, not through strength, rather by bending one's self, and 9) *Yesod*—foundation, connection. The last *Sefira* is *Malchut*—royalty, sovereignty, receiving all the above and then transmitting with glory. These are the ten energies with which God operates and sustains all of creation.

Since the creation of this physical world is a direct transformation of the spiritual worlds above, then all physical reality is just a manifestation of its spiritual counterpart. There exists a parallel spiritual universe to ours. All entities that exist in the spiritual worlds above are projected into our physical world, through adjustments to the limitations of time and space. And just as all the spiritual worlds are reflected in the physical world, so too, to a greater extent, is the inner image of the worlds reflected within man. The difference between the reflection in man and the reflection in the entire universe, is that in every existence in this world other than man, there is reflected but one of the images of the spiritual entities.[28] For example, there are certain animals, the stork, for example,[29] who display the *Sefira* of *Chesed*—acts of kindness for another. Thus, they are a physical manifestation of the *Sefira* of *Chesed* above. However, man is an all-encompassing being, a creature whose image reflects and mirrors the entire system and structure of all worlds.[30]

As to the creation of man, the Torah says,[31] "Let *us* make man, in *My* image and form." Man is likened to God, for just as God sustains and gives life to all worlds through the ten *Sefirot*, the same is true of man; God created man to have contained within him the entire inner structure of creation. It is not just one of the spiritual realities that is reflected in man, rather the entire range of inner dimensions of creation is reflected in this all-encompassing being that we call man. Every human being is created with

ten attributes, which are analogous to the ten *Sefirot*. Man is created in the image and form of God; namely, the ten *Sefirot*. A
human being is a microcosm of the spectrum of *Sefirot*,[32] for each
Sefira is connected with another part of the shape in the Primordial man.[33]

"Let *us* create man" means, allow the entire creation, all the
physical energy, as well as all the spiritual energy, to partake in
the creation of man. Humans have contained within them all the
forces of creation.[34] The entire creation is in a sense like one person, while man is a microcosm of it all. Man is analogous to the
world, while the world is analogous to man.[35] Hence, the Talmud
says, "Man is likened to a small world."[36]

Furthermore, the physical structure of the human body is a
paradigm of the inner structure of the worlds. The pattern of the
human body is homologous with the order of the ten *Sefirot*. Man
is a replica of the image of "man" above.[37] Every individual organ
in the human body is congruous with the particular *Sefira* that it
represents.[38] Each distinct part of the physical body represents a
different *Sefira* in the Primordial man, or perhaps, a combination
of many *Sefirot*.[39] For example, the right hand of a human being
represents the *Sefira* of *Chesed*—kindness, while the left hand
represents *Gevurah*—strength.[40]

Since a human's body and soul reflect the inner image and
make-up of all worlds, and the entire structure and system of the
divine energy flow, that is, the ten *Sefirot*, are reflected in man,
so it is that with every step a human being takes in this mundane
world, he creates a ripple effect in all the worlds above. Not only
do man's actions affect the entire physical universe (as scientifi-
cally proven), but they affect all the spiritual worlds above as well.
The Mishnah says, "Know what is above you."[41] "Know," said a
Chassidic master,[42] "that all that is above is a reflection of you;
you create what is above. Know that what is above, comes from
you."[43]

Most people are not conscious of this notion, nor do they want
to be conscious. For most, this is an overwhelming thought. Most
people attempt to deal with their immediate situation and main-

tain a status quo. If a person experiences negativity in his life, he will try his best to handle the situation. But with this concept in mind, one realizes that it is not a situation one simply finds himself in; the negativity one experiences is in a sense one's very own creation. A human being creates the situation he operates within. A person who is in tune with these thoughts, realizes that every step he takes, affects the entire balance of the world. With every action one takes, positive as well as negative, one tips the scale either way.[44] Thus even when he does an action as trivial as body movement, such as dancing, he is creating spiritual unifications in the worlds above. His dancing here below causes a ripple effect throughout all worlds. This does not mean to say that this exists only for a select few; on the contrary each person has the same effect. It is only that not all are conscious of this phenomenon. For example, when one waves his right hand over his left, this causes the *Sefira* of *Chesed*—kindness, which is analogous to the right hand, to overwhelm the *Sefira* of *Gevurah*—strength, which the left hand represents. The same is true with all the organs of the body; through every physical action below, one affects the spiritual worlds above.

For a *Tzadik*, a master, who is completely aware and attuned to his own inner quintessential make-up, his dance becomes a very consequential and noble act. It is a holy act below, which has an effect upon the upper worlds as well. Since he is a *Merchavah*—a chariot, a vessel in which God's inner plan of creation can manifest itself, his hands, in a sense, become the "hands" of a holy chariot. His hands manifest the *Sefirot* of *Chesed* and *Gevurah*, his feet, the "feet" of the *Sefirot*, until his entire body is a vessel for the manifestation of the will of God.[45]

Yichudim is the act of drawing Godliness down into this world. It is the momentous act of unifying the entire creation in one harmonious deed, and of connecting the spiritual with the physical. When one thinks of *yichudim*, what immediately comes to mind is that the way for one to accomplish this would be through deep meditation, through experiencing a spiritual, lofty feeling, and in this way, merging the spiritual worlds above with this world.

However, in truth, sometimes by doing what may seem a simple trivial act of kindness, one produces an effect through all the worlds that is greater than any meditation or prayer possible.

There is a Chassidic tale which was made famous by the Yiddish writer I. L. Peretz.[46] The story is as follows: There was once a Chassidic Rebbe who lived in a town in which the people were mostly simpletons. The Rebbe was known to be a holy man, a miracle worker. The townspeople believed him to have direct access to heaven. Every year in the week before Rosh Hashanah (the Jewish New Year), all the people of the town would assemble in the synagogue in the early morning hours to recite *Selichot* (a prayer for forgiveness), and each year the Rebbe was nowhere to be found, not in his home nor in the synagogue. The townspeople claimed that he simply went up to heaven.

A skeptic once visited town before Rosh Hashanah, and decided that he was going to find out exactly where the Rebbe went on those early mornings. So, the first thing he did was to get himself invited to the Rebbe's house as a guest. The week before the holiday came, he snuck into the Rebbe's room and hid under the Rebbe's bed, anxiously waiting. The entire night went by and the Rebbe had not yet gone to sleep; he was sitting and studying Torah. When the morning hours were approaching, the Rebbe retired for a short nap. Immediately after awakening, he rose and left the room. The skeptic came out from under the bed and followed the Rebbe. The Rebbe went over to the corner where the tools were lying and picked up an ax. The Rebbe took the ax and walked into the forest where he began to chop wood. When the Rebbe had chopped a bundle of wood, he placed it on his back and headed in the opposite direction of town, deeper into the forest. The Rebbe walked until he came to the edge of the forest, where there was a small village. The Rebbe walked into the village, went over to a broken-down home, knocked on the door, and went inside. The skeptic went over to the window to witness with his own eyes that which was transpiring. Imagine his surprise when he looked through the window, and saw an elderly woman lying in a bed, freezing from the cold, and the Rebbe placing the wood he had chopped into the oven, starting the fire, and wait-ing until it had warmed the home. The Rebbe repeated the same routine throughout the entire village. After he finished, the Rebbe hurried back to the synagogue where his congregants awaited. When the Rebbe entered the synagogue followed by the skeptic, the townsmen raced over to the skeptic, and asked him, "Nu so, you followed the Rebbe. Is it not true that the Rebbe goes to heaven?" The skeptic turned to them and replied, "If not higher."

By doing an act of simple, pure, altruistic kindness, the Rebbe created the most profound levels of *Yichudim* possible.

In another story,[47] the holy Rebbe, Reb Leib, known as the *Shepole Zaide* (the Grandfather of Shepole), customarily traveled from town to town without ever having a permanent home. [It was once a practice by many holy men to travel, and not have a permanent place of residence. They lived in a state of *galuth*—exile, for just as God, since the destruction of the Holy Temple, had no permanent home, the holy men also did not.[48]] The Rebbe came to a town where a Jew had been thrown into jail because he was not able to pay his taxes to the *paritz*, the owner of the estate. This particular landowner was an evil man with a diaboli-cal custom; if someone did not have the money to pay, he would throw them into a pit and starve them, then, after the prisoner was hungry and dying, he would dress him in the fur of a bear, and force him to dance with a caretaker, and whoever would outlast the other would be the winner. If the prisoner danced longer, he could go free, and if he wanted to, he could beat the caretaker. However, if the caretaker won, which occurred most of the time, they would then throw the prisoner to hungry dogs. When the Rebbe heard of this Jew's situation, he felt sickened and sorrowful; however, he didn't know exactly what he could do to help. That night as he lay in bed, he heard a voice speaking. He turned and saw Elijah the prophet, who then said to him, "I want you to go to the prison, and take the place of the prisoner, and dance in his stead." The Rebbe answered, "I am surely will-ing to go and sacrifice my life for his; however, if I were able to dance, I might be able to save my own life as well." So Elijah taught the Rebbe to dance. The night prior to the scheduled dance between the prisoner and his caretaker, the holy Rebbe went to the jail, bribed the watchman, and lowered himself into the pit. The Rebbe explained to him why he had come; they changed clothing, and the Rebbe sent him home to his family. In the morning, when they came for the prisoner, they took the Rebbe instead. They placed the bear's fur on the Rebbe, and they began dancing. To everyone's surprise, the prisoner outdanced the caretaker, and was set free. Chassidic legend has it that the *Hup Kazak*, a melody that is attributed to the Grandfather of Shepole, was the tune to which he danced that night.[49]

That night the Rebbe created the greatest unifications in all worlds; he performed the foremost of holy acts: he danced to save the life of a human being.

NOTES

1. Rabbi Yehudah Ha'Chassid. *Sefer Chassidim*, Chapter 768. The mystic and codifier of *mitzvot*, Rabbi Eliezer Ezcary, (1522–1600) sixteenth century, writes in *Safer Cheredim*. Chapter 38: 18, that there is a mitzvah, a commandment, that whoever has a nice voice, and is able to sing well, to sing songs to God. "Honor the Lord with your wealth" Proverbs. Chapter 3. Verse 9. The Midrash interprets the verse "Honor . . . with your voice. See: Rashi. Ad loc. See also Rabbi Yoseph Caro. *Shulchan Aruch Orach Chaim. Beit Yoseph*. Chapter 53.

2. Talmud, *Berachot* 63a.

3. *Proverbs*. Chapter 3, verse 6.

4. This indeed includes the thought that if one has a pleasant voice or is musically inclined, he should utilize these talents for the service of his creator. Rabbi Moshe Yichiel Elimelech of Levertov, *Safer Shemirat Hada'at*. Aimrei Tal. Ma'amar Nigun, (Bnei Brak Israel: Ginzei MaHaritz. 1986.) p. 16.

5. See: Talmud. *Berachot* 35b, where it says that although people tried to live like the sainted Rabbi Shimon Bar Yochay, they did not succeed. (Rabbi Shimon did not need to go out and labor in order to have his needs taken care of, because God himself provided his needs in the cave. See: Talmud, *Shabbat* 33b).

6. The Lubavitcher Rebbe. *Likutei Sichot*. (New York: Kehot Publication Society. 1964) Vol. 3, p. 907.

7. *Avot—Ethics of our fathers*. Chapter 2. Mishnah 12.

8. *Tzavoas Horivash*. (New York: Kehot Publication Society. 1982.) Chapter 94. *Kesser Shem Tov*. (New York: Kehot Publication Society. 1987) Chapter 282. See also:

Rabbi Tzadok Hacohen of Lublin. *Tzidkat Hatzadik*. (Bnei Brak: Yehadut. 1973) Chapter 179. In the name of the *Zohar*.

9. Da'at is connection. *Tikunei Zohar*. Tikkun 69. See: Rabbi Schneur Zalman of Liadi. *Tanya*. Chapter 3.

10. *Psalms*. Chapter 107 verse 5.

11. *Kesser Shem Tov*, (New York: Kehot Publications Society. 1987) p. 25a.

12. The simple answer is that soul does not literally mean the spiritual soul; it just means man's psyche, his spirit. However, the Baal Shem Tov explains it literally.

13. Rabbi Nachman of Breslov. See: Eliezer Shtainman. *Be'er HaCahassidut Kisvei Reb Nachman*, (Israel: Mochon Kemach.) p. 189.

14. See: Talmud. *Chagigah* 27a.

15. See: *Kol Sippurei Baal Shem Tov*. (Bnei Brak Israel. Pe'er HaSefer. 1976.) Vol. 4, p. 170.

16. *Shulchan Aruch*. *Orach Chaim*. Chapter 6: 4. Rabbi Avraham Gombiner. (1634–1682.) *Magen Avraham*. Ad loc. Rabbi Tzadok Hacohen of Lublin. *Yisrael Kedoshim*. (Bnei Brak: Yehadut. 1973) Chapter 5, p. 12. Rabbi Chayim Volozhine. *Nefesh HaChayim*. Likkutei Maamorim, p. 383.

17. *Avot—Ethics of our Fathers*. Chapter 6. Mishnah 11.

18. Eliezer Shtainman. *Yalkut Meshalim U'sipurim*, (Israel: Keneset. 1958.) p. 35. In the name of the Baal Shem Tov.

19. *Avot—Ethics of our Fathers*. Chapter 2. Mishnah 4.

20. Rabbi Yehudah Yudel Rosenberg. *Tiferet Maharal*. (New York: Ateret. 1975), p. 10.

21. See: The first Chabad Rebbe. Rabbi Schneur Zalman of Liadi. *Tanya*. *Shar Hayicud V'emunah*. Chapter 9. He writes that for humans to say that God is beyond one's finite comprehension, is so removed from what God really is, that it is as if someone would say about a deep thought that they can not grasp that it is such a deep thought, that they can not grasp it in their hands. It is self-explanatory, and for someone to say that they can not grasp it with their hands, is simply making a fool out of himself. What, after all do hands have to do with thoughts? The same is true with God. For humans to say that God is beyond our understanding is so far removed from what God truly is, it is as if one says, the thought is so far removed from comprehension, that we can not grasp it with our hands. God is beyond any definition, even the definition of being infinite.

22. The holy Arizal, Rabbi Yitzchak Luria, was the first to lay out a detailed description of the theory of *Tzimtzumim*. See. for example: *Etiz Chayim*. *Mevoh Shearim*. *Shar Ha'akdamot*, although its roots are found already in the Zohar. See. *Zohar* Part 1: 15a. *Zohar Chadash* Vaetchanan. 57a. (See also: *Midrash Tanchuma*. Parshat Vayakhel. 7. *Midrash Rabbah Leviticus*. Parsa 29:4, where the word *Tzimtzum* is used with regards to a Godly revelation.)

23. There is an argument between Kabbalists, with regards to the Ein Sof. Rabbi Moshe Cordovero, (*Pardas Rimonim*. Shar 3. Chapter 1. By the same author. *Or Ne'erav*. (Israel: Kal Yehudah. 1965.) Part 6. Chapter 1, p. 43.) says that 'Ein Sof' applies to God's essence of being, as He is for Himself. However, Rabbi Menachem Azaryah De Fano (1548–1620) argues (See: *Pelach Harimon*. Shar 4. Chapter 4. *Yonot Elim*.

Hakdamah) that "Ein Sof" applies only to God's will, to God's first cause. And there is no term for God Himself. God is above being infinite. [See: The fifth Chabad Rebbe. Rabbi Shalom Dovber *Yom Tov Shel Rosh Hashono. 5666*, (New York: Kehot Publication Society. 1984.) p. 166.]

24. The reason for *Tzimtzum*, (contraction, concealment of the Ein Sof) is that Ein Sof is infinite, and the world as we know is finite. Since infinite cannot be contained within finite, it would completely overwhelm it, so the "Ein Sof" needs to contract through *tzimtzumim*, and in that way exist within this finite world. However, it is our finite minds that have conceived of this explanation; perhaps in a world that is infinite, there is a way for the infinite to co-exist with the finite. To God this could be logical, just as it is to us totally illogical! Infinite is above logic, above definition. Who says that there must be a *Tzimtzum*? The answer is as follows: God created the world in a way that makes sense to the human intellect. (See: Rabbi Shalom Dovber the fifth Chabad Rebbe. *Sefer HaMaamorim 5658* (New York: Kehot Publication Society 1984) p. 120.) (Thus, Rabbi Yakov Emdin [*Matpachat Sefarim*. Chapter 9: 64.] argues that the idea of *Tzimtzum* is a rational idea, but this argument can make sense only when we know that God created the world in this way.) In other words, the *Tzimtzum*—concealment, appears only in the perception of man to be real, while in God's perspective, so to speak, there is no concealment. And all that exists is He. In this way, man, through observing God's creation, can draw parallels for his own life experience, and through studying the system of the world, learn to construct and create his own unique world. For example, a person observing the contraction of God's essence in order to co-exist with the finite, understands that to truly co-exist in a relationship, one must contract his own space and allow for another to share that space.

25. Although this universe is in Seder Hishtalshelut, in the pattern of evolution, nonetheless, the creation of the physical is *Ex Nihilo*—something from nothingness, because the transformation from spiritual [albeit a finite, defined spiritual] to physical is such a vast transformation, that God "needed" another total *Tzimtzum*, a concealment, a contraction. This had to be as potent as the first concealment, when the idea of finite was first created and revealed. Thus, this universe is called a creation of *Ex Nihilo*.

26. Ten being the number of completion. See: Rabbi Meir Ben Gabbai (1480–1547), *Avodot Hakodesh, Cheilek HaYichud* Chapter 14. The same author. *Derech Emunah*. Response 3. Rabbi Moshe Cordovero. *Pardas Rimonim* Shar 2. Rabbi Yoseph Ergas. *Shomer Emunim*. Part 1: 51. Rabbi Shem Tov Ben Shem Tov. (?–1430) *Safer Ha'emunot*. (Jerusalem: 1969) Shar 4. Chapter 16. Rabbi Shabtai Sheftel Horowitz. *Shefa Tal* (Brooklyn: 1960) Shar 1. Chapter 5. See however: Rabbi Yitzchak Israeli (855–955) *Safer Hayesodot*. (Jerusalem: 1968) Part 2. Maamor 3, pp 75–76.

27. The concept of ten Sefirot is first mentioned in *Sefer Yetzirah*, and briefly in *Midrash. Rabbah Numbers*. Parsha 14: 12. There are those who assert that in the beginning of the Torah, in Genesis, the Torah alludes to the ten Sefirot. See: *Midrash Hagodol. Genesis* in the beginning. *Ramban. Genesis*. Chapter 1:1. *Rabbeinu Bachya. Genesis*. Chapter 1:2. Rabbi Yoseph Albo (1380–1435) *Safer Haikkarim*. Maamor 2. Chapter 11. See also Talmud *Chagigah*. 12a. 'With ten concepts God created the world.' As explained by the *Maharsah*. These ten ideas allude to the ten Sefirot. The Mishnah. *Avot*, (Chapter 5. Mishnah 1.) says, "With ten utterances God cre-

ated the world," which some suggest means the ten Sefirot. See: Rabbi Dan Yitzchak Abarbenal. (1437–1508) *Nachlot Avot.* On this Mishnah. See also: Rabbi Moshe Cordovero. *Pardas Rimonim.* Shar 2. Chapter 3. By the same author. *Shiur Komah.* (Jerusalem: 1966) Maamarot. p. 16. *Ma'arechet Elokut.* (Jerusalem: 1963) Chapter 12. And chapter 13. Rabbi Chaim Vital. *Eitz Chayim.* Shar Ha'malachim. Chapter 6. Rabbi Moshe Isserles *Toraht Ha'olah.* Part 3. Chapter 4. In addition, there are the ten names with which God is called in the Torah. (See: *Avot D'Rebbe Naton.* Chapter 34: 2.) According to Kabbalah these ten names, correlate to the ten Sefirot. See: Rabbi Moshe Cordovero. *Pardas Rimonim.* Shar 20. Rabbi Yeshayah Halevi Horowitz. *Shalah Hakodosh. Shenei Luchot Habrit.* (Jerusalem: 1963) Beit Hashem. 1: 5a. Rabbi Shem Tov Ben Shem Tov. *Safer Ha'emunot.* (Jerusalem: 1969) Shar 4. Chapter 18.

28. A human being can know what exists above, by observing what is below. Above is the source, while below are its branches. *Safer Hayashar.* (Bnei Brak: Mishar. 1989.) Shar 1.

29. *Leviticus.* Chapter 11, verse 19. *Rashi, Chassidah.*

30. This is also the reason that only man has the true freedom of choice. Because every other creation is a direct manifestation of a higher spiritual reality, its behavior is a direct reflection of its spiritual counterpart's behavior. Each creation is a shadow of its true existence. Man, however, who is created in the image of the entire creation, is a manifestation of the entire inner image. So just as man has the capacity to be kind—*Chesed,* he also has the ability to act with strength—*Gevurah,* etc. Man has the capabilities, figuratively speaking, of his creator. Just as God can choose freely how to act, man can also choose his own destiny freely. See: *Midrash. Rabbah Genesis.* Parsha 21. Chapter 5. *Rambam Hilchot Teshuvah.* Chapter 5. Halacha 1. *Genesis* Chapter 1. Verse 26. The commentary by Rabbi Ovadyah *Seforno.* (1470–1550.) Rabbi Dovber. The second Chabad Rebbe. *Torat Chaim Bereishit. (1)* (New York: Kehot Publication Society. 1974.) p. 75a. Rabbi Shalom Dovber. The fifth Chabad Rebbe. *Sefer HaMaamorim 5660,* (New York: Kehot Publication Society. 1985) p. 10. [The greatest good is God, thus the greatest gift of kindness God can bestow upon man, would be to be "like God," and that is indeed the power to choose, to form your own destiny. See: Rabbi Moshe Chayim Luzzatto. (1707–1747) *Derech Hashem.* Part 1. Chapter 2.]

31. *Genesis.* Chapter 1. Verse 26. See: Rabbi Saadiah Gaon *Emunot Vedeyot.* Maamor 2: 6. *Rabbienu Bachya Genesis.* Chapter 1. Verse 26. *Reb Avraham Ben HaRambam. Genesis.* Chapter 1. Verse 26. They all explain that the simple reason that it says "let us" is because of humbleness, referring to oneself in plural, as in saying, we instead of I.

32. Rabbi Yitzchak of Acco (1250–1340) *Meirat Einayim.* Parshat Mishpatim. 23: 21.

33. See: the introduction by Elijah the master prophet to *Tikunei Zohar.* Where each Sefira is connected with another body part, although only allegorically.

34. All spiritual worlds. See: Rabbi Chaim Vital. *Sharei Kedushah.* Chapter 3. Shar Biet. Rabbi Yoseph Yavetz (1434–1507) on *Avot.* Chapter 4. Mishnah 2. As well as all forces within the physical world. See: Rabbi Moshe Cordovero. *Shiur Komah.* (Jerusalem: 1966) Torah. Chapter 4, p. 21. Rabbi Shimon Ben Tzemach Duran. *Magen Avot.* (Jerusalem: Makor Publishing.) Part 2. Chapter 1, p. 8b. Rabbi Mordecai Yoseph of Izhbitz. (1801–1854) *Mei Hashiluach.* (Israel: Mishor. 1995.) Part 1, pp. 12–13. Rabbi

Meir Leib Ben Yechiel Michael Weiser. Known by his initials *Malbim*. (1809–1897) *Genesis*. Chapter 1. Verse 26. Rabbi Pinchas Eliyohu Ben Meir of Vilna *Sefer Habrit*. (Jerusalem: Yerid Hasefarim. 1990.) Part 2. Maamor 1. Chapter 10.

35. Rabbi Shimon Ben Tzemach Duran. *Magen Avot*. (Jerusalem: Makor Publishing.) Part 3, p. 68a. Rabbi Meir Ben Gabbai (1480–1547) *Derech Emunah*. Response 1. Rabbi Yoseph Ergas. (1685–1730) *Shomer Emunim*. Part 1. Number 65. Rabbi Moshe Chayim Luzzatto. *Kinhot Hashem Tzivokhot*. p. 3. Rabbi Menasha Ben Israel. *Nishmat Chayim*. Maamor 1. Chapter 1.

36. *Nedarim*. p. 31b. *Midrash Tanchuma*. Parshat Pekudei. Chapter 3. *Tikkunei Zohar*, Tikkun 69. See also: *Avot D'Reb Natan*. Chapter 31: 3, in which it's shown how many details of the greater world are reflected in man. See also: *Orchot Tzadikim*. (Jerusalem: Orot Chayim. 1986.) (Author unknown, although some attribute this classic to the teacher of the Rambam.) *Shar Yirhat Shamoyim*. pp. 281–286. Where the author demonstrates how the physical structure of the body is analogous to the structure of the world. See also: *Rambam. The Guide To The Perplexed*. Part 1. Chapter 72. Rabbi Yehudah Halevi. *The Kuzari* Maamor 4. Chapter 3. Rabbi Avraham Azulay. *Chesed Le'Avraham*. Part 4. Chapter 5. Rabbi Shem Tov Ben Yoseph Ibn Falaquera. (1225–1290) *Safer Hamevakesh*, (Reprinted Jerusalem: Mekorot. 1970) p. 100. Rabbi Yehudah Ben Yitzchak Abarbanel. *Vikuach Al Ahavah*. (Israel: 1968.) p. 18b. By observing the physical body, one comes to comprehend the physical nature of the world. And by observing the soul, one comes to perceive the spiritual worlds within. See: Rabbi Yoseph Ibn Tzadik. (twelfth century philosopher) *Safer Ha'Olam Hakatan*. (Breslau: Schatzky. 1903) Maamor 2, p. 23. Rabbi Yechiel Ben Shemuel of Pisa. (c. 1493–c. 1566) *Minchath Kenaoth*, (Jerusalem: Makor Publishing. 1970.) p. 87. Rabbi Avraham Ibn Ezra. *Exodus*. Chapter 25:40.

37. The word, person, in Hebrew, Adam, means similar, for man below is similar to the "man above." Rabbi Menachem Azaryah De Fano. *Asarah Maamorot. Maamor Aim Kal Chai* Part 2: 33. *S'fas Emes*. Adam. p. 26. Rabbi Yeshayah Halevi Horowitz. (1560–1630) *Shenei Luchot Habrit. Shalah HaKodesh. Shenei Luchot Habrit.* (Jerusalem: 1963) 3: 1. 20: 2. 301: 2. Rabbi Meir Ben Gabbai. *Tola'at Yakov*. (Jerusalem: Mokor Chaim. 1967) Sod Berchat Asher Yatzar, p. 12. Thus, by observing one's own body, one can comprehend God. See: Rabbi Bachya Ibn Pakudah. (1050–1120) *Chovot Halevavot*. Shar Habechinah. Chapter 5. Rabbi Shem Tov Ben Yoseph Ibn Falaquera. *Safer Hanefesh*. (Jerusalem: Mekorot. 1970) Hakdamah. By the same author. *Igeret HaVikuach*, (Jerusalem: Mekorot. 1970) p. 13.

38. The philosophical explanation for the Torah's use of human terms, for instance the hands of God, the eyes of God, etc., is based on the famous Talmudic dictum with regards to the entire Torah, "The Torah speaks in the language of man." (Talmud, numerous places, *eg.* Talmud *Berachot*. 31b.) The same saying, the philosophers use with regard to God Himself. And the reason that the Torah uses human terms for God is to allow the issue to be more understandable for a human's comprehension. See: *Exodus*. 19:18. *Rashi* in the name of the *Mechilta. Midrash Tanchuma*. Parshat Yisro. Chapter 13. *Rabbienu Bachyah*. *Exodus*. 19:18. Rabbi Bachya Ibn Pakudah. (1050–1120) *Chovot Halevavot*. Shar Hayichud. Chapter 10. *Rambam. Hilchot Yesodie HaTorah*. Chapter 1. Halacha 9. *Rambam. The Guide To The Perplexed*. Part 1. Chapter 26. See

also: Rabbi Yoseph Ibn Tzadik. *Safer Ha'Olam Hakatan.* (Breslau: Schatzky. 1903) At the end of Maamor 3, p. 60. Rabbi Yoseph Albo *Safer Haikkarim.* Maamor 2. Chapter 14. However, no one argues that the Torah means these terms literally, although this idea of interpreting the Torah literally seems suggested in the critique by the *Raavad.* Rabbi Avraham Ben David Of Posqueres. (1120–1198) on the *Rambam Hilchot Teshuvah.* Chapter 3. Halacha 7. See, however *Kesef Mishnah,* by Rabbi Yoseph Caro. Ad loc.

39. Accordingly, when the Torah speaks of God as having eyes, hands, ears, etc., the Torah is speaking of the idea these concepts represent. The famous parable given in mystical thought, (See: Rabbi Yoseph Gikatalia. *Shaarey Orah.* (New York: Mariah. 1985.) Shar 1, p. 4. Rabbi Moshe Cordovero. *Pardas Rimonim.* Shar 22. Chapter 2.) is of a person writing somebody's name on a piece of paper. It is understood that there is no inner connection between the words on the paper and the person the name refers to. The words, however, can indeed serve as a reminder of that person. The same is true with God; these "human" terms serve as a reminder of the attributes of God, of the Sefirot that correspond to eyes, hands, and the like.

40. The physical structure of the body is analogous to the ten Sefirot. See: *Ma'arechet Elokut.* Chapter 10. Attributed to Rabbi Todros HaLevi Abulafia. (1220–1298) Rabbi Yoseph Gikatalia. *Shaarey Orah.* (New York: Mariah. 1985.) Shar 1. p. 4. See also: Rabbi Moshe Cordovero. *Pardas Rimonim.* Shar 6. Chapters 1–2. Shar 7. Chapter 1.

41. *Avot—Ethics Of Our Fathers.* Chapter 2. Mishnah. 1.

42. The Magid of Mezhirech. Rabbi Dovber. (?–1772) *Maggid Devarav LeYakov.* (New York: Kehot Publication Society. 1979.) Chapter 198. *Tzavoas Horivash.* (New York: Kehot Publication Society. 1982) Chapter 142. See also: Rabbi Chayim Volozhine (1749–1821) *Nefesh Hachayim.* (Bnei Brak Israel: 1989.) Sharr 1. Chapter 4, p. 6.

43. In a similar vein, "God is your shadow." *Psalms.* Chapter 121. Verse 5, which means that God mimics man's actions. The way you act to others is how God will react to you. Rabbi Yisrael Baal Shem Tov. *Kesser Shem Tov.* (New York: Kehot Publication Society. 1974) Hosofot Chapter 60. Rabbi Levi Yitzchak of Berdichov. (1740–1809.) *Kedushat Levi.* Parshat Nosa. Rabbi Chayim Volozhine. *Nefesh Hachayim.* (Bnei Brak Israel: 1989.) Sharr 1. Chapter 7, p. 26. See also: *Midrash Shemuel. Avot.* Chapter 3. Mishnah 17. See also: The third Chabad Rebbe, The *Tzemach Tzedek. Igrois Kodesh* (New York: Kehot Publication Society: 1980) p. 324. See also: Rabbi Yechiel Ben Shemuel of Pisa. *Minchath Kenaoth,* (Jerusalem: Makor Publishing. 1970.) pp. 84–85.

44. Talmud. *Kedushin.* 40b. *Rambam. Hilchot Teshuvah.* Chapter 3. Halacha 4.

45. Rabbi Yoseph Gikatalia. *Shaarey Orah.* (New York: Mariah. 1985.) Shar 1. p. 4. See also: Rabbi Meir Ben Gabbai. *Avodot Hakodesh. Cheilek HaTakhlit.* Chapter 26 and chapter 65.

46. I. L. Peretz. 1975, if Not Higher. In *Selected Stories.* New York: Schocken books).

47. It is said that the Baal Shem Tov stated that whenever one tells stories of Tzadikim, it is as if he is engaged in the mystical study of *Maaseh Merchavah,* Divine Chariot. See: *Shivhei HaBaal Shem Tov,* (Jerusalem. Machon Zecher Naftali. 1990.) p. 233. Number 160. Indeed a Tzadik is a Merchavah, a Chariot for God's will.

48. This is the mystical concept of *Shechina Begalutha*—God in exile. This idea is also mentioned in Midrash. See: *Midrash Rabbah Numbers*. Parsha 7. Chapter 10. *Sifri* Parshat Massei. 35: 34. Talmud. *Megillah* 29a. Thus, one emulates God. In addition, experiencing exile causes forgiveness of sin. See: Talmud. *Sanhedrin*. 37. *Berachot*. 56a. *Rambam*. *Hilchot Teshuvah*. Chapter 2. Halacha 4.

49. Rabbi Yehudah Yudel Rosenberg. *Tiferet Maharal*, (New York: Ateret. 1975.) p. 10.

9
Bitachon/The Power of Trust
Inspiring Transformation

'Exile will be transcended with song.'[1]

When King David completed composing what is perhaps the greatest book of praise of all time, the Book of Psalms, he turned to God smugly, boasting, "Is there any creature in Your entire universe who has sung, and sings Your praises more than I?" At that moment, a toad leaped from the waters, sat upon a rock before the great King David, and croaked, "I sing more praises in one day than you can sing in a full lifetime."[2]

All of creation sings God's praises.[3] The song of Nature is such that each segment of the universe behaves according to God's plan, and each element acts in harmony with all other elements; the universe is like a symphony orchestra playing a continuous song of praise. As a Chassidic master once said, "Every blade of grass sings poetry to God. When one sings without ulterior motive or impure thought, and without seeking reward, then one is able to hear this song."[4]

Each element in this world has a tune that accompanies it, each existence with its sympathetic spiritual rhythm.[5] There is a heavenly rhythm in the spiritual worlds above that parallels, and is the supernal source of, this physical world.

Truly, all of reality is alive; there is no inanimate or lifeless creation, although they may appear that way to the human eye. In every dust of sand, every kernel of grain, there exists a spark of God that animates and gives it life. A great kabbalistic master would rebuke his disciples when seeing them break off a twig from a branch. One can detect life and movement even on a subatomic level, where all the particles interact and are being created and destroyed continuously. Once these particles are created, they do not remain static, but continuously move in rhythmic motion. Sound, that is, music, is produced by a wave with a certain frequency; thus, with each movement, new sound waves are created. In this sense, every particle is singing songs.

"If not for the noise created by the activity of 'Rome', man would hear the sounds of the sun."[6] Most people are so engrossed and preoccupied with the "sounds of Rome," that is, feeding and nourishing their physicality, that they become insensitive to the inner sounds of creation. A person hears what he wants to hear; for example, if you arrive at a busy airport, knowing that someone is waiting for you, then your hearing will be keener for the sound of your name, despite the surrounding noise. This is because your mind selectively turns off all other noises, and listens for your name being shouted. Most people, consciously or subconsciously, elect to be attuned only to the "sounds of Rome." However, there are those who through proper meditation become sensitive to the sounds of the spheres above. A sixteenth century Kabbalist wrote that he heard of a person in India who actually went deaf, from the sounds generated by the motion of the sun.[7] Although these sounds are very subtle, in heightened states of consciousness, even the smallest, faintest of sounds can ring like claps of thunder.

Sounds are made by other objects; even abstract thoughts have a tune that they sing. Even heresy has its own tune, which inspires and gives life to the heresy, a tune from which it receives its energy. Nonetheless, the closer a concept is to Godliness, to the spiritual worlds above, the more exalted the tunes are, and the more holy their notes. Therefore, the most elevated of tunes are expressing man's yearning to be close to God, a tune which inspires the person to spiritual movement.[8]

Moreover, every moment in time has its tune, which accompanies and inspires that moment. A Chassidic Rebbe would, for every segment of the day, have a different tune that accompanied the particular moment. He had a tune that he would sing only during the weekdays, and he had tunes which were sung only on the holy Shabbat. He had a special tune that he would sing while he was taking off his weekday clothes and putting on his Shabbat clothes, and he had a tune which he sang while taking off his Shabbat clothes, to dress into his weekday clothes, and so on.[9]

Everything in this world, an object, an idea, or a moment, has a unique tune that it is connected to and inspired by, the same is true of every individual person: There are melodies for every single one of us. In particular, there are certain melodies that one is especially connected to and inspired by, tunes which are entwined with one's soul. There are happy tunes, and there are sad tunes; there are slow, meditative tunes, and there are tunes with a quick, brisk rhythm. Every individual human being has a melodic style of that he becomes inspired and awakened by; these melodies are intimately connected to the source of that person's soul.[10] Each soul has its own unique melody, which he alone is connected to and inspired by. A celebrated poet once wrote, "I hear . . . singing, the varied carols I hear . . . the carpenter singing his as he measures his plank or beam, The mason singing his as he makes ready for work, or leaves off work, The boatman singing what belongs to him in his boat, the deckhand singing on the steamboat deck. . . . Each singing what belongs to him or her and to none else. . . ."[11]

When one considers this idea that each moment in time has a tune that inspires and gives life to that moment, one tends to think of joyous occasions, the best of times, when all is going well. The Midrash however says, "With every breath one takes, he shall praise God."[12] Even in the worst of times, one should sing God's praise. "To you, God, it is admirable to sing during the day, as well as in the night."[13] Not only during the day, when life is full of light and is beautiful, when everything looks bright, is it most appropriate to sing God's praise,[14] but even in a time of night and darkness, when things are not as clear and simple, one shall aspire to sing God's praise.[15]

The Torah says,[16] "To the children of Kehot he (Moses) did not give chariots (to carry the tabernacle) for a holy task was upon them, (the holy ark, the altar, and so on) with their shoulders they shall carry." A question immediately arises as to why the Torah has to say explicitly "with their shoulders they shall carry." If it would have only said "with their shoulders," one would have known that it meant "to carry," for what else could they have done with their shoulders? The Midrash explains[17] that the Hebrew word for "carry" can yield another interpretation as well; it can mean to sing (as in carrying a tune). Thus, the Torah is saying, "They shall sing while they carry (the holy articles) on their shoulders." A Chassidic Rebbe once remarked, "It is indeed true that the word for carrying can also imply singing; however, there must be an inner connection between the idea of carrying on shoulders and singing, which the Torah is also alluding to. The Torah is telling us, he said, that one should always sing, even if one is carrying a heavy burden on his shoulders. Even when one is experiencing difficulties, one should attempt to sing."[18]

Being a happy person is contingent on developing a relationship with positivity, and having an optimistic view of life. The ability to sing, even in the most difficult of times is emphasized; with songs of hope, and melodies which impel one to serve God with joy and gladness of the heart. A Chassidic Rebbe once said that there is a difference between the manner in which *Chassidim* dance today in a time of exile, and the way people will dance in the time of the redemption. They are alike in that the dance is in a circle; however, today everyone participating in the dance begins at the furthest end of the circle, and then moves towards the center, until all are face to face, going back and forth continuously. However, at the time of the redemption, the dance will be in one continuous circle.[19] The difference is that today in exile, when

Godliness is not revealed, there are times during the day when one is inspired, and there are times in the day when one is not; the spiritual status of a person fluctuates. Therefore, the way *Chassidim* dance is through distancing themselves, and then coming close again, and repeating this routine over and over again. However, in the time of the redemption, when Godliness will be revealed, the dance will be in one continuous circle, with man's "face" perpetually facing towards His "face."[20]

Studies have shown that music can be therapeutic.[21] When a person is not feeling well physically, music can be soothing and comforting. In order to utilize the power of healing music, one has to sensitize oneself by opening up to it. One has to be discerning in the music one chooses, as not all music fits everyone or every illness. There is a harmonic energy that requires to be triangulated between the person, the ailments and the music.[22]

There are two statements in the Talmud with regards to a person's approach in overcoming difficulty. One statement is by Rabbi Akiva in which he says, "All that God does is for good."[23] The other is by Rabbi Nachum Gam Zu who states, "This too, is for the best."[24]

Once as Rabbi Akiva was traveling, and evening was approaching, he went into the nearest town and knocked on doors with the intention of finding a spare bed for the night. However, to his dismay, not one person showed him any hospitality, and he had to return to the fields to sleep that night. When Rabbi Akiva traveled, he took with him a rooster to wake him in the morning, a donkey to ride upon, and a lantern to light his path at night. As he was settling down to go to sleep in the fields, a wind came along and extinguished the flame in the lantern; following this, a fox approached and ate his rooster; and a short while later, a lion came to the clearing and ate his donkey. The next morning when he entered the town, he was told that at night, a band of thieves had come into town and robbed all of the townspeople. Only then did he realize that all that had occurred the previous night was for his own benefit. The fact that he was not invited to sleep in town was in order that he would not be robbed; the flame was extinguished so that the robbers would not see him, and the rooster and the donkey were killed, so that they would not create noise and alert the thieves to someone's presence in the fields.[25]

The Talmud relates a story that occurred to Rabbi Nachum Gam Zu.[26] Once, the people of Israel needed to send a gift to the ruling king, and they concluded that their best representative would be the sainted Rabbi Nachum. So they presented him with a bundle filled with gold and diamonds, and sent him off to the king. On his way, he stopped over for a night at an inn; while he slept, the innkeeper looked into his sack. When he saw the gold, he decided to replace the gold with sand. He figured that the old Jew would never realize what he had done until the next morning when he left the inn, and then, if he were to come back to claim his gold, the innkeeper would vehemently dispute his charge. That is exactly what he did. The next day when Rabbi Nachum realized what was in the sack, he said, "This too is for the best," and he continued on his way. When he presented the gift to the king, and everyone saw what was in the sack, they were prepared to execute him for embarrassing the king in such a manner. However, just then, one of his advisers spoke up. (The adviser was actually the prophet, Elijah, dressed in the garb of a royal adviser.) He said, "Perhaps this is a magical sand, as the sand in the times of Abraham, of which it is said, that the sand turned into arrows when it was thrown by Abraham during war." So they decided to give it a try, and miraculously, the sand metamorphosed into spears and arrows.

The difference between these two anecdotes is the difference between two levels of a person's belief in a better future.[27] The first level is when one realizes that although the present may not be so positive, the reason that he is now suffering is only for the purpose of receiving a greater good in the future. Perhaps in the world to come, or even of attaining a greater good in this world. For instance, in the story of Rabbi Akiva, where everything went wrong at night in order that he would not be robbed, the "negative" was only the means to a greater positive in conclusion. Thus everything God does is ultimately for the best.[28] However, there is yet a higher level in seeing the good in everything, and that is when you can realize the purpose and the essence of good within the bad itself. "This too is for the best."

When the son of the sainted Rebbe of Barditchav passed away, the Rebbe immediately began dancing and singing joyous tunes. When his disciples asked him how he could dance when his own son was lying dead, he answered that he was happy for the soul of his son, for it entered this world in purity, in holiness, and exited this world in holiness.[29] The Rebbe saw the good even in the greatest of catastrophes.[30]

What exactly does this suggest? Does this mean to say that if one believes that things will work out for the best, that it will indeed be so? Who is to say for certain that this will be the outcome? And why should a person believe that? What is the basis on which to place such a level of trust?

Before we can fully understand this, we must attempt to make clear the basic idea of *Bitachon*, and explain what *Bitachon* is.[31]

We speak of *belief* in God and of *trust* in God. What is the difference between the two? An obvious difference would be that believing in God translates as believing in God's existence. We speak here of the God of the philosophers, "the prime mover," the God of science, an abstract, removed energy force; *Bitachon*, on the other hand, means believing in a God who is the God of religion, the God of worship and love, a God with whom man can enter into a relationship. Trust means that one believes that God sustains and is the provider of the universe, and thus is a God of goodness and kindness.[32] And the "nature of the good is to do good."[33] Our belief in this means that we trust in God to provide us with the best outcome possible. This is what is known as trust.

In trust itself, there are two levels. One is a level that is perhaps more familiar to Western society. When people are experiencing hardships and are going through difficult times, they feel comfortable knowing that they are in the hands of God. This does not necessarily mean that they are expecting a positive result; it is only that they trust in God's judgment. They may reason that if they are not deserving of these hardships, surely they will go away; and if they feel they are deserving, they feel comfortable knowing that the situation they find themselves in is God's doing, and that surely God knows what is best for them. A person may go through life feeling like a character in an existentialist novel; he may feel the absurdity of it all, not really knowing what is occurring to him, who, if anyone, is conducting and guiding his destiny, if indeed there is a destiny. One may feel like he is constantly being watched and judged, without ever knowing by whom or for what reason. *Bitachon*, however, means that one feels at ease knowing that there is indeed a judge of the world. One submits and, in a sense, surrenders his predicament to God, and thus feels comfortable in the knowledge that he exists in God's world, and that it is God who judges the world in His master plan.[34]

A higher level of *Bitachon*, which is described in classical Jewish philosophy, is when one's trust is so strong that he "knows" that God will transform his moment of difficulty into something positive. His *Bitachon*, his trust in God, is to the extent that he knows with certainty that the end will be good.[35]

How is one to be so confident that God will do good with him in a revealed way? Perhaps one does not deserve it. How can one be certain that all will be good?

This certainty comes from the *Bitachon* itself. When one really hopes and trusts that the outcome will be good, it will indeed be good.[36] There is a Chassidic adage, "Think positive and it will be positive."[37] Positive thinking here in this world below prompts a positive reaction from above.[38] When a person has a positive outlook in life, things will generally work out. When a person is lacking trust, and has negative expectations from life, he is weak and lacking in confidence. These feelings make the person vulnerable to hardship; the mere feeling of hopelessness creates a situation of hopelessness.[39] However, when a person has a positive perspective on life, then there is possibility and less fear. A famed sage of the Talmud, upon entering the town where he lived, heard a great commotion; people were screaming and shouting, for something terrible had occurred. He turned to his disciples, who were walking with him, and said, "I am sure this is not from my home."[40] With *Bitachon* one opens themselves to possibilities, and to positive experiences.

A higher level of *Bitachon* means a change in perspective. It does not eliminate pain and suffering,[41] but it does allow for a positive light to shine. The dealing with suffering is optional; if one dwells on the negative, then the pain is perpetuated; however, if one moves on with life, and includes the pain as a lesson, then the pain becomes a positive building block. The negativity is transformed into something positive. Hence, *Bitachon* alters one's perspective, as he is now coming to life's experiences with the ultimate partner, that is, God.

Melody can be a path to achieve *Bitachon*. How does it work? The Talmud says,[42] one shall have the words, "Happy is the man who trusts in You,"[43] on his lips continuously. The easiest way to remember these words is to put them into a repetitive song; wherever one is, he can hum these words to himself.

Another way in which melody serves as a means of achieving *Bitachon* is that music can serve as a "relaxing agent." When a person listens to music, he calms down. Music inspires a comfortable mood, and a sense of being at ease.[44] Through music, one can reach a level of *Bitachon*, where one feels at ease knowing that he is in God's hands.

Song, as was explained earlier, is a "revealing agent"; a song reveals the essence of soul, the soul of man that is part of God. In this way too, song inspires *Bitachon*. When a person sings a song, he awakens the essence of his soul, which is connected with God. Thus, when singing a song, one feels a sense of security knowing that his life is taking place in the presence of God.[45]

A great Chassidic Rebbe once instructed his grandson not to sing melancholy tunes, only songs of joy,[46] for when one sings songs of joy, one creates a context of joy in his life. We have explained that our relationship with God is a two way path, and that what we receive from above is a mirror image of how we act below. If we think positive thoughts and behave in a joyous fashion, God will respond with reasons for us to be joyous, thus *Bitachon* is generated through song.

Silence, the ostensible opposite of song, stands on a high spiritual plane, and for a person to control his emotions and remain silent in the face of adversity is a tremendous virtue.[47] Indeed, through silence a person can reach great spiritual heights.[48] Nonetheless, it is with song that a human being can attain even higher levels.[49]

The holy Rebbe of Kotzk once said that there are three ways that a human being can respond to suffering: the lowest level is with tears; a more elevated level is with silence; and the highest level yet is when one can transform his distress into a beautiful melody. Rabbi Shlomo, the Rebbe of Radomsk (1803–1866), once observed that when Aharon was rebuked, the Torah says,[50] "and Aharon held his peace" to show his great spiritual stature.[51] However, King David says "Thus my soul shall sing praise to You, and not be silent."[52] David is deemed to have reached a still higher elevation. He was able to transform his sorrow into song.[53]

Silence can be quite expressive, though seemingly devoid of content. Silence, at times, may be eloquent as a demurer and deafening as a passive resistance. In the face of sorrow, King David sang. When one is compelled to express sorrow, one may weep or remain stoically silent, both natural and human expressions resulting from one's tenacious bond with one's ego, one's self. King David existed on an unparalleled plane. His entire being was relinquished to the Being of the Divine. His self and his expressions were merely manifestations of a Godly will.

When faced with challenge his response was a mirroring of Divine expression. This is a level surpassing all others: when one's song is the song of the Creator and all expressions Divine.

NOTES

1. *Tikunei Zohar. Tikkun 2.*

2. *Midrash. Yalkut Shimoni. Psalms.* Chapter 150: 6.

3. See *Zohar.* Part 1. p. 123a. "All which God created sings His praise." See also *Zohar* Vayakhel. p. 196a. In Psalms, King David continuously expresses the idea that all of nature sings God's praise, e.g., *Psalms.* Chapter 148. Chapter 19: 2. There exists

an ancient text called *Parek Shirah*, which tells of every individual part of creation singing his particular song. Each existence has his unique song to sing. This text is printed in *Sidur Beit Yakov* by Rabbi Yakov Emdin, towards the beginning of the book; and by Rabbi Moshe Metrani. *Beit Elokim*, at the end of the book. They both explain that the meaning of nature's singing can be explained in three ways: A) It is an angel that sings, for every physical existence has an angel (an energy), which is its life force. B) It is man who sings his songs. C) Or perhaps even it is they themselves (nature) who sings.

    4. Rabbi Nachman of Breslov. *Likutei Moharan*. Part 2: 63.

    5. Rabbi Nachman of Breslov. *Likutei Moharan*. Part 2. 8:10. All of nature indeed also has its own tune. Rabbi Yonathan Eibeschuvetz. (1690–1764) *Tifferet Yonathan. Parshat Bereishit.* 2: 5. He writes that nature sings songs while it is sprouting. See also. Rabbi Moshe Yichiel Elimelech of Levertov. *Safer Shemirat Hada'at.* Aimrei Tal. Ma'amar Nigun, (Bnei Brak Israel: Ginzei MaHaritz. 1986) p. 25. Rabbi Chaim Ibn Attar. (1696–1743) *Or HaChaim*. Numbers. Chapter 16. Verse 30.

    6. Talmud *Yuma*. 20b, with regard to the music of the heavenly spheres. See: *Midrash Tehillim* Chapter 33. Verse 1. See also: *Midrash Rabbah Genesis*. Parsha 6. Chapter 12. Rambam. *The Guide to the Perplexed*. Part 2. Chapter 8. *Rabbi Avraham Eben Ezra. Job.* Chapter 38. Verse 7. Rabbi Yonathan Eibeschuvetz. *Yarot D'vash*. (Jerusalem: Levin–Epshtain.) Part 1, p. 33a. Rabbi Shimon Ben Tzemach Duran. *Magen Avot*. (Jerusalem: Makor Publishing.) Part 2. Chapter 2. p. 14b. Part 3, p. 52b. Rabbi Yehudah Ben Yitzchak Abarbanel. *Vikuach Al Ahavah*, (Israel: 1968.) p. 21a. Rabbi Yisrael of Modzitz. (1848–1920) *Divrei Yisrael*. Parshat Mikketz. Maamor Echad M'Remazei Chanukah. [Movement, any movement, generates waves, which in turn produce waves of sounds.]

    7. Rabbi Eliyohu Ben Moshe Di Vidas. *Reshit Chochmah*. Shar HaAhavah. Chapter 10.

    8. See: Rabbi Nachman of Breslov. *Likutei Moharan*. Part 1. 64:5.

    9. See: The sixth Chabad Rebbe. Rabbi Yoseph Yitzchak. *Sefer Hasichot 5704,* (New York: Kehot Publication Society. 1986.) p. 95. See also by the same author: *Likutei Diburim*. (New York: Kehot Publication Society. 1980) Vol. 1, p. 103.

    10. The second Chabad Rebbe Rabbi Dovber. *Shaarei T'shuva 2*, (New York: Kehot Publication Society. 1983), p. 15.

    11. Walt Whitman, *Leaves of Grass. The Portable Walt Whitman*, (New York: Penguin Books. 1977) p. 182.

    12. *Yalkut Shimoni. Psalms*. 150: 6. *Midrash Rabbah. Deuteronomy*. Parsha 2 Chapter 37.

    13. *Midrash Rabba. Genesis*. Parsha 6. Chapter 2.

    14. Indeed one *must* sing God's praise when all is going well. See: Talmud *Sanhedrin*. p. 94a. Furthermore, Rabbi Chayim Yoseph David Azulay writes (*Avodat Hakodesh. Tziporan Shamir*. 10: 155) that he who sings praise when a miracle occurs shall surely have his sins forgiven.

    15. Rabbi Yoseph Yavetz (1434–1507) was one of the many who were expelled from Spain, and thus knew suffering intimately. He writes that one shall praise God despite their hardships, not only at a time of difficulty, but because of it. As the Psalmist sings, (*Psalms* Chapter 30. Verse 2.) "I exalt God because (He has caused me) to be

destitute." *Chasdei Hashem*. The Hakdamah. (Printed in Kal Sifrei Reb Yoseph Yavetz. Israel: 1990) The Talmud teaches, that one should aspire to sing and praise, even when one is enduring a (seemingly) harsh judgment. See: Talmud: *Berachot*. 60b. Jerusalem Talmud. *Berachot*. Chapter 9. Halacha 5. See also: *Psalms*. 101:1. *Metzudas David*. Ad loc. The Baal Shem Tov, says, "you shall praise God, from the mere fact that you have the capabilities to praise." *Tzavoas Horivash*. (New York: Kehot Publication Society. 1982) Chapter 132.

16. *Numbers*. Chapter 7. Verse 9. *Rashi* Ad loc.

17. *Midrash Rabbah*. *Numbers*. Parsha 6. Chapter 10.

18. See: Eliezer Shtainman. *Be'er HaChassidut*. *The Rebbes of Poland* (Mochon Kemach. Israel.) The Motzitzer dynasty. p. 207.

19. Talmud. *Taanit*. 31a.

20. The first Chabad Rebbe. Rabbi Schneur Zalman of Liadi. *Sefer Hamaamorim*. 5565. (New York: Kehot Publication Society. 1987.) *Oz Tisamach*.

21. It has been argued for thousands of years by Jewish Sages, that music can heal a person's health, and particularly his nerves. See *Samuel 1*. Chapter 17. With the commentary by the *Radak*. *Rambam Shemonah Perakim*. Chapter 5. Rabbi Shem Tov Ben Yoseph Ibn Falaquera. *Safer Hamevakesh*, (Reprinted Jerusalem: Mekorot. 1970) p. 86. Generally, music is used to relax and calm. See ibid., p. 12. See also. Rabbi Moshe Yichiel Elimelech of Levertov. *Safer Shemirat Hada'at*. Aimrei Tal. Ma'amar Nigun. (Bnei Brak Israel: Ginzei MaHaritz. 1986.) pp. 5–7.) Rabbi Nacman of Breslov. *Sichot HaRan*. Chapter 273, p

22. Rabbi Moshe Yichiel Elimelech of Levertov. *Safer Shemirat Hada'at*. Aimrei Tal. Ma'amar Nigun, (Bnei Brak Israel: Ginzei MaHaritz. 1986.) p. 7. See also: Robert Jourdain. *Music The Brain And Ecstasy*. (New York: Avon Books Inc. 1998.) Chapter 10. pp. 300–302, where the writer explains that although music heals, nonetheless the listener must be musically sensitive. He also writes that each person is affected by different styles of music.

23. Talmud, *Berachot*. 60b.

24. Talmud, *Taanit*. 21a.

25. Talmud, *Berachot*. 60b.

26. Talmud, *Taanit*. p. 21a.

27. The Lubavitcher Rebbe. *Likutei Sichot*. (New York: Kehot Publication Society. 1974.) Vol. 2, pp. 393–395.

28. *Mesilat Yesharim*. Chapter 19. Rabbi Moshe Chayim Luzzatto writes that this idea is similar to a situation in which a doctor must amputate a limb of the body. It may seem cruel, but it is ultimately for the good, although it is not good in itself.

29. Heard at a Chassidic gathering.

30. Nevertheless, this idea did not stop the Rebbe from experiencing tremendous pain, and thus the need to be consoled, as the letter of condolences sent to him by Rabbi Schneur Zalman of Liadi indicates. (See: *Tanya*. *Igerret HaKodesh*, letter 28.) This is a true equilibrium, which man shall aspire to reach. Man must reconcile both opposing views, the view of his physical existence, and the view of his soul, his spiritual existence. On one hand, one must delve deeper than the surface of reality, and see within the physical its spiritual dimension. In the case of death, one must see the good and positive within it, the soul's view. And on the other hand, since man lives

in this physical world, with a physical body, which can not be completely transcended, he experiences death on its physical plane and therefore needs condolence. Moreover, Jewish Law speaks harshly against one who shows no sadness in the face of death. (*Rambam. Hilchot Aveilut* Chapter 13. Halacha 12.) In other words, although the body may be a hindrance for the soul's maximum expression, it is, nonetheless, here on this physical universe where the ultimate purpose of existence, creation, is. [See: Rabbi Yoseph Albo (1380–1435) *Safer Haikkarim.* Maamor 4. The end of Chapter 32.]

31. In *Sharrei Teshuvah.* Shar 3. Number 32. Rabbienu Yona of Gerondi writes that *Bitachon is* a mitzvah. (See also: Rabbi Eliezer Ezcary *Safer Cheredim* Chapter 9: 21. Rabbi Tzadok HaKohen of Lublin. *Safer Hazichronot.* (Bnei Brak: Yehadut. 1973.) Page 48.) However, most authorities do not regard *Bitachon* to be one of the 613 *mitzvot.* The question is, why indeed isn't *Bitachon* a mitzvah? One may argue that just as belief in God's existence, according to many opinions, can not be counted as a mitzvah, because belief in God is a prerequisite to all *mitzvot,* one must first believe in God's existence before he can accept His commandments. (Rabbi Dan Yitzchak *Abarbenal. Rosh Amanah.* Chapter 4. *Mifalot Elokim.* Maamor 1. Chapter 3. Rabbi Chasdai Cresces. (1340–1410) *Or Hashem.* Hatza'ah in the beginning. The third Chabad Rebbe. Rabbi Menachem Mendel. *Derech Mitzvosecho.* (Israel: Kehot Publication Society. 1986), *mitzvot Tefilah.* Chapter 1.) Thus, in a sense, belief in God is higher than a mitzvah; it is the foundation on which *mitzvot* can be built. The same is true with *Bitachon*— trust, which is an extension of the concept of belief. Believing in God's existence is Emunah, and believing *in* God is *Bitachon.* See: Ramban. *Emunah Ubitachon.* Chapter 1. Rabbienu Bachya. Kisvie Rabbienu Bachya. *Kad Kemach. Bitachon.* (Jerusalem: Mossad Harav Kook. 1995.) p. 72. Rabbi Eliyohu Ben Moshe Di Vidas. *Reshit Chochmah.* Shar HaAhavah. Chapter 12. They write that there can be no *Bitachon*—trust, without Emunah—belief. See also: *Orchot Tzadikim.* Shar Hasimchah. (Jerusalem: Orot Chayim. 1986.) p. 85. One can argue that just as prayer (as explained in chapter 6.) is the back bone of *mitzvot,* so it is with *Bitachon. Bitachon* is very important to Torah, for it is the foundation of our relationship with God. Furthermore, the entire Torah in a sense is called *Bitachon.* See: Rabbienu Bachya. Kisvie Rabbienu Bachya. *Kad Kemach. Bitachon,* (Jerusalem: Mossad Harav Kook. 1995.) p. 77. In the name of a Midrash.

32. This is so, although one can *not* say what God is in a positive sense. Nonetheless, we can speak of His relationship with the world. (See chapter 8, in the footnotes.) Thus, we can call God a God of goodness and loving kindness. What we do know is that God is an absolute perfection; thus, there is no reason that he needed to create this world, so when he did create the world, it must have been a true altruistic act of kindness. It is for this reason that some Kabbalists say that the reason that God created the world is in fact, 'To do kindness with others,' so God can bestow His kindness on creation. See: Rabbi Yitzchak of Acco (1250–1340) *Meirat Einayim.* Parshat Haazinu. 32: 26. Rabbi Chaim Vital. *Eitz Chayim Shar HaKellalim.* In the beginning. Rabbi Yeshayah Halevi Horowitz. Shalah Hakodosh. *Shenei Luchot Habrit.* (Jerusalem: 1963) Beit Yisrael. 1: 21b. Rabbi Eliyohu Ben Moshe Di Vidas. *Reshit Chochmah.* Shar HaTeshuvah Chapter 1. Rabbi Yospeh Ergas. *Shomer Emunim* Part 2. Number 13. Rabbi Moshe Chayim Luzzatto. *Derech Hashem.* Part 1. Chapter 2: 1. See also: Rabbi Saadiah Gaon, *Emunot Vedeyot.* Maamor 1. Chapter 4 at the end. Rabbi Chasdai Cresces. *Or Hashem.* Maamor 2. Kellal 6. Chapter 2. Rabbi Yehudah Ben Yitzchak Abarbanel.

Vikuach Al Ahavah, (Israel: 1968.) p. 38b. In Chabad thought it is argued that ulti-mately there is no "reason" for creation. The world was created out of God's "de-sire" to have a dwelling place for Himself on this earth. (See: *Midrash Tanchumah*. Parshat Nosa. Chapter 16.) True desire is above and beyond reason. See: The Luba-vitcher Rebbe. *Likutei Sichot*. Vol. 6, (New York: Kehot Publication Society. 1972.) p. 21. Footnote 69. (See also: Rabbi Saadiah Gaon *Emunot Vedeyot*. Maamor 1. Chap-ter 4 at the end, the first reason for creation.) Nonetheless, according to all, the mere fact that there is a creation, that there exists an existence other than God, is an act of kindness, giving space for another reality to exist. The Lubavitcher Rebbe. *Sefer Ha'maamorim Meluket*. (New York: Kehot Publication Society. 1993.) Vol. 4, pp. 82–83.

33. The second Chabad Rebbe. Rabbi Dovber. Maamor *Atah Echad*. (New York: Kehot Publication Society. 1965.) p. 4. In the name of *Eitz Chayim*. Rabbi Naphtali Hirtz Bacharach. (seventeenth century.) *Emek Hamelech*. *Shar Shashuei Hamelech*. Chapter 1. Rabbi Schneur Zalman of Liadi. *Tanya*. *Shar HaYichud VaEmunah*. Chapter 4. Rabbi Yoseph Ergas. *Shomer Emunim*. Part 2. Number 14. In *Psalms* Chapter 16. Verse 2. It is written, 'You [my soul] have said to the God; You are my Master. My good comes only from You.' Which, according to the Talmud, means that there is no true goodness existing on this world except that which comes from You ie; God. Jerusa-lem Talmud. *Berachot*. Chapter 6. Halacha 1.

34. See: Rabbi Yakov Emdin. *Migdal Oz*. (Israel: Eshkol. 1978) Aliyat Ha'bitachon, p. 151.

35. Rabbi Bachya Ibn Pakudah. (1050–1120) *Chovot Halevavot*. Shar HaBitachon. Chapter 2. (The seventh reason.) Rabbi Yoseph Albo (1380–1435) *Safer Haikkarim*. Maamor 4. Chapter 46.

36. Rabbi Yoseph Albo. *Safer Haikkarim*. Maamor 4. Chapter 46. Rabbi Yehu-dah Loew. *Nesivot Olam*. *Nosiv Habitachon*. Chapter 1. See *Psalms*. Chapter 32. Verse 10. "He who trust in God, kindness *will* surround him." *Kesser ShemTov*. (New York: Kehot Publication Society. 1987) Part 1. Chapter 130. Rabbi Dovber of Mezritch. *Likutei Amorim*. *Or Torah*. Tehilim. (New York: Kehot Publication Society. 1972), p. 136. *Likutei Yekotim*. Chapter 207. Thus, strong belief in an idea causes a reaction accordingly. See also: Rabbi Michal of Zlotchov. (1731–1786) *Malchei BaKodesh*. (Is-rael: Mechon Zechut Avut. 1998.) Parshat Noach. Rabbi Avraham Yeshoshua Heschel. (1745–1825) *Ohev Yisroel*. Parshat Noach.

37. See: Rabbi Yoseph Yitzchak, the sixth Chabad Rebbe *Likutei Diburim* Vol. 1. p. 159. The Lubavitcher Rebbe. *Likutei Sichot*. Vol. 36. (New York: Kehot Publication Society. 1996.) pp. 4–5. Therefore, says a great Chassidic Master, when a punishment has to be given, *Bitachon* must first be removed. See: *Kesser Shem Tov*. (New York: Kehot Publication Society. 1987) Part 1. Chapter 382. This concept of "Think positive and it will be positive" is alluded to in the Talmud. See: Talmud Horihot 12A. See: The Lubavitcher Rebbe. *Igrot Kodesh* (New York: Kehot Publication Society: 1988) Vol. 3, p. 364.

38. See: Chapter 8. Footnotes 42–43 where it was explained that the face above is a mirror image of the face below.

39. Rabbi Yehudah Loew. *Nesivot Olam*. *Nosiv Habitachon*. Chapter 1.

40. Talmud. *Berachot*. 60a.

41. Although there were and are holy men who were so disconnected from all physicality that they were at the level of oblivion. However, this is not the norm, or is it expected from all.

42. Jerusalem. Talmud *Berachot*. Chapter 5. Halacha 1.

43. *Psalms*. 84:13.

44. See: Talmud. *Berachot*. p. 57b. See also commentary by *Maharsah*. Shelosha Mashivin.

45. Rabbi Moshe Yichiel Elimelech of Levertov. *Safer Shemirat Hada'at*. Aimrei Tal. Ma'amar Nigun, (Bnei Brak Israel: Ginzei MaHaritz. 1986.) p. 4.

46. See: *Igrois Koidesh. Admur Hazaken. Admur Haemtza'ee. Admur Hatzemach Tzedek*, (New York: Kehot Publication Society. 1987.) p. 324 and 326.

47. See: *Avot—Ethics of our Fathers*. Chapter 1 Mishnah 17. Talmud. *Kedushin*. 71b. *Megillah*. 18a.

48. Rabbi Eliyohu Ben Moshe Vidas. *Reshit Chocmah. Shar HaKedusha*. Chapter 11. Rabbi Nachman of Breslov. *Likutei Moharan*. Part 1. Chapter 64: 3.

49. The service of the Priests in the temple was a loftier level than the service of the Levites, for they performed in silence, while the Levites sang. (See *Zohar*. Part 2. p. 259b. Part 3, pp. 39b. 177b. Rabbi Dovber. The second Chabad Rebbe. *Torat Chaim Shemot*. (New York: Kehot Publication Society. 1974.) p. 228a. By the same author, *Biurei HaZohar*. (New York: Kehot Publication Society. 1955.) p. 122a.) It would seem that silence is greater than song; however, there are two levels of silence. A) Silence from speech (song stands higher than this type of silence), and B) Silence which is above speech, which stands on a higher rung than the greatest expression of speech, that is, song. A supreme level of love creates a sense of unity, very often not reflected in a pang of feeling, rather, in a sense of being at one with. The Priests represented this higher form of love. A state of being, rather than a feeling. At its highest levels silence, is a serenity that unites with the 'place' where God can be found.

50. *Leviticus*. 10:3.

51. Aharon was rewarded for his silence. Talmud. *Zevachim* 115b. *Midrash Rabbah. Leviticus* Parsha 12. Chapter 2.

52. *Psalms*. 30:13.

53. Rabbi Shlomo Yosef Zevin. *A Treasury of Chassidic Tales on the Torah*, (New York: Mesorah Publications Ltd. 1992.) p. 324.

Index

ABOUT THE AUTHOR

Rabbi DovBer Pinson was born and raised in Brooklyn, New York. Rabbi Pinson is currently studying in Kolel. He lectures and writes on Jewish mysticism, philosophy, and history, and is the author of *Reincarnation and Judaism: The Journey of the Soul* (Jason Aronson Inc.).